"A brilliant wake-up call for individual leadership and personal responsibility. Nothing is more urgent and important than integrity and wisdom in the borderless world, and no one offers better perspective and action steps for successfully managing change than Denis Waitley. His *Empires of the Mind* will endure as timely, yet timeless, building blocks to reinvent ourselves in our business and personal lives."

—HARVEY MACKAY
Author, *Swim with the Sharks Without Being Eaten Alive*

"The bottom line is that great human beings do great things, and this book promises to have tremendous impact on helping people become great human beings. It was an honor to read the book and I encourage everyone to read it."

—HYRUM W. SMITH
Chairman and Chief Executive Officer
Franklin Quest Company

"In our search for meaning in business, family, and community life, this refreshing work opens our minds to the incredible power within to conquer ignorance, prejudice, and mediocrity."

RYAN C. AMACHER, PH.D.
President
The University of Texas at Arlington

"This book is both an inspiration and a superb survival guide for leaders and managers facing the new and unprecedented challenges of the 21st century. Lucidly and excitingly written."

—NATHANIEL BRANDEN, PH.D.
Author, *The Six Pillars of Self-Esteem*

"Denis Waitley's brilliant insights and laser-specific strategies can help anyone transform the chaos of crisis in modern life and business into remarkable success and deep fulfillment. This is must reading for every executive, professional, and leader. *Empires of the Mind* is a treasure that will be your 21st-century success guide."

—HAROLD H. BLOOMFIELD, M.D.
Psychiatrist, co-author, *The Power of 5*

"Denis Waitley's psychology of winning changed my life. Following his philosophy and working with his disciples, I have been able to make significant impact on the nation's future leaders as they have developed at the Air Force Academy. Currently, I draw on Denis's strength to help me make decisions affecting America's athletes, many of whom achieve world-class status."

—COLONEL TOM WILKINSON, USAF (RET.)
United States Olympic Committee

"The concept of personal responsibility and suggested action to incorporate it into one's life would be the best preparation for future change."

—Christine Gibbons
Director, Continuing Education and Summer School
John Carroll University

"Denis Waitley helps change our perception of change, which is usually viewed negatively. There is no limit to what a person can do—those with vision can and will succeed."

—Karen Flock
Director, Management Development Center
University of Tulsa

"Denis Waitley's emphasis on how self-mastery and self-responsibility are the only guarantees for success is right on target."

—Linda K. Bowman
Director, Extended Education Division
Western New England College

"This is one of the most compelling resources out today on the changing world we live in and the necessary steps each individual can take, both personally and professionally, to ensure a positive future. Well done, Denis Waitley!"

—Mary Lou W. Webb
Dean of Management and Professional Development Division
Portland Community College

"It's a good hands-on way to take a better look at change and its effects. He uses easily understood terms to explain more complex conditioning procedures. If you can think it—you can be it!"

—Linda Franta
Coordinator of Special Events
Henry W. Bloch School of Business and Public Administration
University of Missouri, Kansas City

EMPIRES

OF THE

MIND

EMPIRES

OF THE

MIND

LESSONS TO
LEAD AND SUCCEED IN A
KNOWLEDGE-BASED
WORLD

DENIS WAITLEY

WILLIAM MORROW AND COMPANY, INC. ◆ NEW YORK

It is the policy of William Morrow and Company, Inc., and its imprints and affiliates, recognizing the importance of preserving what has been written, to print the books we publish on acid-free paper, and we exert our best efforts to that end.

Library of Congress Cataloging-in-Publication Data

Waitley, Denis.
Empires of the mind : lessons to lead and succeed in a knowledge-
based world / Denis Waitley.
p.   cm.
ISBN 0-688-14033-5
1. Leadership. 2. Industrial management. 3. Success in business.
4. Career development. 5. Continuing education. I. Title.
HD57.7.W335 1995
658.4′092—dc20   94-38533
CIP

Printed in the United States of America

First Edition

1 2 3 4 5 6 7 8 9 10

BOOK DESIGN BY CAROLINE CUNNINGHAM

❖

*To Larry and Bunny Holman, the visionaries and leaders
who inspired and empowered this odyssey*

·

*To the Wyncom family, each a winner and example of
unleashed potential*

·

To Susan, my soulmate and lifelong partner

PREFACE

This book is a reveille call to individual leadership. Each of us must be willing to stand out while fitting into society. We must be team leaders, not just team members. We can no longer say: "Why don't they do something?" We must say, instead: "Here's what I am doing to solve the problem, by thinking globally and acting locally."

Success in our culture has been associated mostly with material wealth, fame, and social status. I call our preoccupation with showing others the fortunes we've built the Edifice Complex. Many people spend their lives erecting monuments to their progress or building empires. At the end, most of us discover that what others really cared about was a shared vision, not a selfish vision.

For a vision to be inspiring and worth sharing, it needs to bring out the best in all of us, not pander to the worst in us. In order to gain the respect of others, we must first earn it. We must be respectable. In order to be a role model, we must first set a positive example. In order to lead others, we must first lead ourselves.

In the past, change in business and social life was incremental, and a set of personal strategies for achieving excellence was not required. Today, in the knowledge-based world, where change is the rule, a set of personal strategies is essential to success, even survival. Never again will you be able to go to your place of business on autopilot, comfortable and secure that the organization will provide for and look after you.

You must look in the mirror when you ask who is responsible for your success or failure. You must become a lifelong learner and leader, for to be a follower is to fall hopelessly behind the pace of progress. The power brokers in the new global arena will be the knowledge facilitators. Ignorance will be even more the tyrant and enslaver than in the past.

Look into the mirror with me and reflect upon the vast potential within. Challenge your time-worn prejudices and assumptions as I do. Understand that the empires of the future will not be built of concrete, with walls of stone, turrets, armies, and gates. The empires of the future will be empires of the mind.

ACKNOWLEDGMENTS

❖

Special thanks to Al Marchioni, Will Schwalbe, Zachary Schisgal, and the other dedicated and talented members of the Morrow team for their always professional, proactive, and creative leadership.

Thanks to Donna Carpenter and Wordworks for "reengineering" my rough manuscript.

Thanks also to Dr. Ken Davis, Dr. Barry Adams, Robert C. Larson, Oliver Nelson, Doug Widner, and to all at Wyncom who are adding mortar and substance to this ongoing process of building empires of the mind.

CONTENTS

Rip Van Winkle is alive and well. I saw him this morning in the mirror when I was shaving. It's as if I'd been asleep for nearly half a century and suddenly awakened to find a world I never imagined, not in my wildest dreams!

ONE

SELF-LEADERSHIP AND CHANGE

1 ❖ How do you respond to sudden, unforeseen changes or challenges?

2 ❖ Are you:　A: Pragmatic, set in your ways?

　　　　　　 B: Flexible, adaptable to alternatives?

3 ❖ When did you complete your education?

THIS IS A BOOK ABOUT SELF-LEADERSHIP TO HELP YOU IMPROVE YOUR career and achieve your personal goals. What worked yesterday won't work today.

Why?

- Yesterday natural resources defined power. Today knowledge is power.
- Yesterday hierarchy was the model. Today synergy is the mandate.
- Yesterday leaders commanded and controlled. Today leaders empower and coach.
- Yesterday leaders were warriors. Today leaders are facilitators.
- Yesterday leaders demanded respect. Today leaders encourage self-respect.
- Yesterday shareholders came first. Today customers come first.
- Yesterday managers directed. Today managers delegate.
- Yesterday supervisors flourished. Today supervisors vanish.
- Yesterday employees took orders. Today teams make decisions.
- Yesterday seniority signified status. Today creativity drives process.

- Yesterday production determined availability. Today quality determines demand.
- Yesterday value was extra. Today value is everything.
- Yesterday everyone was a competitor. Today everyone is a customer.
- Yesterday profits were earned through expediency. Today profits are earned with integrity.

More changes are crammed into every day of our lives than our great-grandparents experienced in decades—and this process is just beginning. Consider for a moment that a musical birthday card has more computing power than existed on the planet before 1950, the year I graduated from high school.

In his book *Powershift,* Alvin Toffler predicted a whole new power structure at every level of our future society. With knowledge now the key raw material for creating all economic wealth, the new power struggles will reach deep into our minds and our personal lives.[1] That's why we believe the only empire that will survive in the 21st century will be the empire you build within your own mind.

CORPORATE "CULTURE SHOCK"

The culture of the American corporation is changing dramatically. Companies that cling to the old ways and attitudes are doomed to extinction.

Old Corporate Culture

- Maximum short-term return on invested capital for shareholders
- Replaceable employees, expedient methods
- Environmental waste, aging factories, assembly-line production
- Central line authority, manage one-on-one

New Corporate Culture

- Meet ever-increasing customer demands
- Rapidly changing world markets
- Highest quality products and services
- Educated, dedicated, skilled, performance-compensated teams who transmit their core excellence and value in their contribution
- Maximum long-term return on invested capital for shareholders

The source of power has shifted from capital resources to human resources, from natural resources to knowledge resources, from position status to relationship process, from shareowner clout to customer clout. The new global leaders will be people who can transmit knowledge and power to each member of an organization. They will be those who can accept the challenge and responsibility of using this new empowerment to build empires in their minds, offering vast inner and material rewards.

THE NEW EMPLOYEE EMERGES

As employees, which most of us are, we have but two choices today: to be a team leader of a winning team or face being cut. Employers too have two choices: empower the few who will be your new team leaders, or they will exercise their free-agent rights and join another team that does have the vision, culture, synergy, and leadership to win. A team, in short, that has embraced the new culture.

The New Employee Paradigm
- Autonomy and empowerment—minimal supervision, maximum training
- Meaningful work—environmentally safe with a mission to help society
- Career path—opportunity to grow and move up the ladder
- Incentives—compensation based on performance standards
- Flexible schedule—consideration of family and cultural pursuits
- Team leader—able to be a standout while remaining a team player

THE PARADOXICAL PROVERBS

Change of all kinds—economic, social, cultural, technological, political—is happening at accelerating rates. In some areas of human activity, it's not just accelerating but exploding. None of this shows any sign of slowing in our lifetime. Throughout this book, we'll be riding the wave of change, offering what we believe are the critical strategies you need to become a self-leader. Many of these strategies will be in the form of what we call paradoxical proverbs. They're proverbs in the sense of being short definitions of what you must do to take command of change. They're paradoxical in that they appear to contradict much of what we've long assumed to be true.

Our first paradoxical proverb is:

You must welcome change as the rule but not as your ruler.

During the past twenty years, I've traveled an average of four days a week, studying change. I've roamed from Fortune 500 boardrooms to the locker rooms of Olympic athletes. I've gone from NASA control rooms to high school lunchrooms. During the past few years, I've been crisscrossing the country searching for examples of self-leadership in the knowledge era. Some of the most interesting input has come from the more than 150 seminars I have conducted together with my colleagues, Tom Peters and Stephen Covey. The program, called Lessons in Leadership, is sponsored by major business schools and colleges of continuing education in nearly every state in the union.

Each three-hour seminar is attended by a thousand or so executives, small business owners, entrepreneurs, and middle managers—who invariably ask the same questions: How can we deal with change? How can we survive and succeed when the only rule is change? What new strategies and tactics do we need to become victors instead of victims?

A SOCIETY AT RISK

Today's America seems a society that has everything going for it, yet with too little coming together. We seem to have been shoved into a race we didn't choose and whose finish line we can't picture. Most of us have houses but not the domestic lives we wanted. We have photo albums and videotapes of our children but not the spiritual strength that underpins healthy families. We're extremely busy, sometimes frantically busy, but we don't quite know where we're going. We cope with the urgent but keep putting off what we sense is truly important. We try to squeeze in lots of fun, sometimes expensive fun, but we're not really happy. Some of us are doing the right things at the wrong time; some are doing the wrong things all the time.

Most of us believed that the computer would give us more time for leisure and personal pursuits. More significantly, however, the computer has brought us competition from everywhere in the world, competition of a global order. American plants are rusting as foreign competitors dominate one industry after another, from machine tools to motorcycles, from consumer electronics to steel.

This onslaught threatens industries that were, until just recently, considered America's bright hope: industrial robots, fiber optics, biotechnology, even personal computers and semiconductors.

Many of us fail to make the connection between rising global competition and America's declining living standards. One way to see this is to look at the declining percentage of middle-income households in all age groups. Census Bureau figures show that the average family income of Americans in the 25-to-34 age group plummeted by 17 percent from the middle 1970s to the middle 1980s. This happened even though many families that had lived on one salary now needed two. Many industries that pay the highest wages suffer most from our lack of competitiveness—another blow to middle-income families.

The eventual outcome of this global economic restructuring is anything but clear. What *is* clear is the force behind the competition: the inexorable yearning of people throughout the world to improve their own standard of living. They too want a seat at the banquet table—together with cars, vacations, and comfortable, well-equipped houses.

One of the biggest changes in our lives might be called time starvation. Ever greater effort seems needed merely to stay even; we must produce more and more with less profit, less time, less margin for error—because customers everywhere have come to expect instant quality. Global competition makes yesterday's world records today's entry-level requirements. No one seems to have enough time. In buying a home or investing our money, when setting up a business meeting or learning to operate a computer program, a dismaying degree of complexity confronts us. There are forms to fill out, experts to consult, second opinions to solicit—and more seminars and training sessions to attend. How *will* we cope?

THE NEW LEADERS EMERGE

Consider the computer's impact. Designed as a tool for managing complexity, it also *adds* complexity, just as new freeways add more traffic. The computer enables us to sort, store, and retrieve material with ever-increasing speed. But the faster data can be analyzed, the faster decisions can be expected—and the greater the pressure to reach them. And the computer's efficiency is hardly lost on our competitors. They install, program, and use them to produce goods and services of the same quality as ours—and for less money.

Thus the competitive edge will belong not to those who use computers but to those who know how to inspire more productivity and excellence from each individual. We are about to enter a new century of unprecedented human growth and development. We must reexamine and reevaluate the way we think, the way we respond to life's daily challenges in what will be a time of even more astonishing change. We need a fresh, enduring strategy for viewing our potential and mapping out our goals—goals that are truly worthwhile, believable, and achievable.

What can make this happen? Only arming ourselves with strategies for ruling when the only rule is change. This is especially critical in light of the globalization of our world and its relentlessly increasing complexity. The players everywhere are more knowledgeable and sophisticated. The pace is far faster. The stakes are higher and the playing field is anything but level. Victims of rapid change understandably dislike all this. Threatened by the new technologies, the growing complexity, the turbulent economy, and the fierce global competition that have changed their way of life, they long for the good old days. But those days are gone forever—washed away by the floods of change.

The new leaders in the new empires of the mind will welcome change rather than try to resist it. They will have learned how to make change work for them rather than against them. And they will have developed unique strategies and skills that enable them to create opportunities from challenges.

The new leaders actually benefit from change—some of which they create themselves. Like surfers, they ride the waves, using their power to take them where they want to go. Rather than trying to resist change, they seek harmony with it. In response to rapid change, the new self-leaders introduce it in the form of new methods that increase effectiveness and efficiency, create new products and new services, lower costs, and encourage ideas to enhance productivity. They learn how, why, and where things are changing so they can exploit the possibilities. Instead of fighting for market share, they create new markets. They respond to global competition by determining what they and America are best at, then doing it.

This book will be your guide to the new epoch—what we call the knowledge era. It will help you develop a strategy for leadership to advance you to your profession's cutting edge. It will explain how to continue your education without going to school and how to rid yourself of obsolete thinking that stifles your creativity. It will help you learn to avoid repeating old mistakes. Here's another paradoxical proverb for the knowledge era.

You must learn from your past mistakes, but not lean on your past successes.

No society has ever survived its own success. No geographical empire or civilization has reached the top and stayed there permanently. All leading societies, industries, and countries of the past rested on their laurels—and were knocked off their pedestals.

When I gave a seminar for savings and loan executives several years ago—at the depth of the S&L crisis—I was joined by John Madden, former head coach of the Oakland (now the Los Angeles) Raiders turned sports commentator. Colorful John summed up the essentials of winning and losing. "You're only as good as next season. You never get your hand stamped to get back in the dance. When you win the Super Bowl or the gold medal, you think to yourself that you've arrived, and the tendency is to enjoy the view from the top. But when you're on top, you become a target and are benchmarked by all your competitors—who want what you have. That's why it's so difficult to repeat, two-peat, or what we call three-peat as a world champion in anything."

SURVIVAL OF THE WISEST

In this sense, the game of life is similar—and we need a new concept of leadership for that larger game. Leadership used to center around power and being number one. It often meant standing victoriously over a fallen adversary or competitor. As we enter a new century, it's obvious that this must change. The leaders of the present and the future will be champions of cooperation more often than of competition. While the power to maintain access to resources will remain important, the "survival of the fittest" mentality will give way to survival of the wisest, a philosophy of understanding, cooperation, knowledge, and reason. The real leaders will get what they want by helping others get what *they* want. Interdependence will replace independence. The world now has too many people, too few resources, and too delicate a balance between nature and technology for leaders to operate in isolation.

We will have no lasting peace until there's a "piece of pie in every mouth." The expectation of tomorrow's bigger, better pie, of which everyone will enjoy a larger piece, is what prevents people from struggling to the end over the division of today's pie. As students of the art of self-leadership, we must acknowledge that we Americans are a vital but single organ of the larger body of the world's population. One segment of human beings can no longer succeed—perhaps even survive— without the others.

KNOWLEDGE: INSTANT GLOBAL ADVANTAGE

"Knowledge portability" is a term you'll hear often in the future. It's shorthand for saying that the geographic boundaries to knowledge have been erased. The computer and telecommunications—fax machines, modems, etc.—have made possible instant information access throughout the world. Therefore, anything of high quality can be made anywhere. Companies are restructuring, relocating, and reengineering to eliminate their own boundaries and hierarchies. So too must individuals reinvent themselves in order to adapt to a fast-forward world in which Chicago is only seconds in communications from Warsaw, and Paris is no farther from Osaka. One CEO put this bluntly: "Unless we manage change, we're going to change management."

In addition to my American travels as a productivity consultant and lecturer on leadership, I spend every summer in Asia. Beginning in Hong Kong, I visit mainland China's free economic zones, then push on through Malaysia, Singapore, Indonesia, Taiwan, Thailand, Vietnam, and the Philippines. Recently, I took along our children, the last of whom will soon graduate from college and enter the work force. I wanted to "scare them back to life."

It was an eye-opening experience for them. When Tom Peters, Harvey Mackay, Ken Blanchard, Peter Drucker, and I lectured in those countries, two thousand to five thousand people would turn out for each speaker. Most were under twenty-five; some were actually teenagers. I told my children that in order to get that kind of audience in

America, we'd have to give away a new car and spike the show with some rap or rock group. But here were younger Asian generations, packing themselves into the halls to hear a bunch of self-styled leaders talk about success.

In Asia, young executives' idea of a good time is an intense discussion about competition, technology, change, and success. A joke I heard in one Asian country makes a relevant point. *Q:* What do you call someone who speaks two languages? *A:* Bilingual. *Q:* Then what do you call someone who speaks more than two languages? *A:* Multilingual. *Q:* And what do you call someone who speaks only *one* language? *A:* American! This consistently prompts a roar of laughter. But I don't laugh—this joke is painfully revealing. We live in a fiercely competitive market, which is multicultural, knowledge-based, and globally oriented. Unless we learn how to ride the wave of change, we'll flounder or drown in its backwash after it has broken over us. The national treasury of little Taiwan has a surplus of over $80 billion, the equivalent of approximately $60,000 for every man, woman, and child there. Our United States has a *deficit* of approximately $60,000 per person.

THE DINOSAUR MENTALITY

In order to move from a nation of victims to a nation of victors, we must change our beliefs and our behavior. We can't continue repeating the mistakes of extinct societies and expect salvation through a lottery ticket. Either we lead or we get out of the way. To follow is to fall hopelessly behind the emerging nations, companies, and individuals—and perhaps be trampled by them.

Hundreds of thousands of years ago, our planet was populated by dinosaurs, many of which were immensely powerful. Then something happened; virtually all the giant beasts perished within a relatively short period. Scientists don't know the cause for certain, but agree that whatever *did* happen, the dinosaurs could not adapt to change. Unless many giant companies adapt, they will become the dinosaurs of the 21st century, and millions of "worker dinosaurs"—individuals who will become obsolete because they lack the knowledge or skills to compete in the new knowledge era—will share that fate.

KNOWLEDGE AS POWER

The new power will be in the ability to adapt, to assume responsibility, to have a shared vision, to empower others, to negotiate successful results, and to assume control of your behavior and your life. *Knowledge is power.* That statement should be displayed in every office, factory, service center, and school in America.

If knowledge is truly power, why don't more Americans grasp this and put it into practice? Why do so few continue their education after they've graduated from high school or college? Why do fewer than 10 percent of us buy and read nonfiction books? One reason is lack of self-esteem. Great numbers of people don't believe they're worth the time and effort needed to learn about new subjects or study those they know in greater depth. You've heard the explanations. (I hope you've never offered them.) "I was never good in school." "I'm not very academically minded." "Books have nothing to do with the real world."

Many Americans also believe that information found in books, computer programs, and training sessions has no value in the business world. How self-deluding! As the new tools of productivity become the interactive computer combined with telecommunications, the people who know how to control the new technologies will acquire power, while those who thought that education ends with the diploma are destined for low-paying, low-satisfaction jobs. In almost the blink of an eye, our society has passed from the industrial age to the knowledge era, in which knowledge and information are the keys to opportunity and advancement.

But another explanation of learning avoidance is plain laziness. Most people prefer to do just enough to get by. Reading and learning seem too much like hard work. They'd rather get home than get ahead.

Actually, people would increase their learning *and* earning power immeasurably by spending half as much time reading as they waste gaping at television. The things we fear in life are those we know the least about—which is why knowledge and action conquer fear. Knowledge starts with keeping an open mind and with the hard work of self-improvement. As someone once said, there is no knowledge that isn't power. All we learn teaches us how to think in different ways. Some of the greatest inventions and creations were born of individuals who were working on something else, when—in a flash of insight—they found the key to their masterpiece.

"NEWSPEAK" IS HERE

Remember George Orwell's *1984,* the classic novel about the essence of totalitarianism? Big Brother, the supreme dictator, systematically reduced the number of words the citizen-slaves could use. The fewer the words, the fewer the ideas, the narrower the thinking, the less power in people's minds and therefore at their disposal. Big Brother mandated a cryptic, crippled language called "newspeak."

Frighteningly enough, Orwell's vision is coming true in America—although not by government dictate. Linguistic experts estimate that the average citizen's vocabulary is decreasing by roughly 1 percent a year. The English language has over 450,000 words. Most of our daily conversations are made up of a mere *400* words—of which some of the most commonly used are *I, me, my,* and *mine.*

One of the most important qualities of successful leaders is an ability to express thoughts and knowledge. Research by management and human resource experts confirms that no matter what the field of employment, people with large vocabularies—those able to speak clearly and concisely, using simple as well as descriptive words—are best at accomplishing their goals. Well chosen, carefully considered words can close the sale, negotiate the raise, enhance relationships, and change destinies. The power of knowledge is immense, and language skill is a key that unlocks that door.

According to UCLA's Brain Research Institute, the human brain's potential to create, store, and learn may be virtually unlimited. "Throughout our lives, we use only a fraction of our thinking ability," concluded a prominent Russian scholar named Ivan Yefremov. "We could, without any difficulty whatever, learn 40 languages, memorize a set of encyclopedias from A to Z, and complete the required courses of dozens of colleges." If this is true, why don't most people learn and accomplish more? As mentioned earlier, one painful reason is their belief that they're not worth the time and effort. Low self-esteem is a devastating inhibitor of growth. The only way to obtain knowledge is through study—which for most people is like paying taxes. It's an activity they don't like and won't tackle unless absolutely necessary.

The United States has the world's richest supply of free educational materials. Our libraries and university extension programs bulge with enough data on virtually every subject to make anyone willing to spend the equivalent of a half-hour every evening both knowledgeable and successful. CD-ROM and interactive computers have made it possible to store entire libraries on saucer-sized discs. This is a primary reason why the Asian nations, which place a much higher priority on continuing education, are pushing us from the scientific and economic summit. They produce 95 percent of the television sets we use to waste our hours—hours, incidentally, not only lacking in value but also generating boredom and apathy.

THE NEW INTELLECTUAL ENTREPRENEURS

"Today, knowledge has power," advises management expert Peter Drucker. "It controls access to opportunity and advancement. Scientists and scholars are no longer merely on tap, they are on top. They largely determine what policies can be considered seriously in such crucial areas as defense and economics."[2]

The information revolution is a revolution in power. More and more of it is vested in people with knowledge and enhanced mental ability. Just as the industrial revolution catered to line managers with manufacturing and materials experience, the knowledge revolution rewards "intellectual entrepreneurs" with strong technical and economic educations. This is not entirely new. Socrates argued that knowledge is the sole good and ignorance is the single evil—and that ancient Greek philosopher also believed individuals should cultivate strong personal character and many personal virtues. But the application to the 21st century does require new forms.

LIFELONG LEARNERS

We all yearn to shape our own lives, fashion our own destinies. But most of us find ourselves in the same dilemma from our teens onward. How do we really want to spend our days? What choices should we make? What can we do that will fill our lives with meaning and bring us the adventure and rewards we seek? How do we know we've chosen the right career and the proper goals? Where have our leaders gone? Who should be our role models now?

These heavy questions can't be taken lightly. We mustn't let our first jobs after high school or college determine our lives from there ever after. Nor should we let our parents, professors, or friends choose our careers—or let money alone make our long-range decisions. Most people allow their jobs—an external factor—to set their courses. This is like the chicken in the chicken-and-egg conundrum. Starting with the egg—the internal factor—is much more likely to assure success. *We must take the first step toward meaningful goals and a life strategy—by being true to ourselves.*

The truth of this proposition can be seen by stepping back to look at the whole person. Why are most people better equipped for, and more motivated by, their hobbies than for their life's work?

You must continue to gain expertise, but avoid thinking like an expert.

The acquisition of knowledge is a lifelong experience, not a collection of facts or skills. Not long ago, what you learned in school was largely all you needed to learn; you could rely on that knowledge for the rest of your life. With knowledge expanding exponentially, this is no longer true. Hundreds of scientific papers are published daily. Every thirty seconds, some new technological company produces yet another innovation. Your formal education has a very short shelf life.

In this world, with ever more to know, leaders need—and many are demonstrating—a new attitude toward learning. Although most are too busy managing to spend much time in classrooms, they continue learning by teaching themselves, absorbing new ideas and knowledge largely on the run. Their love of learning springs from a natural curiosity and their risk-taking nature affects the way they learn. It leads them to dig deeper, to want to know not just *how* but also *why*. Interestingly enough, the people who do know why often have many people with *know-how* working for them.

Thus lifelong learning means far more than formal classroom knowledge. In a world in which working with people is essential, it also means deepening your understanding of yourself and others. A shared belief emerged from a recent round-table discussion among a group of innovative American business leaders. All the leaders, while innovating in their business lives, were doing the same in other spheres of their lives. They agreed that their subordinates' executive growth depended on personal growth, and that those who believed they had completed their education were on a fast track to personal obsolescence. Lifelong learning, once a luxury for the few, has become absolutely vital to continued success.

But while there are dangers in trying to become a leader without thoroughly knowing your field, there are also dangers in thinking of yourself as an expert—especially the danger of losing your sense of wonder. Instead of being driven by curiosity, you become driven to defend what you've previously researched, invented, created, marketed, or published. Reciting safe answers now, you stop saying the liberating words, "I don't know." Leaders who continue learning throughout their lives never forget they always have more to learn. Although their knowledge and experience may have made them teachers, they continue to think of themselves as students.

The most compelling reason to avoid thinking like an expert even while continuing to acquire expertise is that your assumptions may damage your ability to generate and work with new ideas. In later chapters we'll take leadership lessons from some of the most creative thinkers and leaders—which will enable us to manage change in a world in which the only rule is change.

T W O

SELF-LEADERSHIP AND
RESPONSIBILITY

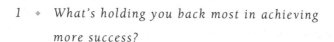

1 ◆ *What's holding you back most in achieving
more success?*

2 ◆ *What are the have-tos in your life?*

3 ◆ *What do you control and what don't you
control on a daily basis?*

THROUGHOUT THE FIRST HALF OF MY LIFE I ASSUMED THAT RESPONSIBILity was widely understood. My travels of the past twenty years—interviewing, lecturing, observing, and listening—have convinced me it is a vanishing concept. Responsibility is the forgotten side of freedom. In Asia, I talked to thousands of young men and women, many desperate to seize educational and economic opportunities and to escape the oppression of their governments. They told me what they most wanted was what America represented to them—the freedom to be as uncommonly successful as they wanted to be—and they were willing to work to attain that. But when I interview immigrants who have spent some time in America, I find that their greatest cultural shock comes from discovering that many Americans are trying to escape *to* the very things they were escaping *from.* While the immigrants yearn to be free to work and grow according to their own visions, many Americans prefer being cared for by the government.

RESPONSIBILITY DEFINED

Responsibility is badly in need of redefinition. For a start, let's look at the *American Heritage Dictionary*'s definition.

Responsibility, n. 1. The state, quality or fact of being responsible. 2. A thing or person that one is answerable for, a duty, obligation or burden. *Responsible,* adj. 1. Legally or ethically accountable for the care of or welfare of another. 2. Involving personal accountability or ability to act without guidance or superior authority. 3. Being the source or cause of something. 4. Capable of making moral or rational decisions on one's own, and therefore answerable for one's behavior. 5. Able to be trusted or depended upon; reliable. 6. Based upon or characterized by good judgment or sound thinking. 7. Having the means to pay debts or fulfill obligations. 8. Required to render account; answerable.

My friend and colleague Stephen Covey defines it in his own way. "Look at the word *responsibility*—response-ability—the ability to choose your response," wrote Stephen in his best-selling *The Seven Habits of Highly Effective People.* "Highly proactive people recognize . . . responsibility. They do not blame circumstances, conditions, or conditioning for their behavior. Their behavior is a product of their own conscious choice based on values, rather than a product of their conditions, based on feeling."[1]

"Have-To's" Are a Choice

Everyone likes to talk about freedom of choice. After all, that's one of the principles on which our nation was founded. But we often tend to feel that much of what we must do in life has been forced on us. Is that true?

Must you go to work, for example? The ultimate answer is no. You can choose to lie in bed, fake an illness, move in with someone willing to support you or apply for long-term government assistance. Must you pay taxes? Not really. You can earn too little to qualify, try to fool the IRS, give up your citizenship, go to prison, or invest in tax deferral programs that last until your death—after which your heirs can pay your taxes. You have to work late tonight? Not exactly. You don't *have* to. Many people feel compelled to work late at the office. However, those who understand positive self-determination *choose* to do that occasionally because they feel they have commitments that require important things to be accomplished. Leaders realize that working forty hours a week is usually enough to make a living—and also understand that their success depends on a good deal more.

We really don't have to do much of anything. We choose to do the things we do because they're profitable to us and the best choice among the alternatives. People who feel they *must* do things usually forfeit many available options and alternatives, losing control of their lives in the bargain. But those who are aware that they have the power of decision—that they exert control over what happens to them—can choose more effective responses to change and to life's offerings. (Note the word *response* again.) Incidentally, the second category of people is also generally happier.

Unfortunately we're living in an age of eroding responsibility. Although most people are willing to fight for the credit when good things happen, fewer and fewer want to accept responsibility for their own actions.

You must accept responsibility for your actions, but not the
credit for your achievements.

You may recall a *Time* magazine cover story not long ago that portrayed America as a land of sore losers, spoiled brats, blame-fixers, and crybabies. Compared to the qualities we ascribe to the pioneers who founded this nation not so many generations ago, those are sad charges.

The "Why me?" so often heard today should be "Try me!" "Try me, I can handle it." "Give me the chance and I'll do the job." Blaming others—parents, bosses, companies, immigrants, fate, weather, bad luck, the government, or the horoscope—is a mark of a juvenile mind. The mature mind asks what is within *me* that caused this to happen. "What did I fail to consider? What can I do better next time?" Instead of contemplating what's ticking inside them, blame-fixers focus on what's going on around them. It's always easier to assume the faults lie elsewhere.

Rather than remorse and apology or determination to face the consequences, the common response to lapses and failures is to blame one's upbringing or other circumstances. Today's philosophy often seems to be, "It's not whether you win or lose, it's how you place the blame!" In our age of euphemism, the drug addict has become "chemically dependent." The delinquent is suffering from "a behavioral disorder caused by preexisting conditions." And ever-greater numbers of murderers plead insanity, convincing ever-greater numbers of juries.

THE IMMUTABLE UNIVERSAL LAW

But one way or another, our actions cause consequences. "To every action," as Sir Isaac Newton observed, "there is always opposed an equal reaction." Good begets good and evil leads to more evil. This is one of the universe's eternal, fundamental truths: the law of cause and effect.

It means that every cause (action) will create an effect (reaction) approximately equal in intensity. Making good use of our minds, skills, and talents will bring positive rewards in our outer lives. Assuming the personal responsibility to make the best use of our talents and time will result in an enormous gain in happiness, success, and wealth. This is true of everyone.

However, scarcely one person in a thousand puts his or her time to anywhere near its potential good use. Most of us fritter away much of our lives watching the game from the sidelines. Nor is there any ultimate advantage in taking praise or rewards away from others. Every time we think we can cheat our boss, fellow workers, friends, family members, or peers, we hurt ourselves most of all. Every less-than-properly-responsible act toward others slashes most deeply into our *own* opportunity to grow and prosper.

The truly successful leaders, those who have built financial empires or accomplished great deeds for society, are those who have taken personal responsibility to heart and to soul. By being true to themselves and others, they achieve success, wealth, and inner happiness. In the end, we ourselves—far more than any outsider—are the people with the greatest ability to steal our own time, talents, and accomplishments.

Responsibility psychology is a field of study pioneered by Abraham Maslow and carried on by Carl Rogers, William Glasser, Viktor Frankl, David McClelland, Albert Bandura, Nathaniel Branden, and other prominent scientists. It holds that irresponsibility and the lack of values leads to abnormal behavior, neurosis, and mental deterioration. Treatment for victims of those afflictions focuses on showing them that they are responsible for their present actions and future behavior, although they need not be hung up on the past.

This school of psychology is optimistic about human growth and potential. Its practitioners have found that when neurotics are helped to assume personal responsibility, the prognosis for recovery is good. Case after case has demonstrated that responsible self-control leads to sound mental health.

LOOKING FOR THE "GOAT"

Alcoholics Anonymous and other recovery programs recognize that an individual must admit that there is a problem before he or she can begin to change. Admission of a problem can't come with a finger pointed at other people or external conditions. It means accepting responsibility for one's difficulties and making a genuine effort to change.

I'm fond of a story from the Old Testament book of Leviticus about a sacred ceremony called "The Escaped Goat." When the people's troubles became overwhelming in those early days, a healthy male goat was led into the temple. The tribe's highest priest placed his hand on the animal's head and solemnly recited the long list of the people's woes. Then the goat was released—and it ran off, supposedly taking the human troubles and evil spirits with him. That was some four thousand years ago, but the concept of the scapegoat remains in full force today. Blaming someone else or something else for our problems is nearly as old as civilization—and stays consistently young. When Adam ate of the apple, he quickly pointed at Eve. "The woman you've put here with me made me do it," he said.

THE DISPOSABLE ASSETS

We live in a land of incredible abundance. Americans enjoy material riches and a civic and legal inheritance that people of other countries continue to die for, as the massacre of Chinese protesters in Beijing's Tiananmen Square reminded us. To those willing to think about it, satellite projections of conditions in Eastern Europe, Africa, Haiti, and other tortured regions continue to remind the world of priceless rights that most Americans take for granted. But like so many successful societies in history, we are squandering our resources and past rewards faster than we're replenishing our investment for future harvesting. That has become obvious to almost everyone but ourselves. It's dangerous enough to simply rest on one's laurels. Worse than that, we may actually be engaged in pawning them.

Perhaps the major explanation for Japanese success in building their industry out of World War II's ashes is their willingness to work very hard for the sake of *future* rewards. Their tolerance for sacrifice gives them an enormous social and financial force. Japanese workers save an estimated 20 percent of their spendable income, more than triple the percentage of American savings. In Japan, this is called discretionary income, signifying recognition of a choice to spend or to save it. In America, we call it disposable income. And we do hasten to dispose of it—in pursuits, moreover, that tend to relieve tension instead of achieving a goal.

We protest for individual liberty and social order in the same breath. We strive for material wealth, hoping that spiritual riches will come with it as a bonus. We plead for more protection from crime but demand less interference in our social habits. We want to cut taxes and build our own empires—at the same time, we want our government to provide more financial security. But we can't have it both ways. If we want results, we must pay the price. So far we've been dealing with the symptoms. The secret is in changing the cause.

THE FOURTH "R"

The various separate causes of most of our social problems are underlaid by one major cause. Throughout my twenty years of traveling—of interviewing students, teachers, parents, business and civic leaders, astronauts, former POWs, Olympic champions, factory workers, clergy, and health professionals—one message has come through loud and clear. It is that reading, writing, and arithmetic are critically important—but of little use without responsibility, the fourth and missing "R." I believe the greatest single cause of American problems is the irresponsible obsession with immediate sensual gratification.

We want love without commitment. We want benefit packages without productivity requirements. Increasingly, we want children who demand little more from us in the way of leadership than our pets do. This is selfishness and narcissism in action.

Pain, sacrifice, and effort—the attitudes and resolve that truly made America great—are increasingly unacceptable to many. If at first you don't succeed, the hell with it. If it feels good now, just do it, baby. To achieve emotional security, each of us must develop two critical abilities: the ability to live with change and uncertainty, and the ability to delay immediate gratification for the sake of long-range goals.

ROOTS AND WINGS

As the father of six birth children and an adopted daughter, I know that the greatest gifts parents can give their children—and that business and other leaders can give their team members—are roots and wings. Roots lie in core values and feelings of self-worth. Wings grow from acceptance of responsibility, which enables our children to fly freely as independent adults. The loss of roots and wings too often leads to pursuit of "loot and things," and other tragic results.

HOW TO BE DIFFERENT

In a very real sense, we all become hostages of hundreds of restrictions of our own choosing. As children, we either accepted or rejected the teachings and lifestyles of the significant adults in our lives. As teenagers and young adults, many of us felt a need to conform to the standards of our peers. While fooling ourselves into thinking we were being different, we were actually as regimented as an army calling cadence and marching in full-dress uniform.

To be responsible leaders, we must understand that being different is admirable and valuable if:

* It means higher personal and professional standards of behavior.
* It means putting more time and effort into everything you do.
* It means taking calculated risks.

Life's greatest risk is depending on others for your security, which can really come only by planning, acting, and making choices that will make you independent.

UNHOOK YOUR PREJUDICES

When you're totally truthful with yourself, what do you say is holding you back from achieving your goals? Do you make certain excuses again and again? Are any of these among them?

* I don't have what it takes.
* I don't have the right education.
* I don't have the contacts or the clout to break into this field at that level.
* I don't have enough talent.
* I'm too old.
* I'm too young.
* I don't want the responsibility.
* I'm trapped in my present job.
* My field's too competitive.
* I don't have enough credibility.
* I don't have enough capital.
* I'm not a self-starter.
* I'm before my time.

If any of these lines sounds familiar, you should realize that all are prejudices standing between you and your ideas and goals.

Talking to leaders, one line comes up again and again. "Everyone told me I was crazy, but I went ahead and did it anyway." Everyone told Fred Smith he was crazy to start an overnight package express service. "There's no market for it," some warned. "The Civil Aeronautics Board will never approve it," insisted others. "You'll never be able to find reliable couriers." "If there were a market for such a service, the major airlines would already be offering it." Needless to say, Smith did it anyway, which is why you and I—by the thousands and thousands—send Federal Express packages every day.[2]

If someone hasn't told you lately that your ideas are crazy, you haven't been doing much independent thinking. Self-leadership doesn't rest on playing it safe or on always doing things the same old way. Leadership ideas that solve problems and create opportunity come from creative trial-and-error thinking. They require us to challenge our assumptions, think outside previous boundaries, and take constant risks.

In short, they require us to unhook our prejudices.

You must stick to your convictions, but be ready to abandon your assumptions.

A prejudice is a judgment or opinion reached before the facts are known or maintained after the facts have changed. Ridding our thinking of prejudices is more critical than ever because they limit our ability to respond effectively to change.

Prejudice limits vision. It keeps us focused on what already exists or on something that we imagine exists when it does not, rather than on what might exist. Prejudice stifles creativity. It insists that there is only one correct way of looking at problems when there are often many ways. Prejudice prevents problem-spotting. Often leaders solve problems that aren't even clearly identified—they're simply "the way things are" and therefore the way people believe they have to be. Before Fred Smith visualized Federal Express, people didn't consider the lack of an overnight express service a national problem. They simply thought, "I'm in trouble. This package is supposed to be on Smithers's desk in Denver tomorrow. I sure wish there were some way of getting it there by then."

Prejudice restricts the inflow of information. Prejudiced people choose to believe that they have all the relevant facts rather than open their minds to other ideas.

THE VIRTUE OF PORTABLE IGNORANCE

Tom Wolfe once observed that what a good journalist needs most of all is "portable ignorance," an ability to put aside what he or she "knows" in order to receive other points of view without prejudice. In the knowledge era, developing portable ignorance is essential to becoming a self-leader. Left to their own devices, our minds tend to see the world in familiar patterns. It's (temporarily) easier to cling to assumptions without determining whether they have a factual foundation. Thus we lose our curiosity, our sense of wonder. People who've become prejudiced pay less and less real attention to the environment. They don't look for new patterns, notice anomalies, or ask *why*.

Opportunities rush by without notice. Ridding the mind of prejudice never comes naturally—and the older we get, the harder it usually becomes.

TEST YOUR ASSUMPTIONS

Here's an exercise for helping measure your prejudice quotient. Supplying your typical responses to the following statements—rather than those you know to be correct—will give you a rough idea of where you stand.

1. I'd rather know the truth than be right.
2. I often seek contrary feedback from my spouse, colleagues, friends, and others.
3. I'm often accused of asking too many questions.
4. I believe the opinions of others are helpful most of the time.
5. I like routines and tend to stick by them.
6. I don't believe in seeking counseling unless I've got a serious problem.
7. I make it a point to see things from the other person's point of view.
8. I work on trying to look at things with a totally open mind.
9. People find it easy to share their failures and their vulnerable spots with me.
10. I listen unconditionally without prejudgment.
11. I tend to make up my mind quickly with only a little information.
12. I'm objective.

What do your responses reveal? While everyone is close to other points of view at times, your success as a leader depends on how able you are to think with a fresh mind—and only you can take steps in that direction.

If you're self-employed, your closed-mindedness may go unnoticed by others. No one really knows how you think, solve problems, or create opportunities for yourself; people see only the results or lack of them. If you're a leader, your team members have probably recognized your prejudices long ago. They may not speak up about it, but their reaction probably reduces their output. Current, unbiased information and feedback are critical in the knowledge age, but your team members may be screening information to cater to your biases.

THE PRICE OF SUCCESS

Years of study and some painful personal experiences have convinced me that fear of the costs of success are among the reasons prejudiced people resist change. For success *does* have its costs, including:

1. Taking responsibility for giving up bad habits and invalid assumptions.
2. Taking responsibility for setting an example in our own lives.
3. Distancing ourselves from a peer group that isn't helping us succeed and therefore tends or wants to hold us back.
4. Leading ourselves and others down a new and unfamiliar path.
5. Working more to reach a goal and being willing to delay gratifications along the way.
6. Being willing to face criticism and jealousy from people who would like to keep us stuck in place with them.

These are among the perceived costs of success that prompt people to escape from the present by occupying their minds with past memories or future expectations. Leaders, by contrast, are not dismayed by the cost of success. They get started and build positive momentum. Determined to pursue their potential, they look forward to an endless dialogue between their talents and the claims of life.

THREE RUTS IN THE ROAD TO EXCELLENCE

Heading the list of "prejudice ruts" that self-leaders must avoid are: The Rut of Average, the Rut of Conventional Wisdom, and the Rut of Group-Think.

The Rut of Average. We live in a society in which average is good enough for most. Punching in at 9:00 A.M., workers begin a countdown until 5:00 P.M. For many managers, too, the job seems an interruption between weekends. "Don't work too hard" is a popular slogan. The employee who works longer and harder is often ridiculed. The businessman or businesswoman who assumes all the risks and responsibility is resented. Excellence is almost frowned upon. The right to become unequal by choice—to climb toward a pinnacle—is submerged in an insistence that all individuals are entitled to equal results. While few are upset when millions are won on the lottery, more people feel ambivalent toward the man or woman who has made a fortune through uncommon efforts. It's almost as if the "winners" are irritating reminders of what each of us might be if we were willing to stop hiding in our peer group.

Mediocrity's only socially redeeming feature is regularity—constancy. It's muddling through from birth to death with the least inconvenience, giving no highs, no lows, just medium—which rhymes with tedium. A new soft drink—Okay—seems symbolic of this condition. It's not very tasty but not very bland, not too sweet or too sour. It doesn't have much color but it isn't quite transparent. It's neither strongly carbonated nor totally flat. Nothing special, nothing outstanding, just Okay, the drink for the majority—of which we should be opposite. Instead of average, we should all strive to be the best we can be.

The Rut of Conventional Wisdom. Conventional wisdom is nothing more than the consensus of opinion until someone replaces it with something better. When conventional wisdom held that the earth was flat, people who had invested heavily in that paradigm tried to discredit new explanations because they'd lose face if it was proven wrong. The same is true with our energy policy, new methods of construction, farming, the welfare system, the tax system—and with leadership itself. Not very long ago, the prevailing leadership paradigm was the power of central authority. Management by command and control seemed everlasting—which is why shifting from power over others to *empowering* others is proving so difficult.

Remember the state of the automobile industry twenty years ago. The deep estrangement between labor and management was viewed as inevitable. Management's underlying assumption was that America's blue-collar workers were lazy and contentious by nature. For its part, organized labor viewed management as incurably uncaring and greedy. Then came the Japanese automobile onslaught, topped off, in the 1980s, by the construction of Japanese factories on American soil.

The Japanese didn't buy the conventional American wisdom. A study by Columbia University's Business School found that their companies "generally outperformed their American counterparts in terms of quality products, the absenteeism rate, the relationship [between] workers [and management] and their relationship with customers." Coming at a time when American companies were moving manufacturing operations overseas because they couldn't get things right here, the report was particularly embarrassing. The Japanese were beating us at our own game, on our own turf, with American workers. But the American automobile manufacturers woke up and, to their credit, reassumed leadership. First, they admitted that conventional wisdom was obsolete in the knowledge era and that labor-management relations had to be improved. Ford made quality job number one. Chrysler reinvented itself from the ground up and General Motors designed its new Saturn manufacturing plant around the need for active worker participation in decision-making. And as I write this paragraph, the Big Three are enjoying their greatest comeback in history.

The Rut of Group-Think. Leaders often appear to be outsiders to the areas in which they excel. Samuel Morse, the inventor of the telegraph, was a portrait painter. Robert Fulton, inventor of the steamboat, was a schoolteacher. Galileo was a tailor. Bill Gates, who founded Microsoft, was a college dropout. Golda Meier, Israel's first woman prime minister, was a divorced grandmother from Milwaukee. Before joining Jack Goeken to found MCI, Bill McGowan owned a small company that manufactured testing devices.

What accounts for the success of so many outsiders? That they were never infected with group-think has much to do with it. "Everyone said we were crazy," Bill McGowan observed. "But I didn't come from the telephone industry so I didn't have any preconceived notions. What seemed impossible to them didn't seem strange to me. We looked over the papers in the Federal Communications Commission library and we couldn't find anything that said AT&T had a right to a monopoly in telephone service."

Group-think is powerful in all professions, organizations, industries, and societies. It's the idea that "this is how we do things around here, so fall in step and march to the cadence."

YOU'RE THE CEO

Just as companies must dissolve their boundaries and erase their hierarchies, so must you, the individual, reinvent yourself to meet the knowledge era's changing demands. From the day you read this, I urge you to live by another paradoxical proverb:

You must act self-employed, but be a team player.

What this means is that you're your own chief executive officer. Start thinking of yourself as a service company with a single employee. You're a small company—very small, but that doesn't matter—that puts your services to work for a larger company. Tomorrow you may sell those services to a different organization, but that doesn't mean you're any less loyal to your current employer. Taking responsibility for yourself in this way *does* mean that you never equate your personal long-term interests with your employer's.

The first step is resolving not to suffer the fate of those who lost their jobs and found their skills were obsolete. The second is to begin immediately the process of protecting yourself against that possibility—by becoming proactive instead of reactive. Ask yourself how vulnerable you are and what you can do about it. "What trends must I watch? What information must I gain? What knowledge do I lack?" Again, think of yourself as a company—for this purpose a research and development company—and establish your own strategic planning department. Set up a training department and make sure your top employee is updating his or her skills. Start your own pension plan knowing that *you* are responsible for your own social security. Entrusting the federal government with your retirement is like hiring a compulsive gambler as your accountant.

You're the CEO who must have the vision to set your goals and allocate your resources. Since your primary concern is ensuring your viability in the marketplace, you must think strategically in every decision. This mindset of being responsible for your own future used to be crucial only to the self employed, but it has become essential for us all. For today's typical Americans are no longer one-career people. Most will have five separate careers in their lifetimes.

But although you must become your own life's CEO and always act as if you were a company of one, being a team leader is equally important for your future. We'll examine why in more depth later in the book. Here, it's enough to remember knowledge portability and information accessibility. It's no longer possible to achieve alone in our world of accelerating change, where the new global village has become the local neighborhood. Rather than become dependent on others, however, we should become *interdependent,* treating everyone we meet as a potential customer, someone with whom we may develop a strategic alliance in the future.

WHO'S IN CHARGE?

Although many things in life are beyond anyone's control, you do have a great deal of control—more than most of us are willing to acknowledge—over many circumstances and conditions. Here are a dozen of the most important:

1. You can control what you do with most of your free time during the day and the evening.
2. You can control how much energy you exert and effort you give to each task you undertake.
3. You can control your thoughts and imagination, channel what you think about.
4. You can control your attitude.
5. You can control your tongue; you can choose to remain silent or choose to speak. If you choose to speak, you can choose your words and your tone of voice.
6. You can control who you choose as role models, and who you'll seek out for mentoring counsel and inspiration. You can control who you spend your leisure time with—and, to a great degree, with whom you communicate.
7. You can control your commitments, the things you absolutely promise yourself and others that you'll do.
8. You can control the causes to which you give your time and ideas. This is what I call the purpose behind the purpose.
9. You can control your memberships.
10. Fate is partly the hand you're dealt. You can't control that, but you can control how you play your cards.

11. You can control your concerns and worries—and whether you'll choose to take action about them.

12. You can control your response to difficult times and people.

THE OTHER "LADY IN THE HARBOR"

I've long been a champion of equal rights for all—and of equal responsibilities for all. Rich Meiss, an associate in Minneapolis, and I have formed a nonprofit foundation called The Center for Personal Responsibility. Our initial project is sponsoring an essay contest for primary and secondary school students to describe verbally or in a graphic illustration their ideas for a new monument called "The Statue of Responsibility." As you've guessed, it's meant to complement the Statue of Liberty.

Together with Viktor Frankl, who wrote the classic *Man's Search for Meaning,* I've lectured about the need for such a symbol for years. The idea sounded frivolous to many in the 1970s, 1980s, and early 1990s. But America's current condition has turned the seeming frivolity to somber concern.

Lately, I like to put myself in an imaginary time machine and arrive at the year 2020—with an unsettling premonition:

> Together with my great-grandchildren, I'm aboard a huge hydrofoil tour boat, taking off from San Francisco's Pier 39 for a 45-minute excursion around the new Statue of Responsibility on Alcatraz Island. Looking back at the city skyline, we see the Sumotomo and Hong Kong Bank centers, formerly the Transamerica and Bank of America buildings. Other landmarks have undergone similar transformations. The Mark Hopkins, Sir Francis Drake, Fairmont, Hilton, and Mansion hotels are now called the Peninsula, Shangri La, Mandarin Oriental, Royal Garden, and Miyako hotels.
>
> In 1884, France gave us the Statue of Liberty as a gesture of friendship and a lasting reminder of the precious liberty that we citizens enjoy under a free form of government. In 2020, 136 years later, the Asian Common Market offered us a reminder of the investment in that liberty by giving us the Statue of Responsibility. It seems both ironic and entirely appropriate that this new monument was erected on Alcatraz Island, a rusting reminder of freedom forfeited by irresponsibility. At the base of the statue, I read a

telling inscription: "If you take good things for granted, you must earn them again. For every right you cherish, you have a duty to fulfill. For every hope you entertain, you have a task to perform. For every privilege you would preserve, you must sacrifice a comfort. Freedom will always carry the price of individual responsibility and the just rewards of your own choices."

I hope our generation understands this message so the statue need never be built. If it *is* built, I hope it's because we remembered freedom's obligations before it became too late. The saddest will be if the monument is for reminding us, after our economic colonization, of the forgotten lessons from our immigrant ancestors. Meanwhile, Rich Meiss and I hope our essay contest reaches schoolchildren's minds and hearts.

ACTION REMINDERS

Here are some action steps to help you gain more personal responsibility in your business and personal life:

1. Carry this affirmative motto with you: My rewards in life will reflect my service and contribution.
2. Invest in developing your own knowledge and skills. The only real security in life is inside us.
3. Take fifteen minutes each day for yourself alone. Use them to ponder how you can best spend your time for achieving what's most important to you.
4. Set your *own* standards rather than comparing yourself to others. Successful people know they must compete with themselves, not with others. They run their own races.
5. Learn to depend on yourself. Don't rely on other people, material rewards, or a prestigious job title to give you your self-worth. No one can take away your self-respect when it comes from within.
6. "No excuses, Sir" is a West Point motto. When you make a mistake or fail at an assignment, avoid making excuses or blaming others. If a commitment can't be met, always call immediately with a reason instead of making excuses after the fact.

7. Use another motto for your self-analysis: Life is a do-it-yourself project. When your subordinates or teammates bring you a problem, first ask them what *they* think should be done to resolve it. Be certain to assign responsibility for the solution and follow through to the subordinate or team member. Resist taking the easy way out by doing it for them.

8. Let your teammates, subordinates, and children make mistakes without fear of punishment or rejection. Show them that mistakes are learning devices that become stepping stones to success.

9. Be more curious about your world. Observe nature's wonder and abundance. Read book digests, and consider investing in an optical scanner for copying important ideas directly into your data files. Listen to books on audiocassettes while driving. Subscribe to newsletters. Make sure you are on-line with computer network services. Seek out and gain counsel from the most successful people in your profession.

10. Break your daily and weekly routine. Get out of your comfortable rut. Unplug the TV for a month. Take a different route or different mode of transportation to work. Have lunch with people in totally different industries and read publications in totally different fields than your current one.

11. Take the blame for your position in life honestly and openly—and share the credit for your successes with those who deserve it.

THREE

SELF-LEADERSHIP AND BENCHMARKING: YOUR NAVIGATIONAL SATELLITE

1 ♦ *What do you enjoy doing most?*

2 ♦ *What are your greatest natural talents?*

3 ♦ *What are your most favorable personality traits? Most unfavorable?*

IF YOU DON'T KNOW WHERE YOU'RE GOING, AN OLD SAYING HAS IT, ANY road will take you there. And if you don't know where you *are,* no decision can move you intelligently toward a goal or purpose. Knowing where you stand in your profession and industry is critical to becoming a self-leader in the global era.

INDIVIDUAL BENCHMARKING FOR EXCELLENCE

Benchmarking was originally a surveyor's term referring to a point of reference. Robert C. Camp, a leading advocate of business benchmarking, defines it as "the search for industry's best practices that lead to superior performance. The idea is to use the best to become the best."[1] Benchmarking, in other words, is seeking out the best in your field and putting those examples to work for you.

The Xerox Corporation is said to have popularized the term in the business world, using it to describe a 1980 quality program. Two years later, Xerox teamed with L. L. Bean, the Maine-based retailer, to become the first benchmarking effort to win national attention. Seeking increased productivity in its logistics and distribution unit, Xerox looked to L. L. Bean as a model. The result was a 10 percent increase in warehouse productivity, 3 to 5 percent of which Xerox attributed directly to studying Bean. Who could have foreseen Xerox teaming with a sporting goods retailer—or, to take another example, mighty Motorola benchmarking with Domino's Pizza in an effort to reduce cycle time between order receipt and delivery of its cellular telephones?[2]

Benchmarking's popularity is partly due to a requirement of the Malcolm Baldrige National Quality Award that all entries perform it. But the deeper explanation of its growth is the intense global competition forcing companies to seek out the world's best and adapt it to their own situations. Most leading American corporations practice some form of it—and it can and should be adapted to help *individuals* choose and achieve learning goals. How can we know how good we are without comparing ourselves with others? How do we discover whether we're learning enough and fast enough unless we find the pace-setting learners? Benchmarking counterparts at competitive companies can help establish where we stand and what we should be learning in relation to others in our field. Looking at contemporaries in completely different fields gives a fuller view of who is currently best and who might be so tomorrow—and why!

COFFEE, TEA, OR PROFITS!

These questions know no occupational or geographic boundaries. Every Singapore CEO goes through the flight attendant and service programs of government-owned Singapore Airlines, one of the world's most successful and profitable companies. Enhancement of CEO performance in Singapore—the world's most productive country for over a decade—is no accident. Benchmarking shouldn't be based only on our counterparts in other companies; we can also learn from those "above" and "below" us. It's also no accident that members of the top management staffs of the major hotel chains have been taking training in bell service, valet parking, front desk, housekeeping, and concierge services.

Teresa Eyre, Hewlett-Packard's education manager, is quoted in a book entitled *The Learning Edge* thanking benchmarking for giving her company a new sense of the possible in an organization. "We were interested in understanding more about how the roles of managers, particularly middle managers, were changing in complex organizations," said Eyre. "We had read a lot about the new management roles, but we hadn't seen a lot of change in what our managers actually did at work. So we sent teams of middle managers to talk to their peers in other companies about how their jobs were changing. Because Hewlett-Packard is recognized for its successful management practices, it's tempting to believe that our way of doing things is the right way," Eyre continued. "Yet our success depends on our ability to continue to improve."[3]

Typically, the company sends teams of two to four managers to meet with peers in other companies. After exchanging ideas about leadership and organizational practices, the benchmarking teams exchange comments. "We encourage managers to look for ways to generalize beyond their specific observations, such as what conclusions they can draw about leadership in general," Eyre elaborated. "Then we encourage them to examine their own practices relative to these conclusions. Benchmarking can help managers develop concrete mental pictures of people doing things that may be different from how we do them here."[4]

If you want to become or stay the best, you must know more than what your competitors are up to; you must know the best business practices, wherever they exist. The most reliable way to investigate a competitor's product is to disassemble it. In 1990, Apple Computer found out the hard way that it had been surpassed. After Apple introduced its first portable computer, Compaq Computer came out with a six-pound notebook. "We took it apart and were stunned because we realized we couldn't make anything similar," an Apple executive told *The New York Times.*[5]

Apple introduced its notebook the following year, 1991, after which Compaq's sales stalled and its market share fell. Late in 1991, Eckhard Pfeiffer, IDTK, told *The New York Times* that past success had blinded Compaq. "The company had been so successful over the past nine years that there hadn't been any doubt that the success formula was working. But it masked the changes that were happening. The company failed to recognize the changes necessary to cope with the environment in the 1990s."[6]

TARGETING THE RIGHT LEADER

For individual benchmarking, it's important to choose leaders with the new leadership philosophy. Flip back to the beginning of the book and look at the lists comparing the old and new leadership styles, the old and new corporate cultures, and the new employee paradigm. One major benchmarking flaw is choosing the wrong competitor for comparison—which is what Compaq had been doing with IBM, a company with enormous problems of its own. Compaq had been exclusively benchmarking the wrong competitor, IBM, instead of Apple.

Jack Welch, chairman of the General Electric Company, stresses that the practice is for pinpointing where you sit *now,* not where you wish or hoped you'd be. It's locating where you actually are and where you need to be five years hence, as well as realistically assessing the chances of getting from here to there. This requires a clear picture of your strengths, weaknesses, and desired destination—which, in turn, requires a clear perspective on your life.

MY CIRCUITOUS "STAR TREK"

Back in 1951, when two seventeen-year-old high school graduates named Bill Anders and Denis Waitley boarded a Greyhound bus for a four-day trip from California to Annapolis, Maryland, I doubt that either knew what they really wanted to do in life. What Bill and I did know is that we'd just passed the mental and physical examinations for acceptance as midshipmen at the U.S. Naval Academy, class of 1955. In high school, I'd known Bill as one of the brightest, most positive and ambitious young men I'd ever met—and he was the same at the Academy. Gifted in mathematics, science, and English, he blended his tenacious desire for knowledge with an easygoing style. Throughout the Academy's rigorous academic and physical program, my friend stood high in our class, always adapting easily to the demands.

For me, the navigation and math classes were the most difficult—specifically using complex tables to compute where ships would be at a certain moment, given their speed, the wind, the drift, and the tide. We fixed our position by taking star sights with a sextant. When you're aboard a ship in bad weather in a remote corner of an ocean, it can be very difficult to find your bearings. It can be equally difficult when you're in an airplane trying to return to a carrier after flying 500 miles out while that carrier has been making 30 knots in another direction. But you must know where you are at all times, not just where you're headed.

Bill Anders chose the U.S. Air Force, while I and others became naval aviators after graduating from the Academy. We'd take off from a carrier and fly at high speeds for hours, low over the water in order to avoid radar. To find our way back, we had to use dead reckoning navigation; strict radio silence meant the ship couldn't beam us a homing signal. Our two alternatives, if we couldn't find her, were to eject and ditch or stay with the plane, fly it into the ocean and never be heard from again. Somehow I always made it back, although my every carrier landing was something of a controlled crash.

At the Academy, I had stood near the top of my class in English, foreign languages, and, of all things, after-dinner speaking. I did considerably less well in electrical engineering, navigation, and the various branches of math. I spent so much time debating and writing that several officers grilled me about why I'd chosen the Academy instead of a liberal arts school, where I could have majored in English or journalism. The answer was that I came from a poor family and wanted an education and to serve my country at the same time. (The Korean War was then in full force.) The service academies offered a very positive and prestigious way to accomplish those goals.

On my summer cruise after freshman year, I served aboard the U.S.S. *Missouri* as an assistant to a very assertive midshipman two classes ahead of mine. The crew-cut man was unusually decisive and self-confident. It would have been hard not to be impressed by his powerful leadership qualities. Even though he was only twenty, I knew he was destined for success.

That September, he was appointed brigade commander, which put him in charge of all 3,700 midshipmen at the Academy. That was H. Ross Perot, who would build Electronic Data Systems and become one of the wealthiest entrepreneurs in American history. Bill Anders, my old friend and shipmate, went on to orbit the moon as an Apollo 8 astronaut, then to a series of high leadership positions, including chairman of the board of General Dynamics Corporation, one the nation's largest aerospace firms.

COURSE CORRECTION

After naval aviation, I turned to a completely different career: writing and lecturing about high-performance human behavior. I embarked on this second calling at the age of thirty-eight, which made me a late bloomer compared with Anders and Perot. Had I been better at observing my interests and assessing my talents, I believe I'd have started earlier in my new field. Had I been able to learn about my aptitudes in high school, they would have shown me that I'd have done better majoring in English, foreign languages, or writing and speech.

Struggling through my Annapolis studies, I graduated in the bottom half of my class. All along—even when I was flying a marvel of high-tech equipment worth several million dollars—I relied on my quick reflexes to get me through. I never really learned how my aircraft operated, let alone how to repair it. If the fire warning light had ever come on, I'd have steered away from populated areas and ejected because I wouldn't have been able to figure out what was causing the malfunction. My naval career was a classic example of flying by the seat of one's pants.

I left the navy thanks largely to a wish to discover my potential and a feeling that I wasn't where I should be for that. You can be in a fine profession with a great organization, you can even see a clear career path there—but if you really want to do your best, you must continually reexamine what you need for that, and what you have to offer.

WHAT ARE YOU HONESTLY GOOD AT?

"The world in general is perishing for a lack of those who love us enough to tell us the truth," writes Richard Bolles in *What Color Is Your Parachute?* If you haven't read that excellent book or its successors, I strongly recommend them. Bolles's statement answers the critics who denounce testing and evaluation because they supposedly stereotype and pigeonhole the tested. On the contrary, a good benchmarking test whose interpreter knows its purpose and limits provides the kind of self-knowledge that is liberating, not limiting. A sharp shift away from substantive curriculum in favor of meaningless, self-gratifying subjects has greatly weakened American schools. The strong shift away from tracking children in school contributes to the same educational destruction. Knowledge about people's aptitudes, interests, values, and emotions helps construct their launching pad for self-actualization.

If you love someone, give that person the gift of the truth about himself or herself. If you love yourself, find out the truth about your strengths and weaknesses.

KNOW THYSELF

When I was chairman of psychology for the United States Olympic Committee's Sports Medicine Council during the 1980s, a sign with the famous KNOW THYSELF motto hung at the Olympic Training Center in Colorado Springs. Hopefuls had read or heard this advice since the earliest Olympic days in ancient Greece. We wanted *our* hopefuls to do the same. Self-knowledge has always been the key to preparing for competition. Our Olympic competitors are given physiological and psychological profile assessments to benchmark them against other world-class athletes and help them develop the habits, skills, and regimens for developing a leader's mind-set.

INTERNAL, NOT EXTERNAL CAREER MOTIVATION

Knowledge of your attributes, abilities, interests, strengths, weaknesses, and traits is essential to becoming proactive in career choice and career change. I like to draw a distinction between external and internal criteria in these crucial matters. The overwhelming majority of job-hunters and career-changers react to purely external pressures and circumstances—above all, to money. Their ideas about what careers pay well are likely to be outdated; and even if you choose a career that *is* lucrative but makes you miserable, you may well end up on the short end of the stick.

A cartoon in the delightful *What Color Is Your Parachute?* has two college students walking in New York's Central Park. "Hey, what are you majoring in?" asks the first. "Physics," says the second. "Physics?

Man, you shouldn't major in physics—computer science is the thing these days." "No, I like physics," the second answers. "Man, physics doesn't pay much," the first insists. "Really?" says the second. "Switch to computer science," the first student persists. "Okay," the second agrees. "I'll look into it tomorrow."

Huge life decisions often turn on such scanty information instead of on the homework to identify one's favorite and strongest skills. After money, the second external factor is ignorant advice, much of which is well-meaning but some of which is downright malicious. The third external is family or social pressure: donning the old school tie to follow in Dad's or Mom's footsteps. The fourth is the perception of the job market as gathered by nothing more substantial than recent advertisements. The fifth is leaving it all to luck.

Most people, locked in a strangely passive attitude, simply fall into their jobs, often with terrible results. We all must deal with external pressures and circumstances, but starting with them instead of with the internal factors—our own minds and hearts—is a kind of mad reversal of priorities.

DOING WHAT COMES NATURALLY

Where to begin your personal benchmarking? In my seminars throughout the country, I talk about dusting off your childhood in order to see whether the adult you is headed in the right direction. A series of remarkable studies by British behavioral scientists over a twenty-eight-year period is very relevant here. In the first study, released about twenty-one years ago, a collection of seven-year-old children was interviewed in depth about their likes and dislikes, their outlooks and opinions, their vision of their personal futures. What did they most like doing? What did they want to do as grown-ups? The interviews were filmed and shown on the BBC, the object of this exercise being to track childhood attitudes into adulthood.

That first study was entitled *Seven-Up*. Seven years later, a documentary of new interviews with the same children—now adolescents— was called *14-Up*. This was followed by *21-Up, 28-Up,* and, most recently, *35-Up,* when the subjects were well into what they had done and would be doing with most of their lives.

This extensive study confirmed that what we love and do well as children continues as our latent or manifest talent as adults. Surprisingly—or predictably, for those who work in human motivation—all the subjects eventually engaged in a profession or pursuit related to the interests they had had when they were seven through fourteen years of age. Although most had strayed from those interests during adolescence and early adulthood—in some cases, going in entirely different directions—virtually all found their way back toward their childhood impulses, even if only in their hobbies, by the age of thirty-five.

So an excellent benchmarking exercise is to spend a weekend with the key people in your company and/or the significant people in your family and dust off your childhood memories. Let yourself go. Remember what you really wanted to do as a child.

In my own youth, a recurring fantasy—starting when I was about nine and continuing for many years—put me on the stage of a dazzling New York theater, bowing to an appreciative audience after a performance of some kind. I was wearing a tuxedo. My mother, father, grandparents, and sister and brother were smiling at me from the front row. Not very long ago, I found myself in a tuxedo before an audience in New York's Carnegie Hall. My parents and family weren't in the front row, and instead of performing in the direct sense, I was—I hoped!—educating. But everything else about the setting was nearly identical to my dream. It was almost déjà vu.

Igor Sikorsky developed the helicopter when he was in his middle fifties. Before that, he built the first four-engine airplane and pioneered transoceanic air travel with his American Clippers. Sikorsky is reported to have had a dream as an eleven-year-old: Inside a large flying ship he'd built himself, he was walking along a panel passageway lit by soft blue lights. Some thirty years later, his friend Charles Lindbergh was at the controls of one of his big flying ships. Deciding to take a stretch, Sikorsky, the co-pilot, headed back toward the passenger cabin and found himself walking along a panel passageway inside a big flying ship lit by soft blue lights. His childhood dream flashed back in instant recall.

FROM AVOCATION TO VOCATION

The next step in assessing your interests is considering your current ones. What do you most enjoy after work? What do you most want to do on weekends and vacations? What are your hobbies? Your extracurricular activities? Your favorite kinds of books? Examination of your avocational interests might reveal a gem of potential you can apply to your vocation. I strongly suggest you don't unthinkingly relegate what you love to do for yourself solely to hobbies. You might make it, or at least integrate it into, your life's work.

YOUR INTERESTS MAY NOT BE YOUR TALENTS

Next comes an assessment of your natural gifts. After twenty-five years of observation, I'm still surprised by how few people try to make a connection between what they're good at and what they "do."

CONDUCT AN INTERNAL AUDIT

Imagine that an insurance company is considering a $10-million policy on your life. They ask you to complete a questionnaire—which you do objectively, since you want the insurance.

First identify your character strengths—at least five, if possible. Are you honest? Trustworthy? Do you have good communication skills? Do people enjoy your company? Do you have a natural ability to lead? Are you curious about the world? Eager to lend a helping hand? Do you handle money and possessions responsibly? Are you optimistic and enthusiastic? Do you have a realistic understanding of people's limitations—and of your own? Next identify your physical traits and abilities. Do you have a strong constitution and the capacity to endure hard work? Are you especially well-coordinated? Musical? Good with words? Highly intuitive? Are you mentally quick—alert to details and changes? Exceptionally creative? Do you have strong mechanical and/or mathematical ability? Do you perceive trends easily?

In addition to your own audit, I strongly recommend that you take a natural gifts test and that your team members, associates, and family members do too, regardless of their age.

DON'T SECOND-GUESS YOUR TALENT

Seventy years ago, Johnson O'Connor, a Harvard graduate in philosophy, realized that happy, productive, achieving, pace-setting leaders, professionals, craftsmen, and artists were generally engaged in work for which they had natural ability. This prompted O'Connor to devise a battery of tests for measuring ability—a battery still used by the Johnson O'Connor Research Foundation and, in a slightly modified form, by the Ball Foundation. Landmark studies in the 1980s by Harvard's Dr. Howard Gardner confirmed O'Connor's discovery that intelligence is multiple and varied, not unitary and homogeneous—and that a variety of talents should be tested. Johnson O'Connor and his colleagues identified nineteen of these traits, and no doubt there are more. Each year thousands of my seminar participants make inquiries of the Johnson O'Connor testing centers. Many follow through to take the aptitude tests, whose substantial cost is well worth the investment because they can give excellent leads to individual potential.

The tests are broken down into categories:

Personality determines if a person is objective—best suited for working with others—or subjective and more suited for specialized individual work. Roughly three-quarters of the more than 600,000 clients tested in seventy-odd years have revealed objective personalities.

Graphoria identifies clerical ability and ability to deal with figures and symbols—abilities necessary for performing bookkeeping, editing, and secretarial tasks at high levels of speed and efficiency. Graphoria is usually also a good indicator of how well a person will do in school.

Ideaphoria measures creative imagination and the ability to express ideas, which is needed in fields such as sales, advertising, teaching, public relations, and journalism.

Structural visualization tests the ability to visualize solids and think in three dimensions. This aptitude, often possessed by concrete thinkers who do less well with abstract thinking, is critical for engineers, mechanics, and architects.

Inductive reasoning, which helps form logical conclusions from fragmented facts, is important for lawyers, researchers, diagnostic physicians, writers, and critics—all of whom must be able to move quickly from the particular to the general, perceiving patterns—and the big picture—from a collection of details.

Analytical reasoning is necessary for writers, editors, computer programmers, and others who must organize concepts and ideas into classifications and/or sequences.

Finger dexterity is needed for all forms of manual or mechanical work, including word processing. Also important for creative arts such as sculpting and piano playing.

Tweezers dexterity is the skill in handling small tools with precision, which is vital for professions such as surgery, watchmaking, and assembling microchips. Surprisingly, there is little correlation between this skill and finger dexterity.

Observation, the ability to take careful notice, is tested by showing examinees a photograph of a number of objects, then asking them to identify the slight changes in ten more photos of the same objects. Valuable for artists and painters, keen powers of observation are especially useful for researchers and investigators of all kinds, as in the study of microscopic slides.

Design memory, the ability to remember designs of all kinds, is extremely helpful for everyone who works with plans or blueprints as well as in art.

Tonal memory is the ability to remember and reproduce sounds.

Pitch discrimination differentiates musical tones.

Rhythm memory measures rhythm timing

Timbre discrimination measures the ability to distinguish sounds of the same pitch and volume.

Number memory, the ability to store many things in the mind at the same time, is useful in professions such as the law, medicine, and scholarship—that require summoning quantities of facts and information on which to base judgments, diagnoses, or determinations.

Numerical reasoning, an aptitude for identifying relationships among sets of numbers, is most helpful in bookkeeping, accounting, computer programming, and actuarial work.

Silograms measure the ability to learn unfamiliar words and languages. Vital for translators, this skill is also important for speech teachers, language teachers, and persons doing written translation work.

Foresight is the ability to keep the mind on a distant goal and visualize paths and obstacles. Market research analysts, sales forecasters, political scientists, diplomats, politicians, and corporate leaders are among the many who need foresight.

Color perception, the ability to distinguish colors, is obviously essential for fashion designing, multimedia graphic artists, painting, interior decorating, and advertising—and for all professions and crafts involving art and layout functions.[7]

Most people tested by the Johnson O'Connor and the Ball foundations have three to five strong aptitudes; few have more than seven. My test confirmed that I'm probably in the right profession because my strengths lay in ideaphoria, analytical reasoning, observation, and silograms. I took a lot of math in high school because my father hoped one of the service academies would accept me. Good memory and study habits enabled me to do quite well, but it never came easily or happily—and sure enough, the test showed I was far from a star in structural visualization, finger dexterity, design memory, and other areas related to engineering, mechanics, and mathematics.

While studying economics and anthropology at Stanford, Helen Vogel took the test and found she was a highly structural as well as a subjective personality. Told she would probably succeed in engineering or a similar profession, she ignored the advice and switched her major to English and creative writing. After graduation, she worked in a bookstore and a student loan office—with little satisfaction. Two years later, she returned to school—for engineering. When she'd earned her degree, she went to work predicting, measuring, and reducing noise levels in buildings. She is extremely happy with engineering, and sustains her liberal arts interests by writing short stories, playing the piano, and taking art classes.

Although she had a good position in personnel work, Jane Leader was restless. She took the aptitude tests when she was in her forties, considered the results, and quit her job. The nine hours of testing had revealed she was more objective than 96 percent of all clients ever tested by the foundation. That indicated a natural skill for business management, and Jane's high scores in graphoria, the ability to deal with numbers and details, suggested the same. She opened Nice'n Spicy, a shop specializing in herbs, coffees, spices, teas, and handcrafts. It was a great success and she opened franchises for similar shops in other locations. With a big smile, she says she's really happy in her work for the first time.

Vocabulary Is the New Sword

In some of his earliest tests, Johnson O'Connor found a distinct correlation between vocabulary and career success. O'Connor consultants now stress the continuing importance of vocabulary. "The aptitudes point which direction a person should go," concludes an O'Connor Foundation research paper, "[and] the vocabulary level predicts how far a person will go in his or her chosen career." Another way to say this is that limited vocabulary and feeble ability to communicate keep many people with excellent abilities of other kinds from developing them.

Confirming the much-publicized fall in college entrance test scores of recent years, Foundation records show that the vocabulary skills of eighteen-year-olds declined dramatically between 1955 and 1990. The good news is that vocabulary, far more than any of the basic, natural aptitudes, can be improved with effort and discipline. The O'Connor centers provide several books for those willing to make the commitment. The benefits will be great—and not only in better letters and reports and more interesting conversation. Better vocabulary and word skills will enrich your life in many ways. And the Johnson O'Connor staff reports that the difference between an excellent and a mediocre vocabulary is only 3,500 words.

Although the aptitude tests have been given to children as young as nine, they are probably most effective at age sixteen or seventeen, when high school students are making college or career choices. They are also important to anyone considering a career or industry shift. The earlier you can discover your natural gifts the better—but it's never too late.

Our entire family took the tests, with sometimes startling results. I'd picked one of our daughters to be a veterinarian because of her love for animals. She turned out to be a motivational speaker. The son I saw as a professional athlete is headed for marketing. Another son I was certain would become a researcher is working his way into broadcasting. The daughter I picked for fashion design is a primary school teacher. The daughter I believed would become a businesswoman in Asia is a high school teacher. The daughter I pictured as an actress is a corporate consultant.

I often wish that my older children had been tested much earlier. Aptitude testing revealed that I'd sometimes missed their natural gifts and pegged them wrong—which proves to me that parents and leaders can't do enough to help their team members discover their gifts. Too many parents leave the job to a high school counselor with two hundred or more students to advise. Their counseling is usually based on report cards and casual conversation about career patterns and upward mobility. Then the students go home and often hear a version of the cartoon in *What Color Is Your Parachute?*—something like: "Why don't you go where the money is? The computer field's wide open."

Identifying natural ability is also important for avoiding disappointment, frustration, and anger in career choices. One young son of a surgeon couldn't follow in his famous father's footsteps because he hesitated too much during simple surgical procedures. His father branded this as cowardice. In fact, it was a lack of tweezer dexterity. Structural visualization, another prerequisite for good surgeons, is not passed on from father to son, only from mother to son. Since daughters can inherit structural visualization from both parents, surgeons might better look more to their girls to carry on the family tradition.

It would be irresponsible to suggest that aptitude tests alone should determine career choice. Natural abilities, acquired skills, imitation of role models, youthful experience—all those factors are involved, together, of course, with circumstance. Our major decisions often hinge heavily on family considerations, particularly financial realities, at pivotal ages. Still, it's hard to be rational or wise about developing our lives without taking conscious steps to discover our natural abilities— and as early as possible. Even if we decide to pursue our gifts as hobbies and diversions, that promises less futility than if we ignore them entirely.

Many of our frustrations lie deep within us. We can't explain them even to our loved ones; we can only say, "I don't know why I feel I'm wasting my life, but I do." Exhaustive testing demonstrates again and again that we all have talents. How much more satisfied and fulfilled we feel when we're able to express them creatively and regularly!

To end this appeal on a practical note, I'll mention that the Johnson O'Connor Research Foundation is based in New York City and has offices in many other cities. The Ball Foundation, headquartered near Chicago, has several additional testing centers. And Achievement

Technologies Corporation, one of the best testers of natural ability in the country, is in Denver, Colorado.[8]

MIND AND BODY IN CONCERT

We used biomechanical computer profiling to measure Olympic athletes' physical capabilities, then psychological evaluation to see whether they had the mental toughness—the drive, focus, powers of concentration—to become champions. The ice hockey team that made history by beating the Soviet Union in the 1980 Olympic Games underwent psychological evaluations to help us select young, coachable team players. They were good as individuals. As a team, they became an unbeatable skating machine.

BETTING THE FRANCHISE ON BEHAVIOR

Knowing that scouting reports can miss potential behavior problems that could cause difficulties later, most professional baseball, basketball, and football franchises use behavioral assessments before selecting their draft picks. If professional athletes need behavioral testing, so do business executives and professionals in other fields. I've never had a business problem that wasn't in some way a "people" problem.

Billy Kelley argued the case for testing in "Assessment at the Top," an article in the March 1994 issue of *Human Resource Executive* magazine. Kelley began by quoting Jim Clayton, CEO of Clayton Homes in Knoxville, Tennessee, about hiring someone a year earlier without giving him an assessment test. "To this day Clayton regrets it. 'What we did,' says the self-made millionaire, 'is hire someone who was good at interviewing but not right for the job.' Clayton is hardly the first business person to feel that way and undoubtedly won't be the last. Hiring and promoting executives is a challenging task with no guarantee of success."[9]

Still, many businesspeople are finding ways to increase their chances of hiring or promoting the right person for the right job at the right time. Consultants and industry experts are increasingly turning to behavioral assessments for many reasons. First, the cost—in money and nerves—of hiring or promoting the wrong person is rising relentlessly. And the nature of modern business is equally important. It is changing so fast that the jobs we'll be asking people to perform in just a few years will be quite different from those they're now performing. New managerial and leadership skills are needed to cope with those changes. This is partly why so many major American corporations use some form of testing in their selection process, and why the trend is constantly increasing. With work changing so fast, the premium on *people* grows ever higher.

THE BEST PEOPLE, THE FIRST TIME

Most information on applications for employment is predictably subjective. Résumés present only positive information, some of it exaggerated. Stricter EEOC regulations and the threat of lawsuits for discrimination make it difficult to obtain negative information from an applicant's previous employers. Even former employers willing to comment on an applicant rarely give the real reasons he or she left the old organization. Experienced interviewers can often obtain additional information, but many applicants are more skilled at being interviewed than they'll ever be in the jobs themselves. Behavioral assessment testing is the most objective, economical way of obtaining necessary information for predicting an applicant's probability of success in any position.

The tests provide valuable information about thirty-three characteristics related to success—information unavailable from any other source. Those thirty-three items consist of *interpersonal traits,* which include outgoingness, affiliation, social recognition, exhibition, nurturance, self-sufficiency, suspiciousness, defensiveness, and rebelliousness; *organizational traits* such as conceptual thinking, cognitive structure, order, sturdiness, tough-mindedness, boldness, dominance, assertiveness, and radicalism; *basic personality traits,* including self-confidence, desire for achievement, endurance, conscientiousness, practicality, ability to change, curiosity, aesthetics, abasement; and the *emotional traits* of tension, emotionality, dependence, argumentativeness, impulsiveness, and controllability or the lack of it.

A LEADER'S CRITICAL TRAITS

The Winslow Research Institute in Redwood Shores, California, one of the finest behavioral testing organizations anywhere, has combined its data base from working with Olympic athletes, coaches, and professional teams with another data base on high-performance executives in nearly every field and job description, from technical to sales, from top management to hourly workers.[10] Winslow found that certain core behavioral traits generally define the high achiever and the leader. Prognosis for success is marginal without high scores in:

◆ Self-confidence
◆ Mental-toughness
◆ Conceptual thinking
◆ Ambition to achieve

Candidates who score low or moderately low on any of the above, or whose tests show a high degree of emotionality and/or difficulty of control, may require careful screening and interviewing to predict their probable impact on performance. The most difficult behavioral traits to modify are those related to emotion.

Winslow's very detailed, individually specific reports for position analysis and career development are almost uncannily accurate in predicting performance results. What résumé in the tens of millions of them has ever done that? Many managers decline to use assessment tests based on the misapprehension that they are illegal or invite litigation, but this isn't true. The Labor Department's EEOC and other government agencies have declared that valid and reliable testing contributes substantially to nondiscriminatory selection, placement, and development practices. Testing can also be a strong defense against complaints of, and lawsuits for, discrimination and wrongful dismissal.

Another myth is that applicants can falsify test results by giving answers they believe to be desirable rather than those they know to be true. The fact is that the latest tests use control questions very effectively to detect dishonesty. Experience has shown that from 10 to 30 percent of applicants try to "improve" their answers, usually in hopes of getting the job. When told that their answers are inconsistent, most individuals are honest when they retake the tests and the results are validated.

Much of the information obtained used to be too technical to be useful to the typical manager, but testing programs are becoming user-friendly, even for managers with no background in psychology. Should applicants for all jobs be tested? The general consensus is that only the two or three finalists for a position should be tested, and that current screening procedures should be continued, if effective, for the preliminary selection stages.

In the past, tests were usually limited to applicants for management and sales positions. However, high turnover rates and the rapid increase of hiring costs have prompted many organizations to test for most white-collar and technical positions. In deciding which applicants to test, organizations must consider the importance of the position and the hiring and training costs. Applicants uncomfortable with testing or opposed to it often have high levels of suspiciousness, aggression, or rebelliousness—or a low level of self-confidence. In any case, those possibilities should be explored before hiring. For most organizations, the cost of testing is less than five percent of the applicant's salary for a single month, an insignificant expense in comparison to the cost of hiring and training the wrong person.

Behavioral assessment is also an excellent tool for skill development, and very helpful to those who recognize that they must be life-long learners. In the leading companies I know, behavioral and personality assessments can identify employees' skills and match them with jobs into which they can grow, helping prepare people to assume key positions in the near or even the distant future. The idea is to assess personality and talent, then provide the coaching or mentoring to develop it. But most important is that testing for this purpose spurs the subjects to keep learning.

It's worth noting that personality assessment is not primarily for investigating tastes or styles. The analysis that counts is for helping determine whether *this* person will be successful in *that* job.

FROM PERSONALITY TO EXPERIENCE

With a solid handle on your attitudes and aptitudes, you next should identify educational and training experiences that have given you skills and information pertinent to your goals. Do you have a degree in your field or the field you want to enter? Have you read all the information you can find about how to succeed in that field? Have you completed an apprenticeship? Worked alongside a parent in a similar business? What related skills do you have? Be sure to include areas of self-study, since far from all education is formal.

It helps to list the areas in which you have the most information and skills training. Remember that you don't have to interrupt your career in order to get a degree. Your library may have—or can surely order—reference books entitled *Off-Campus Degrees* and *Non-traditional College Degrees.* Nontraditional should not suggest a diploma mill or a nonaccredited college. There's a big difference between an accredited college and one that is merely "approved by" one or another supposed authority. Avoid all "approved by" degree programs and stick to colleges accredited by the organizations that do the same for the nation's leading universities.

I imagine you'll be very surprised to learn that you can earn a full, four-year degree—even an advanced degree—without setting foot in a classroom. The secret is using your personal computer, audio and videotapes, and correspondence courses—for which your car can become a kind of rolling university, the lectures coming from the tape deck. This route to a college degree—using evenings, weekends, and commuting and/or exercising time—will take longer than four years, but it can be done, and done very well. I think you'll also be surprised by the number and the quality of universities—including the University of the State of New York and other major American institutions, even the Sorbonne in Paris and Great Britain's London University—that offer such off-campus or noncampus degrees.

You'll also want to identify nonscholastic experience that might help meet the challenges of your new goals. Have you worked for many years—even as a volunteer—in the field you're considering? Do you have a hobby in, or related to, the field? Again, making a list of relevant experiences will help you remember them.

A list of potentially helpful people is also a good idea, a list that should extend well beyond your strongest supporters, from whom you can expect the greatest encouragement. It should specify practical ways in which others might help: some who may supply information or advice, others to help secure financing, still others to write letters of introduction and recommendation. One of the most important categories, if you're lucky enough to know such people, is of those who can provide hands-on help or professional assistance. Your larger list should also include your mentors and role models, not only in your company and in your field, but outside them as well—perhaps including your golf or tennis partner and people with whom you exercise. When considering an important move, you can easily make your small talk with these people more meaningful.

Throughout your personal audit, you will want to ask yourself three major questions, of which the first is: *What do I need to know?* I'm continually amazed by how often well-intentioned people make plans without having assembled the needed information. ("When all else fails, read the instructions.") The new computer service programs— America on Line, Internet, CompuServe, and others—make excuses for not having the necessary information sound more and more feeble. Still, be open-minded enough to admit that you may not have all the necessary answers and skeptical enough to accept that what you do know must be field-tested. In approaching a new position, challenge, or business risk, you need solid information in at least five areas.

1. What is the current jargon and what basic concepts does it symbolize? Every activity has its own conversational style and culture. If you work in computers, you know that the jargon changes from month to month. If you're new in the stock market or another investment or financial domain, you'll need to be fluent in its particular set of insider terms.

Learning the local language, especially as used by the most successful, may require vocabulary lessons, which must include a thorough understanding of the underlying concepts and how various concepts relate to one another. Verify your fluency by seeing how easily and appropriately you can use terms in discussions—and how comfortable you feel with them.

2. What is the organizational design? Every enterprise is structured

in its own way—often not in the way it appears on its public organization chart, which is only an approximation. Knowing who's who and
how authority is exercised is vital to survival within any organization,
just as knowledge of the power structure of his or her community is
vital to candidates for political office and knowledge of the appeals
process is essential if you're involved in litigation.

3. What are the most important issues or problems in the field or
confronting a particular enterprise? Every industry, company, and
project faces obstacles or hurdles at every stage. How can they be
crossed, circumvented, or diminished in their impact? For example, in
planning or starting a business venture or introducing a new product
or service, the market must be analyzed and the product's strengths
and weaknesses in that market must be determined—and all factors
that might work against the product must be very carefully considered.

4. How does the information flow? Every enterprise has a distinctive
grapevine in addition to its formal information channels. Find out who
has access to the most current, reliable, and useful information, and
who or what the decision-makers rely on. In other words, locate the
sources used by those most reliably in the know and by those who call
the shots. Read what your role models, mentors, and corporate leaders
read. Keep totally current with trends, data, and new inventions, processes, and theories.

5. What is the protocol for introducing ideas or making changes?
Every enterprise has rules, written or unwritten, for these matters—for
how changes are proposed in an organization, how new members are
accepted into a club, what promotional strategies are appropriate for
introducing new product lines. Explore how the enterprise—or the industry as a whole—works in this sphere.

Needless to say, the quality of your information is all-important, and
not only for when it might be challenged and you would have to explain why you believed it was accurate and/or wise. America is awash
in sound bytes, hype, advertisements of every conceivable kind, and
speculation grounded in biased opinion. These aren't facts—often the
opposite. But your system can't help ingesting them because they per-
meate our atmosphere. To counteract the babble—to acquire genuine,
useful information—you must do more than filter out the communication pollution and the prejudice that, as we saw in Chapter 2, is espe-

cially harmful in the knowledge era. You must try not to rely on hearsay evidence or repeat opinion as fact. Instead, take yourself to libraries, lectures, seminars, and workshops—and review the credentials of the authors and speakers you read and hear. Be open to a variety of opinions and sources, and skeptical enough to check them for accuracy and relevance to your particular needs. Your goal isn't scoring points in political discussions, let alone convincing yourself, but arming yourself with practical knowledge for leaping the hurdles.

Question number two: *Whom do I need to know?* Take a few moments to identify key people from whom you can seek advice about how to reach your life goals. Did you list *successful* persons? I'm also often amazed by how many of us turn to inappropriate people for information and encouragement. A friendly ear isn't enough. Credentials in the form of character and achievement are essential.

For many, role model summons an image of someone for children to look up to. Of course children need good role models—but adults do too. Finding a mentor who represents what you want to do or want to be will give your life and career a huge boost.

The best role model is opposite to a celebrity in the sense that he or she is someone you can get to know personally and closely—preferably someone with a background or career path similar to yours; someone who has been where you are now. This is not to suggest that authors, teachers, and leaders can't also be role models or mentors. A great deal can be learned from people whose ideas are available in print, audio, video and/or computer programs. If you encounter authors or speakers who seem to speak directly to *you,* don't just admire them; really learn from them by studying their work and lives. Still, it's hard for that kind of role model to serve the full purpose, for which you should choose someone with whom you can spend time personally, trading experiences and exploring ideas in direct conversation.

For personal role models and mentors, seek those who have not only achieved external success but whose whole lives, including their personal conduct, merit emulation. Career success can rarely be separated from character; one facet of a person's life invariably affects the other facets. If you are young and relatively inexperienced, your best choices will probably lie among more mature, seasoned entrepreneurs.

When I form a team, I try to put a rookie with a veteran of proven persistence and accomplishment. The combination of youthful desire and rich, seasoned experience can be very powerful. Rookies, who are inclined by nature to be more enthusiastic and excited, often lack patience and sometimes staying power—but they also tend to be more innovative and less set in their ways. As they profit from veteran executives' stores of practical knowledge, the veterans can profit from youthful openness—not yet narrowed by frustration and defeat—to new ideas.

Finally, the third question: *What experience do I need?* Learning about something is a far cry from actually doing it. As we'll see from the discussion of virtual reality in Chapter 6, one of the best ways to prepare for challenge is to practice with the aid of simulation. To simulate is to imitate or assume the character of—something we identify with the training of pilots, astronauts, and athletes. The best simulations require response to stimuli, the more compelling and more demanding of physical reaction the better. American Airlines's simulator in Dallas has the complete cockpit instrumentation of the airline's various aircraft types. Surrounded by and wired to equipment driving audio, visual, and medical technology, American pilots fly the simulator through every kind of weather pattern and emergency situation. They taxi from the ramp, take off, fly to a given city, and land there, seeing all the sights and hearing all the sounds of a real trip—even feeling the pull of gravitational and other forces in their bodies, although they never leave the ground.

YOUR OWN TIME MACHINE

Projecting yourself into a desired future is another valuable simulation. I often ask my seminar participants to visualize an ideal day for themselves five years hence. Where will they be living and how will their day begin? How are they traveling, where are they going, what kind of work are they doing—in what position and with what income? Who are their friends? What moments of the day give them most satisfaction; what do they do purely for fun?

Let your imagination go; let it take you to the question of what you really want from your life. More love? Greater wealth? To be thinner, more attractive, healthier? To break into an entirely new field? To make a significant contribution to society?

With this in mind, ask yourself whether what you're doing now is what you feel you should be doing. Certainly it's providing you with an income, but is it advancing you toward where you want to be? If you haven't determined that, you should be exploring—not vaguely, but on a daily basis, using some of the measurements we've suggested here. Even if you're reasonably satisfied, asking such questions can increase your self-awareness. And if you do know what you really want to do— and it involves changes—ask whether you are *acting* to make your dream a reality.

BECOME AN INVESTIGATIVE INTELLIGENCE AGENT

Observational skills are critical for personal benchmarking. Most of us have read a newspaper account of an event that we witnessed first hand. I'll venture that the written report probably didn't convey the essence of the event as you saw it—which is my point. For the important decisions, second-hand information will always be second best. No one can do your observing as well as you.

I've tried to suggest why it's essential to draw your own conclusions on the basis of the best information available. To this it must be added that only you can gather much of that best information because no one knows your instincts better. That means becoming an active observer instead of passively taking in—or ignoring—your surroundings. If a flight is delayed, you can of course find a seat in the airport waiting area and dig into your briefcase for paperwork. But this is also an excellent time for observing the behavior of other passengers, eavesdropping on conversations—even striking up some yourself. Scanning the newsstands and bookstores will tell you something about what's available, not just the content of that day's articles. What are other people concerned about? What do their values seem to be? Rather than relying on journalists' interpretations, this gets you started on your own mental files about what people are really thinking and feeling. It takes initiative—especially questioning perfect strangers—but not an unreasonable amount of it.

Robert Hazard, CEO of Choice Hotels International, interviews almost everyone he can—and not for his health. Seated next to a stranger in a waiting room or on an airplane, Hazard likes to break the ice by asking what the stranger is planning for his or her next vacation. "People start talking about their travel patterns and I get an outsider's view of my own industry," Hazard says. "That kind of information is invaluable." On a business trip to Phoenix, he asked his barber there the same question—and was awarded with an earful. The barber said that in small towns, he stayed in moderately priced motels, refusing to pay more than $25 a night. But he always stayed in style when he hit the big cities like Las Vegas or San Francisco. Price wasn't a consideration in the big cities. Hazard's leading questions give him key information not always revealed by formal marketing research.[11]

THE NEWS BEHIND THE HEADLINES

John Naisbitt, the author of the *Megatrends* books and *Global Paradox,* benchmarks trends with a method known as content analysis.[12] Content analysis is patterned after World War II intelligence-gathering methods—specifically, the discovery that newspapers smuggled from small German towns had strategic value. Those papers' occasional reports of spot shortages of food or fuel sometimes revealed a more general situation behind the enemy lines.

Content analysis, in short, is based on a recognition that since much change begins at the grass roots, local and regional concerns can provide excellent clues for identifying social priorities and inclinations. Naisbitt Group researchers now scan three hundred daily newspapers, clipping articles about local concerns. Together with the texts themselves, the number of column inches devoted to various issues helps predict basic trends.

For its business intelligence program, a research and consulting organization named SRI International examines publications throughout the world rather than domestic periodicals alone. SRI scientists, engineers, and management consultants in California, Washington, D.C., London, Tokyo, Singapore, and elsewhere volunteer to monitor publications in their respective fields for patterns of change. They report their observations to program coordinators at SRI headquarters in Menlo Park, California, where incoming data is reviewed monthly.

You can do your own content analysis of your mail and the publications you read or review. What are the changes from the previous year—in your local newspaper's listing of job opportunities, for example? What about the junk mail and advertisements? Brief scanning before you discard them can provide valuable clues to developing trends. When you're on the road, local newspapers are a rough guide to regional attitudes and the regional economy. And some taxi drivers are very knowledgeable about community affairs and community trends. Talk to them seriously. Their last passenger may have been a competitor's CEO!

Florence Skelly—formerly of Yankelovich, Skelly and White, now president of Telematics, Inc.—strongly suggests keeping an eye on the popular culture for spotting trends. "Make an analysis. Look at magazines, watch television, go to the movies, watch MTV—but you don't have to do this as a habit, just dip in and out of them. What themes run through current movies, books, magazines, videos? What values are portrayed? That's the trend."[13]

If you can decipher the lyrics, you may find popular music instructive. What are the trend-setters singing about now? Loneliness? Despair or the need for affiliation? Whether love is worth the candle? If you can suspend your own value judgments and listen carefully, you may learn a lot.

Regis McKenna, the Silicon Valley marketing consultant, reads between fifty and one hundred magazines a week, in addition to assorted newspapers. He clips articles and creates files for information he wants to retain.[14] (It's much easier to buy a hand-held optical scanner and scan articles directly into your laptop, which can be done while you're on airplanes or during other "down" time.) Listening to audiotapes in your car is an increasingly popular way of benchmarking individuals and trends. Recorded publications such as the *Hines Report,* a monthly audio service, provide brief updates on business and other happenings in the financial community. Soundview Executive Book Summaries in Bristol, Vermont, offers summaries of almost every major business book published for a quick, easy listen or read. Research subjects are also written up and taped in brief, fast-moving reports. Another service called News Track scans seventy business periodicals, from *Industry Week* to *The Warden Magazine,* and summarizes selected articles for its subscribers.

A good way to broaden your benchmarking intake is to consult *TV Guide,* especially the cable version, then program your VCR to tape educational programs when you're not home or not in a concentrating mood. (Some cable channels, such as the Discovery Channel, Lifetime, and the Family Channel, offer a treasury of information about medical developments and other innovations, as well as about more generally enlightening subjects.) Taping allows you to fast forward through commercials and get straight to the substance. More importantly, it lets you pick your own time for watching: early Saturday morning or Sunday evening for me, but you're your own scheduler as well as the student for this rarely unpleasant form of self-improvement.

Here are some characteristics of creative individuals. The overwhelming majority are:

* optimistic about the future;
* highly curious and observant;
* adventurous with multiple interests;
* able to project their daydreams into the future;
* independent thinkers who use their whole brains (which translates innovative ideas into practical solutions);
* constructively discontent with the status quo;
* open to alternatives;
* able to recognize and break bad habits;
* unwilling to fall in love with a *new* invention or idea, since they accept that ideas are expendable and someone's bound to come up with an even better one.

How many describe you? Challenge yourself to engage *your* positive qualities by putting them to practical use. And here are a few more action steps related to personal benchmarking:

1. Continue your education regardless of your age. On average, adults do 10 percent better in college than younger students—and use of computer discs, video- and audiotapes, and other modern methods means you may never have to be on a campus.
2. Keep a dictionary beside you when you read and look up every word you don't fully understand. Doing that on the spot helps make the word part of your vocabulary forever. And don't depend on your computer's spellchecker for your spelling.
3. Get a good vocabulary primer. An excellent one now offered on audiotape as well as in book form by the Achievement Technologies Corporation has graded degrees of difficulty so you can gradually move up from, say, the achiever to the top achiever

category.[15] Remember, a mere 3,500 words separate the average person from those with superior vocabularies.

4. Consider taking a reputable aptitude test. Check to see if the companies we mention in the back of the book have an office near you. Also check your public or university library.

5. Have lunch once a week with someone at your career level or higher in another company, perhaps in an entirely different industry. If you've never met this person, explain by letter, fax or phone that you want a brief meeting, when convenient, to exchange ideas.

6. Model yourself after people you most admire and respect—not necessarily those you'd most like to be, but those from whom you can learn the most. Think about what you'd want to be if you could start your life again—and about whether you're *now* making the best use of yourself. What practical action—real steps, today and tomorrow—can you take toward fuller expression of your talents?

FOUR

❖

Self-Leadership and Integrity: Your Absolute Bottom Line

———————— ❖ ————————

1 ❖ *If everyone in your organization had your integrity, what kind of organization would it be?*

2 ❖ *Can you think of any situation that calls for dishonesty?*

3 ❖ *What do you think about expecting leaders to be honest in their personal lives, as well as in their professional positions? Is there a difference?*

———————— ❖ ————————

A SIMPLE MOTTO HUNG ON THE LIVING ROOM WALL OF MY GRANDPAR-ents' small frame house, where many seeds for my development were planted. My grandmother and grandfather didn't talk about the lines; they lived them.

> *Life is like a field of newly fallen snow;*
> *where I choose to walk, every step will show.*

They believed you were either honest or you weren't. There was nothing in between, no such thing as partial honesty.

THE LEADER'S STANDARD

Integrity, a standard of personal morality and ethics, is not relative to the situation you happen to find yourself in and doesn't sell out to expediency. Its short supply is getting even shorter—but without it, leadership is a facade.

People unconcerned with self-respect and able to see little value in themselves will not guide their lives with such an internal compass. Unfortunately, their own inner value system is thoroughly mixed up, even inverted. I find real confusion about self-respect among the younger generation, whose comments seem to indicate that they take braggarts, clowns, and celebrities as role models—people who *appear* successful, but are often submerged in show. "Can you believe he/she actually spoke to me?" I often hear students saying about stars. That's not entirely their fault: Our society puts a huge premium on celebrity for celebrity's sake.

SKIN-DEEP VALUES

Learning to see through exteriors is a critical development in the transition from adolescence to adulthood. Sadly, most people continue to be taken in by big talk and media popularity, flashy or bizarre looks, and expensive possessions. They move through most of their years convinced that the externals are what count, and are thus doomed to live shallow lives. Men and women who rely on their looks or status to feel good about themselves inevitably do everything they can to enhance the impression they make—and do correspondingly little to develop their inner value and personal growth. The paradox is that the people who try hardest to impress are often the least impressive. Devotion to image is often for the money it can reap. Puffing to appear powerful is an attempt to hide insecurity. If only we could see many of our celebrities when their guard and pretenses were down!

An essay in *Time* magazine tackled one of our culture's great problems: the tabloid celebration of the famous and the infamous.

> Any moral crusade will run smack into the messages conveyed by America's celebrity-obsessed national culture. A few moments in the limelight can mean big bucks: a book contract, a speaking tour, a TV docudrama. All Fawn Hall had to do was reveal that she helped Colonel Oliver North destroy documents related to the Iran Contra Affair and suddenly actress Farrah Fawcett was on the phone with plans to make Hall the heroine of a feature film. Ethical distinctions are quickly lost as talk show appearances and gala opening night parties become schools for scandal.[1]

The myth that all that counts is bottom-line success often leads to fleeting stardom and ultimate defeat. Ask a thousand has-beens.

THE WAX EMPIRE

In the Roman Empire's final corrupt years, status was conveyed by the number of carved statues of the gods displayed in people's courtyards. As in every business, the Roman statue industry had good and bad sculptors and merchants. As the empire became ever more greedy and narcissistic, the bad got away with as much as they could. Sculptors became so adept at using wax to hide cracks and chips in marble that most people couldn't discern the difference in quality. Statues began to weep or melt under the scrutiny of sunlight or heat in foyers.

For statues of authentic fine quality, carved by reputable artists, people had to go to the artisan marketplace in the Roman Quad and look for booths with signs declaring *sine cera* (WITHOUT WAX). We too look for the real thing in friends, products, and services. In people, we value sincerity—from *sine cera*—more than almost any other virtue. We expect it from our leaders. We must demand it of ourselves.

Integrity that strengthens an inner value system is the real human bottom line. Commitment to a life of integrity in every situation demonstrates that your word is more valuable than a surety bond. It means you don't base your decisions on being politically correct. You do what's right, not what's fashionable. You know that truth is absolute, not a device for manipulating others. And you win in the long run, when the stakes are highest.

> *You must consider the bottom line, but make it integrity*
> *before profit.*

The synonyms for integrity are honesty, trustworthiness, honor, and moral fiber. Implanting this in your consciousness and conscience will put you so far ahead of the rest in the long run that you'll wonder why everyone doesn't do the same. And it's not just in the major decisions that this quality is needed. Complete integrity in little things is no little thing at all.

ELEPHANTS DON'T BITE, BUT FLEAS DO

As has been said many times, "The devil is in the details" and "Elephants don't bite, but fleas do." There are no degrees of integrity. You have it or you don't, just as you're pregnant or you're not. I've long wondered why so many people turn to crime when there are so many *legal* ways to be dishonest. You can usually get away with shading a few points here and there. The IRS won't catch you every time. Cheating on your spouse may be a "safe" adventure for a time. But one day, little details will be noticed and the piper will have to be paid.

YOUR INVESTMENT PORTFOLIO

The dictionary defines integrity in terms of soundness of moral character, adherence to ethical principles, and being unimpaired. Its middle English root is related to *integrate*—to bring together into a whole—and *integral,* complete, whole. Another relative is the mathematical *integer,* a whole number, not a fraction. These references to wholeness rightly suggest that integrity affects all aspects of our lives, which is why I like to refer to it as a healthy investment portfolio filled with blue chip stocks such as honesty, fairness, loyalty, courtesy, cooperation, compassion, generosity, and kindness.

WHEN IN ROME . . .

Today, however, it's hard to avoid the *antithesis* of integrity. Members of Congress bounce checks and use taxpayers' funds for personal use. An FBI agent—the first in history—is arrested for spying. A trusted officer of the CIA is convicted of the same, his greed having fingered for execution roughly a dozen of the CIA's most valuable Moscow moles. Prominent Wall Street investment bankers are convicted of illegal insider trading involving billions of dollars. Savings and loan executives are imprisoned (but many also escaped their just punishment) for defrauding tens of thousands of trusting customers. Welfare, insurance, and health fraud costs billions of dollars. Academic cheating infects even the service academies. The college loan default rate continues to escalate. . . .

Stir these together, add the disingenuous public denials of the politically high and mighty, and you get a hint of the scope of our national malaise. The media is hardly immune. The respected news division of one of the major television networks admits to rigging a truck to explode on impact in a supposed exposé of the truck's defects. (The truck may indeed have been unsafe, but the news division, in effect, lied in order to prove it.) A leading newsmagazine publishes a blatantly misleading photograph of the president on its cover and fails to reveal it has nothing whatever to do with the cover story. A leading newspaper manipulates a front-page photo and the accompanying story—which is even more despicable because it inflames racial animosities even further.

INTEGRITY BEGINS AT HOME

What can we do to increase the dwindling integrity in our society today? Like charity, integrity begins at home. One of the greatest gifts you can give your children is a strong sense of ethical and moral values. Let them accept responsibility for their own actions as early as possible. The more sense of responsibility they develop, the better they will feel about themselves.

Above all, for integrity's sake, teach them graciousness and gratitude and how to care about the rights and welfare of others. Teach your children (and business associates who look to you for leadership) that their true rewards in life will depend on the quality and amount of service they render. Show them, by example, how to treat others as they would have others treat them.

If I were writing a single commandment for leadership it would be: "You shall conduct yourself in such a manner as to set an example worthy of imitation by your children and subordinates." In simpler terms, if they shouldn't be doing it, neither should you.

When I told my kids to clean their rooms, for example, they took a closer look at the condition of my tools and possessions in the garage. When I told them that honesty was our family's greatest virtue, they commented on the radar detector I had installed in my car. When I told them about the vices of drinking and wild parties, they watched from the upstairs balcony the way our guests behaved at our adult functions.

Integrity is easier preached than practiced. We go along for a while setting a good example, but sometimes we tell ourselves we need a break. The trouble is, our children and subordinates get confused. First they think we are being ourselves by modeling healthy behavior. When they see the unhealthy behavior coming from their leaders, they are puzzled and hurt at first, but then they catch on. They learn to play the game of "say one thing, do another." The old cliché holds true: What you are speaks so loudly no one can really hear what you say. But it is even more true that if what you are matches what you say, your life will speak forcefully indeed.

It's hardly a secret that learning ethical standards begins at home. A child's first inklings of a sense of right and wrong come from almost imperceptible signals received long before he or she reaches the age of rational thought about morality. Maybe you're asking yourself what kind of model you are for future generations, remembering that people are either honest or dishonest, that integrity is all or nothing, and that children can't be fooled in such basic matters. They learn by example.

THE INTEGRITY TRIAD

One of the principles of integrity is to defend your convictions in the face of great social pressure. Consider this true story about an abdominal surgery performed in a large, well-known hospital. It was the surgical nurse's first day on the medical team. Responsible for ensuring that all instruments and materials were accounted for before completing the operation and sewing up the incision, she told the surgeon that he had removed only eleven sponges. "We used twelve and we need to find the last one," she reported. "No, I removed them all," the doctor declared emphatically. "We'll close the incision now." "No," the rookie nurse objected, "we used twelve sponges." "I'll take the responsibility," the surgeon said grimly. "Suture, please." "You can't do that, sir," blazed the nurse. "Think of the patient!" The surgeon lifted his foot, revealing where he had hidden the twelfth sponge. "You'll do just fine in this or any other hospital," he said, smiling.

Don't back down when you know you're right.

A second key integrity principle is always to give others the credit that's rightfully theirs, never fearing anyone who has a better idea or is smarter than you. David Ogilvy, founder of Ogilvy and Mather, made this point to newly appointed office heads by sending them a *matrioshka,* the painted Russian doll with five progressively smaller dolls nestled inside. His message to his new executives was in the smallest doll: "If we hire people who are smaller than we are, we'll become a company of dwarves. But if each of us hires people bigger than we are, we'll become a company of giants." And that is precisely what Ogilvy and Mather became, one of the world's largest and most respected advertising firms.

Our third integrity principle is to be honest and open about who you really are. Be yourself. Don't exaggerate your achievements. Don't get trapped in a cover-up of past mistakes, even of personal traits that dissatisfy or displease you. When the going is tough, be tough by facing reality with adult responses. Use the good and the bad as material for personal growth.

We must teach our children and our subordinates self-respect and the supreme value of a clean conscience as early as possible. They are powerful components of integrity.

LESSONS IN LEADERSHIP

I love discussing integrity with high school students. I throw a wallet into the center of the room where we—members of a small seminar—are sitting in a circle. The wallet contains a driver's license, credit cards, photos, and eight $100 bills. I ask the students one by one what they would do if they found the wallet on a deserted street. The answers are uncomfortably revealing. "Wow, that would be awesome!" goes the most typical. "I'd keep the money as my reward and mail back the wallet with the credit cards." Other students invariably suggest not putting a return address on the envelope so the owner couldn't call and ask if there was money in the wallet when it was found. I usually ask how the $800 windfall would be explained to parents and friends. And if word got around—and ultimately back to the owner—would they say, "Losers weepers, finders keepers"?

SITUATIONAL INTEGRITY: A NEW OXYMORON

Then I place the wallet in special situational contexts. What if the driver's license showed that the wallet belonged to your best friend? Or to your mother? What if you recognized the driver's license photograph as that of an elderly neighbor who lived on Social Security and who probably dropped the wallet on her way to the hospital for kidney dialysis, which she needed every week? Most students somberly agree that in those specific situations, it would be best to return the money, too. (One once ventured a slight exception if the wallet belonged to his mother: She'd understand, he assured us, if a few hundred dollars were missing.)

Finally, I ask an even more sensitive—and defining—question: "What if you were at an airport ready to fly off on a student summer tour of Hawaii and Australia. You use the rest room and leave your wallet—containing eight $100 bills—on the sink when you wash your hands. Realizing what you're missing as you board the plane, you run back, explain your emergency to the gate agent and race to the rest room, heart pounding. If you were in that situation, what would you hope?"

"That the wallet's on the sink where I left it," most call out in unison. "And what do you hope is in the wallet?" I continue. "Eight $100 bills and my credit cards and my driver's license," they chorus. "And if a good samaritan like you has picked up your wallet, what do you hope he or she does?" Turns it into lost and found or airport security or a gate agent, they say—with all the money intact. From there, we return to the wallet found on the deserted street. Now the students, many with wisdom-widened eyes, are clear about treating it as they'd want others to behave if the wallet belonged to them. The point has been made: Honesty and integrity are nonsituational—and inner standards for your performance and behavior are the foundation of true self-respect.

NONSITUATIONAL INTEGRITY OR NO INTEGRITY

Specific situations require different management approaches and styles—but how do you feel about the term *situational integrity*? We've seen that if integrity applies only in specific situations, it's not integrity at all but expediency. Do you believe in absolutes or does everything derive from your point of view, your (temporary) advantage? To answer that question with another question, you might ask what your family or your company—or our world—would be like if everyone had your ethics. The choice is yours. We'd either be in terrific or terrible shape. Of course people do cheat to get ahead; you know that. But when you maintain your integrity at all costs, even if you feel you might suffer in the short term, you'll win hands down in the end.

Most importantly, you'll be an inner winner, with victories no one can ever take from you. Is stealing paper clips, note pads, and rubber bands from your office anything to worry about? A person of integrity is not tempted down that slippery slope that can lead to more serious situations, even embezzlement. Is integrity a primary consideration in a practical, profit-making organization? Not to have it courts the risk of sophisticated surveillance equipment, disgruntled employees, and IRS tipsters. Ethics deprivation can lead to inner rot. The company building may be located in a high-rent district. It may be made of the finest steel, chrome, and glass—but it will decay from the inside.

Can you think of a successful relationship without integrity? I doubt it. All are based on mutual trust. Break that trust and you break the relationship. Subvert it and it's almost impossible to put together again. Creating a long-term relationship takes two or more people— whether executives, representatives of labor and management, or husband and wife—who are grounded in and operating on the same nonsituational integrity. Nothing less will last.

When *Fortune* magazine asked the CEOs of many Fortune 500 companies what they considered the most important qualities for hiring and promoting top executives, the unanimous consensus was that integrity and trustworthiness were by far the key qualities. That survey of leading businessmen—not of preachers or motivational speakers— speaks for itself.

Here are some tips to help you further embrace integrity in your personal, business, and family life:

1. Justice and fair play are integrity's core values. Go out of your way to be helpful and make others Number One in your life. A smile will almost always be returned with a smile—and you're none the worse for the wear even if it's not.

2. Set high standards of ethics for yourself and expect others to do the same. Your single most powerful teaching tool is not talking about what's right but quietly doing it. A businessperson or a parent who lectures about obeying the rules but constantly breaks them is making an especially powerful negative statement. The old "Do as I say, not as I do" is severely damaging to children and subordinates.

3. Give of your best in the worst of times. Personal integrity knows no season and doesn't hinge on the weather, the stock market report, or the leading economic indicators. You have it or you don't.

4. As my friend Dr. Ted Engstrom advises in his book *Integrity,*

chart your course by the north star of conscience by doing unto others as you would have them do unto you. Most of the world's religions have long urged the same. "Do not to others what you would not want done to you" is a pillar of ancient Chinese philosophy. Charting your course by the north star means you are stable, constant, resolute. You base your decisions on principle, on your immovable belief system.

5. Respect diversity in culture and heritage. The world's rapid transportation, interactive media, virtual reality, and global communications network means we must learn to live in harmony with other human beings. The dictionary tells us that integrity is wholeness, which implies mutual acceptance. Don't make the futile attempt of trying to be an island. Welcome the foreigner. Work hard at understanding other cultures, languages, and points of view.

6. Read articles and books about integrity and make your car a university on wheels by listening to tapes of self-improvement and business programs. Be willing to be stretched in your thinking. What would you do if you found a wallet with a good deal of money in it? Adults are often confronted by much more serious problems. Ask yourself if you have the solid, bedrock values to get you through any situation without compromise.

Your children and subordinates will do what they see you do. Your job as a leader is enormous, but so are the rewards. A life of principle—of not succumbing to the temptations of easy morality—will always win in the end, leading you to the real wealth of the present and the 21st century.

FIVE

SELF-LEADERSHIP AND CORE VALUES: YOUR DIAMOND MINE

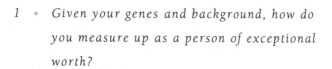

1 ◆ *Given your genes and background, how do you measure up as a person of exceptional worth?*

2 ◆ *How do you measure your own performance?*

3 ◆ *How much success do you deserve?*

Let's take a moment for review. You understand the need to rule change. You've committed yourself to taking personal responsibility for your goals and choices. You see the benefits of being totally honest with yourself and others. Now on to another important step—which will depend on your answers to three questions. First, how much are you worth? Second, what empire do you want to build? And third, do you truly believe you can achieve to your highest potential?

How much are you worth? The typical answers to this question reflect ignorance, confusion, and embarrassment. "Ask my accountant." "Ask my stockbroker." "Maybe $100,000, maybe a few times that." "I don't know, I haven't seen *The Wall Street Journal* today." "How's the economy doing?" "None of your business."

But the essential point is that real worth has little to do with salary, possessions, or position. Without self-esteem, your answer to the question will have to be "Not much" or "Next to nothing." This is why a plethora of self-help books, tapes, and films have recently flooded the market, especially in America.

Self-esteem is among the most overpromoted, misunderstood terms of our day.

SELF-ESTEEM PERSPECTIVE

Self-esteem was coined by a psychologist named William James over a century ago. Convinced it could come only in comparison with others, James described it as feelings of worthiness enjoyed when people concluded they were better than their neighbors or fellows. If someone near you was more talented in something, your self-esteem had to be lower. Today we understand that comparison invites totally inappropriate worry and fear.

Self-esteem was little discussed before the 1960s. Psychology books offered scant information about it except for several observations by Sigmund Freud and Alfred Adler. Freud wrote about "self-regard" and noted that a low measure of it resulted in a helpless feeling of "I can't do anything." Adler suggested that every child started life feeling less worthy than everyone older, including older siblings as well as adults.

Dr. Nathaniel Branden, a friend and colleague, was among the first to do serious research on self-esteem. His *The Power of Self-Esteem,* published in 1969, and later books including *The Six Pillars of Self-Esteem* prompted much more attention to the importance of self-esteem and its effect on our performance. Throughout the 1980s, many more books appeared on the subject, which became hot for popular discussion as well as for scientific studies. One of those books was the 1981 *The Antecedents of Self-Esteem,* in which the author, Stanley Coopersmith, described self-esteem as "a personal judgment of worthiness that is expressed in the attitudes the individual holds towards himself or herself." It was becoming clearer to psychologists that each person must develop his or her idea of what makes them feel worthy.

By the late 1980s, self-esteem was a favorite subject of talk shows, magazine articles, and supposedly sophisticated conversation. It was common to hear statements such as, "My self-esteem was crushed." Or, "How could you let him treat you like that? Where's your self-esteem?" In 1990, the state of California formed a task force to study self-esteem, the first instance, as far as I know, of a government agency making a public issue of that seemingly personal matter. The final report defined self-esteem as "appreciating my own worth and importance and having the character to be accountable for myself and to act responsibly towards others." People with high self-esteem, it stated significantly, tend to be less involved in negative behavior such as drug and alcohol abuse, crime, child abuse, and educational failure.

I am a founding member of the National Council for Self-Esteem, which has also studied the impact of self-esteem on performance in school, the workplace, and personal life. A 1992 Gallup Poll interviewed 612 adults about their feelings about self-esteem. Eighty-nine percent considered it "very important" for motivating hard work and success. Altogether, more than a thousand scientific studies of self-esteem have been conducted, and researchers have tried to measure it with two hundred varieties of tests, many of which ask people to agree or disagree with statements such as: "I am happy with myself." No one is certain that the feeling can be measured, but nearly everyone agrees on its importance.

THE WEEDS OF LOW SELF-ESTEEM

Many people with low self-esteem are evidently trying to avoid or escape from pain. They see themselves as unworthy of success; they believe their lives will always be unhappy. They feed the ranks of those who turn to drugs, alcohol, or crime to escape their negative feelings—responses, of course, that only aggravate the problems.

My own belief is that we're all born with as much potential as we'll ever have, but that early years can squeeze out feelings of self-worth and self-esteem like an electric juicer. Most psychologists say it starts in infancy, when parents are or are not able to respond appropriately to a baby's needs and reflect back to the baby that they see, respond to, and accept the baby as he or she really is. Tiny infants can be made to feel that their demands are excessive, burdensome, not worthy of full attention, and can respond by asking for and, worse, expecting less. Comparison is only part of the equation and this begins as soon as they're old enough to hear parents, peers, and teachers compare them with others. Once started, the erosion of self-esteem often picks up speed in high school. In training videos I produce in various high schools, some students slump in their chairs, staring at their hands. Others reveal how little they think of themselves (as well as their fellow students) by interrupting with "cute" remarks or boisterous chatter. The attempts to hide a fragile self-image are most obvious among those who affect the cool look or who display disdain.

DESPERATE TO BELONG

I remember my own youth, how desperate we were to belong to the "in" group. Sometimes I went to extremes, clowning around in efforts to impress the most popular girls and boys. I felt wonderful when I was accepted, distraught when I was ignored or rejected. With the greater emphasis today on material and physical appearances, young people seem even more driven to vie for their peers' attention and recognition, as if buying or crashing their way into the winner's circle were *the* key to the good life. However, there's a critical difference between having to prove yourself—wanting to be the best to make up for inadequate self-esteem—and seeking to manifest inner worth and value, being your best for the pure exhilaration of excellence. We all struggle with these two forms of expression, myself included. One reason I've spent much of my adult life studying human behavior is that I want answers to the questions for myself, especially the difference between winners and losers—about which I had cause to wonder early in my own youth.

BODY LANGUAGE

An easy way to gauge feeling about yourself is to check how you treat your body. Where does it fit in your lifestyle? I used to look at my own body much like a second car, an older clunker needed only for transportation. For fuel I used bean burritos, french fries, and sugar-laced colas, a variety of items that clogged and corroded. I never considered switching to the premium stuff. Why bother when the point was only to keep going with the fewest possible overhauls?

The change came after I'd been on the lecture circuit every day for several years, and returned from one trip utterly exhausted. This so-called specialist in high self-esteem and winning behavior had allowed his physical self to sag very sadly. Going through the mail during a short break before my next tour, I saw a flyer advertising a healthy human behavior seminar. It would be held in a nearby community, only thirty minutes away. Something told me to learn a thing or two about the old carcass before going back on the road.

I did learn, especially about the evils of junk food and the need for exercise. After a final, rousing lecture on those themes, the facilitator closed the session with instructions for taking a self-awareness test in the privacy of our own homes.

MIRROR, MIRROR

The next evening, while my wife Susan and our children were working on our new computer, I slipped away to the bedroom and turned the lock. Following the instructor's orders, I cut two eye holes in a large paper bag. Then I closed the drapes, stripped bare, and slipped the bag over my head. Adorned only in that "outfit," I stepped to our full-length mirror to begin my self-awareness test, which was essentially monitoring one's response to the spectacle in the glass.

Who was the naked stranger there—a chubby prowler turned exhibitionist? Why did he make me want to laugh and cry at the same time? The person I'd long known, understood, excused, and occasionally adored was gone. As instructed, I touched and pinched, but the muttering was my own idea. The bag indeed helped me see objectively, and what I saw most clearly was flab, bulges, and sags—very depressing creases that needed pressing. "Isn't it amazing how certain angles can make you look so wide!" I reflected.

Shaken, but determined to complete the test, I followed the instructions for those who, as the seminar facilitator had put it, believed their self-esteem was very high. That is to say, I turned around and looked over my shoulder for a rear view. That was too much. "I don't know who you are," I said aloud, "but I wish you'd get dressed and leave."

A MOMENT OF TRUTH

Just then, a familiar shape appeared in a corner of the mirror. So I hadn't locked the door after all! Susan, my wife, had apparently tiptoed in. In any case, she was there now, observing the creature with a bag over its head, touching, pinching, and muttering. Susan, a practical person, thought first of long-range implications. "It's finally happened, hasn't it, Denis?" she said quietly. "You've been on too many airplanes and changed time zones too many times. Have you thought about settling down and taking a teaching job at the university?"

"It's not what you think," I tried quickly. "This is an experiment."

"You're not into one of those new cult movements, are you? You didn't buy a book from some of those weird people at an airport?"

I had to think fast. After all, I was supposedly a distinguished lecturer and author—and more importantly, my wife had respected me, at least until then. It was late October. "Trick or treat, dear," I said too sheepishly. "What do you think?"

Susan pursed her lips. "There's not much treat there—I'll take the trick! Anyway, Denis, be kinder to yourself. If you want to streak in our bedroom, don't cut eye holes in your bag."

VALUE IS INSIDE-OUT

Since then, my diet has radically improved; most of the junk has been pruned. Some of the bulges are gone and I'm working on the others. The ridiculous bag experiment actually worked, since I saw what the instructor wanted me to. It also fit my conviction that in order to change, *you* must take charge. And where better to start than with your body, the most marvelous machine you'll ever operate? Why treat a space shuttle like a broken-down pickup?

THE FOUR LEGS OF VALUE

All positive motivation is rooted in self-esteem—the development of which, just as with other skills, takes practice. And that practice, as with other forms of it, must be carefully structured. Think of self-esteem as a four-legged chair. Imagine you're sitting on it right now, and looking in the mirror. Do you respect the person you see? Is it someone you really want to be? Are you doing what you want to personally and professionally? Are you going where you want to go? *Are you in charge of your life?*

An unhesitating "yes" to a majority of these questions suggests your self-esteem is in good shape. Negative answers indicate you should read on with particular attention.

A Sense of Belonging

Returning to the image of the chair, the first leg of self-esteem is a sense of belonging. We all have a deep-rooted need to feel we're a part of something larger than ourselves. This need, which psychologists call an affiliation drive, encompasses people, places, and possessions. Our instinct for belonging—for being wanted, accepted, enjoyed, and loved by close ones—is extremely powerful.

A Sense of Individual Identity

The second leg, which complements the sense of belonging, is a sense of individual identity. No human being is exactly like another, not even an identical twin. We are all unique combinations of talents and traits that never existed before and will never exist again in quite the same package. Leaders stand out particularly for knowing who they are, having confidence in what they believe, and feeling respect for their present lives as well as for their potential.

A Sense of Worthiness

The third leg of self-esteem is a sense of worthiness, the feeling that I'm glad I'm me, with *my* genes and background, my body, my unique thoughts. Even if others make you feel you belong, even if others praise you, you won't feel very worthy if you violate your own values. (This isn't limited to individuals. One of the basic missions of American corporations is nourishing a sense of worth through improved quality and excellence.)

Without our own approval, we have little to offer. If *we* don't feel worth loving, it's hard to believe that others love us; instead, we tend to see those others as appraisers or judges of our value. People who feel undeserving of love because their self-esteem is marginal easily hurt those who *do* love them. Insecurity generates the jealousy, excessive possessiveness, and compulsion to turn trifles into tragedies that often ruin caring relationships.

These three requisites of self-esteem—a sense of belonging, identity, and worthiness, all of which leaders share—lead us to another paradoxical proverb:

You must view performance as a reflection of your value, but
not a measure of it.

If you were lucky enough to have parents who taught you the importance of responsibility, honesty, initiative, courage, faith, self-control, and most of all, love, please remember to say a frequent prayer of thanks. Many of us were less fortunate—but we can still build our own values by asking ourselves the right questions. Are the trappings of your lifestyle more important to you than your inner values? Is making a good impression more important than being true to yourself? Do you constantly feel you must prove your worth with outer achievements? Do you feel guilty when you're praised or when you indulge yourself in some selfish pleasure?

A sense of belonging, identity, and worthiness can only be rooted in intrinsic core values as opposed to outer, often material, motivation. Without them, we depend on others constantly to fill our leaking reserves of self-esteem—but also tend to suspect others of ulterior motives. Unable to accept or reject others' opinions for what they're worth, we are defensive about criticism and paranoid about praise—and no amount of praise can replace the missing qualities.

A healthy sense of belonging, identity, and worthiness is also essential to belief in your dreams. It is *most* essential during difficult times, when you have only a dream to hang on to.

The Fourth Leg: A Sense of Control and Competence

Early in my career in motivational psychology, I thought the chair of self-esteem balanced firmly on those three legs, especially since they involved intrinsic core values. It took much time and research to realize that a fourth leg—one of the most important—was missing.

There are many reasons why few Americans currently in high school and college believe they were born to win. The supportive extended family—in many cases, even the nuclear family—is disappearing. Role models are increasingly unhealthy. The commercial media bombards young senses ever more insistently with crime, hedonism, and other unhealthy forms of escape. But whatever the explanation, constructive leaders cannot emerge and develop without the creative imagination that serves them like fuel—which is why the apprehension, frustration, and hesitation I see and hear in the younger generation is cause for concern. At the moment, the future they imagine will help drive neither happiness nor success.

The chair's fourth leg is self-efficacy, a functional belief in your ability to control what happens to you in a changing, uncertain world. A sense of worthiness may give you the emotional means to venture, but you need self-efficacy, the sense of competence and control, to believe you can succeed. And that belief can't develop without confidence that you can make a difference.

Self-efficacy is essentially confidence in your personal power—not the power to control or dominate others, but power in the richly creative sense of self-empowerment: of being able to do successfully what you set out to do. With a sense of self-efficacy in place, mind and body join in the journey toward the goal—as an inventor, artist, executive, teacher, nurturing parent . . . anything.

In theory, once a goal is attained it no longer serves the same purpose. An entrepreneur who has found investors willing to advance sufficient capital to launch a new business doesn't keep looking for venture capital. However, self-efficacy is an exception. Empowering you to strive for your goals, it also continues motivating you after you've reached the initial objectives.

That's why it is so important to assign responsibility for small tasks to the people involved. The more success they experience, the stronger their confidence grows—and the more responsibility they want to assume. In an increasingly competitive global marketplace, each member of the work force simply must believe that he or she is a team leader, a "quality individual" who expresses that quality in excellent production and service. With increasing pressures on profit and the need to do more with fewer workers, it's essential to raise the value of the employees' stock in themselves.

Sam Deep is an organizational consultant and trainer; Lyle Sussman is a professor of management at the University of Louisville. Their *Smart Moves* (Addison-Wesley, 1990) offers ten steps to building team members' self-esteem.

1. Document their accomplishments so they can't pretend they don't exist. Never allow team members to lose sight of their accomplishments, and with it their potential for success.
2. Show them how to find opportunity in adversity. Every outcome, no matter how negative, presents options that were not previously available.

3. Assign them tasks that will display their talents. By transferring important responsibility to team members, you demonstrate your confidence in them and give them the chance to succeed in increasingly challenging assignments.

4. Teach them how to get what they want from other people. Teach your people to be assertive rather than too aggressive or too passive.

5. Show them the awesome power of listening, an active strategy for achieving personal success. When your subordinates become better listeners and begin reaping the benefits, they will feel better about themselves.

6. Teach them the advantage of being a sieve rather than a sponge. A sponge soaks up all the water it can hold and, when squeezed, shoots it in every direction. Water passes through a sieve completely; "sieve people" are less rattled by adversity than sponges.

7. Tell them exactly what you expect of them and find out what they expect of you. The reason most subordinates and team members give for not satisfying their management is not knowing what management expects.

8. Criticize performance but not people. The spirit of criticism should be, "I don't like what you did in this case, but I do like you."

9. Praise not only them but also their performance. You don't want merely to keep your people happy; you want them to know what they did right so they can repeat it.

10. Keep them in ongoing training programs. This gives them a vote of confidence, and carefully chosen training will further contribute to their effectiveness and ultimately their self-esteem.[1]

A VALUABLE TIP

My grandmother, who immigrated from England in the late 1800s, filled my childhood with valuable tips for an abundant life, many from scriptures and family lore. She was fond of the origin of acronyms such as *posh,* which came to mean luxurious or first class. *Posh* originated on British ships traveling to sweltering India. In the days before air-conditioning, the more desirable cabins had portholes in the shade—which meant the ship's left side on the outbound voyage and right side during the voyage home. Thus *posh,* short for *P*ort *O*ut, *S*tarboard *H*ome.

Tip is said to have originated in the 1700s in the British town of Broadway—specifically at a country inn where travelers stopped on their way from Chesterfield to Bath, then on to London. When a carriage driver or horseman rode up to the inn, he would toss a coin to the stable boy as an incentive to water down and feed the horses and to clean the saddles or the carriage for the following day. The advance payment for the service to be rendered encouraged the stable hands to make their performance measure up.

Thus *tip,* which was slang for *T*o *I*nsure *P*erformance, grew from a practice designed to ensure good work. A tip about yourself and the quality you're able to deliver should ensure that your work reflects that value. And tips that leaders offer team members, especially tips encouraging self-trust, help ensure that performance measures up to what we expect of ourselves and what leaders expect of us.

SUCCESS BREEDS SUCCESS

In my work with Olympic and professional athletes, I see the following almost daily: The longer he hits his jump shot, the longer she volleys crisply at the net, the more each believes in his or her success. The better we become, the more we trust ourselves—and success at previous tasks tends to have the same effect.

Few people get into their cars pondering whether they can drive safely to their destination. Previous experience has given them faith in their ability to do that. As accomplishments mount, self-confidence and ability grow in other areas as well. The more we accomplish, the larger our view of our enormous capacity for creative growth.

CORE VALUES: FROM INSIDE TO OUTSIDE

Core values radiate like rings, as when a leaf falls in a pond. The self-centered constantly seek approval from and power over others. They try to impress them with their worth rather than express concern for others' well-being. And their outward appearances usually involve ways to hide their real thoughts and intentions.

The paradoxical proverb here is that:

> **You must feel worthy of the best, but not more worthy than the rest.**

The value-centered give of themselves freely and graciously, constantly seeking to empower others. Open and modest, they have no need for conceit, the opposite of core value. Feeling good about who they are, and not needing to talk about their victories or line their walls with celebrity photos, people with core values spend much of their time "paying value," as I call it, to others. When praised, they share the spotlight. When they make mistakes, they view them as learning experiences and accept responsibility.

My friend Nathaniel Branden has taught me—and countless others—that self-esteem can't be bought, won in an arena, measured by a stock portfolio, or displayed in a fashion model's figure or an entertainment star's profile. Self-esteem is a profound belief that you deserve to be happy and successful, combined with a trust or confidence in an ability to manage life's challenges. It is as necessary for human development as oxygen, as basic as the carbon from which diamonds are formed. I used to think that diamonds were so sought after because they glitter, but discovered that they're actually so valuable because they're almost impossible to destroy. Formed at the earth's core and very rare, they hold their value indefinitely.

THE SAGA OF RUSSELL CONWELL

Thoughts of core values and diamonds always take me back to Russell Conwell, one of the original American motivational speakers. Raised on a farm in Berkshire, Massachusetts, Conwell grew up believing in infinite human possibilities.

When the Civil War began, young Conwell raised a full company of volunteer soldiers. His talent as a recruiter helped vault him to the position of captain of that company. One day, a Confederate attack surprised them at Kennesaw Mountain. When the captain—now a lieutenant colonel—was almost mortally wounded and struggling to hold on, a young orderly put himself in harm's way to keep Conwell alive, giving up his own life to do so. Before the youth died, he changed his lieutenant colonel forever by telling him about his deep inner faith. Conwell too chose to live a life guided by inner beliefs.

When the war finally ended, the soldier's soldier began a successful law practice and founded several newspapers. His faith remained unshaken when his wife died while he was still in his twenties. Later, Conwell became a minister and a well-known preacher at Philadelphia's Great Baptist Temple. Summoning recruiting and leadership skills honed in the military, he led a core of committed volunteers who turned a night school in their church basement into Temple University.

This took years of sacrifice and effort. To raise money for books, facilities, and faculty, Conwell became a prominent lecturer and an author of sixteen books. He gave his most famous lecture some six thousand times over two decades. It was the spellbinding "Acres of Diamonds," whose message is as relevant today as it was when he traveled the nation sharing it. I myself first heard the story from the late Earl Nightingale, one of my primary mentors.

It opens when Conwell found himself on the Tigris River with a party of English travelers. The year was 1870. The group's guide was an elderly Arab who had been hired to show them the ancient cities of Assyria. Much more than a guide, however, the old Arab was a consummate storyteller who seemed compelled to weave a tale at every bend of the trail. "And now I will tell you a story I reserve for my particular friends," he said one evening, introducing the "Acres of Diamonds" story that Russell Conwell shared with hundreds of thousands of listeners.

ALI HAFED'S ACRES OF DIAMONDS

Not far from the River Indus, there once lived a Persian farmer by the name of Ali Hafed, who owned a large farm with orchards, grain fields, and gardens. He was a wealthy, contented man—contented because he was wealthy and wealthy because he was contented. One day he was visited by an ancient priest, a wise man from the east. The priest sat by the fire and told Ali Hafed how our world was made.

He said the Almighty thrust a finger into the fog and slowly turned it round and round, increasing the speed until it gradually became a ball of fire. Then, he said, the ball of fire rolled through the universe, burning its way through other cosmic banks of fog and condensing the moisture until it fell in floods of rain upon its surface, which cooled the outer crust. When the melted mass burst out and very quickly cooled, it became granite. That which cooled less quickly became silver—and even less quickly, gold. "And diamonds," said the ancient priest, "diamonds are congealed drops of sunlight." Declaring diamonds the highest of God's mineral creations, the priest said that one stone the size of Ali Hafed's thumb could purchase the whole country. If Ali Hafed had a mine of diamonds, he could place his children on the thrones of countries throughout the world.

Ali Hafed went to bed that night a poor man—poor because he was discontented and discontented because he thought he was poor. "I want a diamond mine," he repeated to himself throughout his sleepless night.

He woke the priest early the next morning. "Will you tell me where I can find diamonds?" he asked.

"Diamonds," said the priest. "What do you want with diamonds?"

"I want to be immensely rich," replied Ali Hafed candidly.

"Then go along and find them, that's all you must do," advised the priest.

"But I don't know where to go," Ali Hafed pleaded.

"Well," said the priest, "if you look for a river that runs over white sands between high mountains, you will always find diamonds in those sands."

"I don't believe any such river exists," Ali Hafed challenged.

"Of course it does, there are many of them," said the priest. "All you have to do is find them."

Ali Hafed went to the window and looked out, his gaze fixed on the mountains that bordered his farm. "I believe you. I will go!" he resolved.

He sold his farm and collected his money. Leaving his family in a neighbor's care, he went off in search of diamonds, starting with the nearest mountains. Next he searched in Palestine. Finally, he wandered Europe. When the last of his money had been spent, he stood in rags at Spain's Bay of Barcelona, watching the waves roll in. Soon the penniless, hopelessly wretched man cast himself into the oncoming tide and sank beneath the water, never to rise again.

One day, continued the old Arab guide, the man who had purchased Ali Hafed's farm led his camel into the garden to drink. As the beast lapped the brook's clear water, Ali Hafed's successor noticed a curious flash in the shallow stream's white sands. Reaching into the water, he withdrew a black pebble with an eye of light that reflected all the colors of the rainbow. He took the curious stone into the house, put it on the mantel, and returned to his chores.

Some days later, he was visited by the ancient priest. The moment the priest saw the gleam from the mantel, he rushed to it. "There's a diamond here!" he shouted. "A diamond! Has Ali Hafed returned?"

"No, he hasn't returned and that's no diamond," the new owner answered. "It's nothing but a stone from out there in the garden."

"But I know a diamond when I see one," the priest insisted. "And I tell you that's what this is, a beautiful diamond."

Together they rushed to the garden stream. They stirred the white sands with their fingers—and lo, discovered more stones, even more beautiful and valuable than the first. Thus was the diamond mine of Golcanda discovered—the most magnificent in history, exceeding even the Kimberly silver mine.

For decades, every shovelful from near that stream revealed gems that would decorate the crowns of monarchs. Had Ali Hafed remained at home and dug in his own garden instead of wandering aimlessly into a life of frustration, poverty, and suicide in a strange land, he would have had acres of diamonds.

If ever a story had a more powerful moral, I haven't encountered it. Perhaps you have already developed the wisdom to know that the diamonds you seek are waiting to be uncovered in your own back yard—the back yard of your mind, where your sense of values and your self-worth are embedded.

The simple truth is that if we have no internalized feelings of value, we have nothing to share with others. We can need them, depend on them, look for security in them—but we can't share or give emotion to anyone unless we possess it. The diamond is inside us, waiting to be discovered, shaped, and polished.

Here are some action tips to enhance your self-esteem and that of the significant others in your life:

1. Be more aware of your physical appearance. You don't have to be the best-looking in any group, just look your best. Being clean says you care about yourself. Make a commitment to join a support group with a proven program that will overcome any habit that reduces the quality of your life.

2. Improve your body language. Stand erect yet relaxed. Walk purposefully but without arrogance. Your jaw and face should be relaxed, your eyes bright and in direct contact with others while in conversation, your pronunciation should be clear, your voice projecting confidence and intensity. Always extend your hand and offer your own name first in any personal encounter—and offer your name first in phone conversations. Smile with your eyes, voice, face, and body language. In every language, a smile is a light in your window that says a caring person resides within.

3. In your day planner, whether it's on paper or on disc, write down and define the success qualities you want to acquire. Help your associates and family members do the same. You may want to focus on one quality a month. It takes about a month of repetition to develop a new habit, about a year of practice to make it permanent.

4. Make a thanks list. Write "I am thankful for the following" at the top of a piece of paper, then three columns for People, Things, and Other. List all the people and things for which you are grateful. In the Other column, consider items we tend to take for granted, such as freedom, health, and opportunity. Read your list twice a day for a week and discuss it with associates and significant family members. When disappointment clamors for attention, review your blessings and your thanks list. Teach the members of your team to like what they have rather than constantly trying to have what they like.

5. Dwell on your strengths and talents. Keep a video record of your professional and personal milestones and achievements—positive memories for reinforcement during difficult times. Also, make a video of the older members of your family and senior members of your company relating their experiences and their expertise. Nothing is more important to rookies and the younger generation than wisdom from people who have been there before. And nothing is more important than featuring dedicated employees who may not be getting the attention they deserve.

6. Communicate unconditional acceptance of yourself and significant others regardless of their current performance. When criticizing specific behavior, be certain to reassure your associates and children of your love. A core of self-acceptance is a powerful defense against needing externals to define self-esteem.

7. Become comfortable giving and receiving compliments and expressions of affection. An ability to accept appreciation is a sign of healthy self-esteem.

8. Be open to criticism and relaxed about acknowledging your mistakes. Your self-esteem is not tied to being always right or to an image of perfection.

9. Since you trust your ability to cope with challenge and change, enjoy life's ironies and humorous aspects. Remain flexible in your responses, eager to contribute inventiveness and innovation.

10. Make the first and last fifteen minutes of your day at home and at the office—the time I call sign-on and sign-off signatures—the most important for all around you. Make it a habit, no less important than brushing your teeth, to start your day on a positive note. Wake up looking forward to a new slate. Send your partner or spouse off with a loving, encouraging thought. Send yourself off to work with a bright outlook. Send everyone at your factory or office forward with the expected results, not the morning newspaper's bad news.

Just as important, use the last fifteen minutes of your office and family day to let others know how much you care for them—by signing off with a reassuring, optimistic sentence or two. Just before leaving the office, think of something in your working environment that brings you satisfaction and pass it on. Do the same at home before going to sleep. I believe this has influenced my family to rise higher in their aspirations. I know it has changed my own life.

SIX

SELF-LEADERSHIP AND VISION: YOUR VIRTUAL REALITY

---

1 ◆ *Looking back, what are your dominant memories?*

2 ◆ *Looking forward, what is your vision of the future?*

3 ◆ *How vivid and real are your "mental movies" of the future?*

TRUE VISION IS INNER VISION, AN ABILITY TO CONVERT PAST EXPERIENCE into positive input and to visualize a desired future. People who can do this become leaders, many also attaining great wealth. Storing every transaction as a learning opportunity, keeping their vision unclouded by negativism from past setbacks, they can see their missions clearly and describe them vividly. This combination of insight, hindsight, and foresight—the ability to filter out failure, reinforce what has worked before, and see accomplishments ahead—attracts followers who share a similar mission but not the vision.

SHARED VISION

Three of the world's fastest growing companies—Blockbuster Entertainment, Boston Chicken, and Discovery Zone—share a common vision path. Boston Chicken, which opens a new store and hires twenty new employees every business day, doesn't see itself as a fast-food outlet. It is in the "home-cooked-meal replacement business, where chicken is the protein of choice." The company's founders, Scott Beck, Saad Nadhir, and Jeffrey Shearer, synthesized ideas they gleaned while helping build Blockbuster Entertainment. It was Scott Beck's foresight that led H. Wayne Huizenga to buy Blockbuster in the first place.

When they left Blockbuster, their vision was to start another national retailing chain, where operating-level managers would have the knowledge and expertise to drive the company forward. The founders would provide vision, capital, and technology, then become facilitators, empowering their team members to see themselves as—and to become—successful entrepreneurs.

When asked about Boston Chicken's astonishing growth rate of over 100 percent a year, a spokesperson for KFC (Kentucky Fried Chicken) responded that Boston Chicken was like a "tugboat compared to the *Queen Mary*." A recent article in *Fortune* magazine pondered that reaction: "Wake up and smell the barnacles, Colonel: The *Queen Mary* has been a floating museum since 1967."[1]

If you have small children, you've probably been to a Discovery Zone center somewhere nearby. The national chain of family-oriented child play centers—which is growing at 200 percent a year—features climbing and other physical recreation activities. It is the brainchild of Donald Flynn, a board member of Blockbuster, which owns 20 percent of Discovery Zone. What drives Blockbuster?

WAYNE'S WORLD

Perhaps you think Blockbuster's huge chain of video rental stores will become obsolete when a phone call and a flick of the remote control will bring pay-for-view to everyone's television set. Think again! With visionary Wayne Huizenga at the helm, the only limit to Blockbuster's future is his seemingly limitless imagination. With annual revenues of well over $2 billion and a worldwide reach expanding at the rate of a new store every 24 hours, the company appears to be in perpetual infancy. Huizenga is also America's only owner in three major sports: football (the Miami Dolphins), baseball (the Florida Marlins), and hockey (the Florida Panthers). He is planning a huge sports and entertainment mecca between Miami and Ft. Lauderdale, with major-league stadiums and indoor/outdoor recreation facilities designed to attract millions of visitors every year.

Huizenga sees his thousands of Blockbuster Entertainment outlets as software showcases for new products. Prospects will come in to test-drive the latest offerings, rent them, and buy the most user-friendly items. In a way, Huizenga's burgeoning empire, which might be called the "Wayne's World" of the future, rivals the world of another great visionary named Disney.

THE "3-D" VISION OF LEADERS

The three dimensions of leadership vision are:

1. Viewing failures as not-to-be-repeated learning experiences.
2. Reinforcing past success to nourish confidence for taking new risks.
3. Imagining future successes as real, despite the unknowns.

In a world in which change is the rule, dealing with failure and mastering misfortune is essential to effective self-leadership. We'll devote a full chapter to this later.

REPLAYING IT RIGHT

Most people fail to project themselves into the future because their previous experiences have been frustrating and they see more of the same ahead. They tend to "instant replay" old lowlights, which offer no vision of eventual victory. Viewing negative experiences as target corrections, leaders, by contrast, constantly replay highlights, helping inspire themselves and their teammates.

Gary Player, one of golf's immortals, gave an impromptu demonstration of this process during a memorable Master's tournament. Player lined up a fairway shot and stroked a solid seven-iron shot that softly deposited the ball thirty feet past the pin. For me, that would have been a sensational shot. For Player, it left a long putt for a birdie and he wanted to correct his "mistake." A quick look at his caddie was enough for the caddie to hand him his eight-iron. Player walked back to where the ball had been and swung through without it. As he watched his imaginary ball land dead to the pin, you could almost hear him thinking, "That's the way to play the shot. Next time I'll get it right!"

REINFORCING SUCCESS

Nations, companies, teams, and families with a tradition of excellence constantly reinforce it in order to keep the vision of greatness in the minds of their veterans and rookies, whatever the current circumstances. These visions can take the form of big-screen video highlights at rallies. They can be daily or weekly bulletins and words of inspiration. Or they can be leaders' mental memories during their solitary minutes and hours.

Larry Holman, to whom this book is dedicated, knows from his own mind how leaders think. His dynamic growth company, Wyncom, Inc., sponsors the "Lessons in Leadership" conferences and teleconferences featuring Tom Peters, Stephen Covey, myself, and others that have become so popular in America and abroad.

Walking back to his office in Lexington, Kentucky, after lunch one day, Larry passed a playground basketball court and an urge hit him hard. "It's been a long time," he thought. "But maybe I can still . . ." After checking to see if anybody in the company was watching, he was on the asphalt court and in the thick of the competition. Pity he hadn't brought his new Converse shoes. Still, he felt "up." He took a bounce pass, head-faked to the inside, pivoted in the opposite direction, dribbled twice, stopped, and launched a jumper from twelve feet. Swish!

A moment later he was at the top of the key. None of his teammates was open so he shot from there. Nothing but net, three points. Larry's team was almost back in the game. A crew of spectators yelled their approval. He slipped past two big defenders. As he left the ground, the basket, twenty-two feet away, seemed big enough to toss a watermelon through. Holman couldn't miss!

But he had to be back at work. He was expecting an important phone call and anyway he couldn't stay there all afternoon in a business suit and wing-tipped shoes—and, as it turns out, with no other players and not even a basketball! Maybe you think Larry was making a fool of himself with his solitary pretending. Not so. The former court star was using a leader's power of recall to reinforce winning highlights. This marvelous ability to retrieve memories as if they were CD-ROM images is essential to innovation and creativity.

PRACTICING THE RIGHT STUFF

Olympians train up to 1,200 days for a few moments of competition. Astronauts simulate until the profoundly unknown is perfectly known, the strangely unfamiliar becomes intimately familiar. I remember my own combat training as a naval aviator. My throat tightened as two enemy interceptors appeared on my radar screen. Knowing that a heat-seeking missile would be locked onto my tailpipe in seconds, I executed an aerobatic maneuver into heavy cloud cover. But I pulled too many Gs and lost control of the plane. With a bad case of vertigo, I was thrown from the cockpit by the centrifugal force of the uncontrollable spin. I fell for what seemed an eternity . . . about four feet, from the flight simulator onto the hangar floor. The door of the simulator had unlocked and I'd forgotten to fasten my seatbelt.

The instructors doubled up in laughter. My peers joined with some choice remarks as I lay sprawled on the control room floor. Even worse were the stares of members of Congress and other VIPs who had come to observe Naval Air Pacific warriors display their superb combat skills. Being more like Chevy Chase than Tom Cruise was hard on my ego, but the fallout included an important leadership lesson. "Just be glad this was the simulator," my instructor said, shrugging "There are no second chances with the real thing!"

What I learned that day—over thirty years ago—I later confirmed again and again. It is that the mind can't distinguish between imagined and real experience. The mind stores as truth everything vividly rehearsed and practiced—which is why it's so vital to store winning instead of losing images. And to correct your mistakes as they are made, focusing on how to do it right next time.

SEEING IS BELIEVING

The power of envisioning should be easy to appreciate. Brilliant performers like Dustin Hoffman and Meryl Streep studied method acting, which is largely training to recall scenes from the past that will evoke relevant images and emotions. These help enrich an actor's interpretation of a current role. If, for example, he or she has a scene in which they must react to abuse, they deepen character and mood by remembering past abuse or something similar in their own lives.

Since the mind can relive experiences as if they are happening, it can also "prelive" experiences that haven't yet happened. This is the secret to goal setting. The more vivid the image, the more real the design for the future. Who you "see" is who you'll be.

THE VIRTUAL LEADER IN A VIRTUAL WORLD

Virtual reality is a computer-created environment with sensors for human reaction within that environment. Immersion in simulated sight, sound, and touch propels the "player" into a virtual world.

Although we usually think of virtual reality as a high-tech video game, it's more than a new pastime. It is used to simulate combat missions and space exploration by putting warriors and astronauts in environments that are mirror images of actual battlefield and space conditions.

One of virtual reality's most exciting applications is in medical surgery. Simulating on virtual patients, surgeons can get the precise feel and sensations of performing delicate procedures. This makes the old methods of training obsolete: observing from a gallery above the operating room or watching a one-dimensional videotape. Microrobotics and virtual reality transmissions on the global information network may soon make it possible for a surgeon to operate on a real patient in a distant hospital. Instead of trying to airlift the patient, the surgeon's brain and expertise—his or her hands and fingers—may be transmitted electronically by satellite dish or cable to any operating room in the world.

In more everyday applications, it's not unusual to see Tokyo couples designing their dream homes by virtual reality. Husbands and wives walk around a simulated kitchen they've selected and equipped with their choice of cabinets and appliances. They can put dishes away to see if there is sufficient space; they can turn on faucets and listen to the running water. Each room can be designed in advance even light fixtures adjusted and clothes positioned in closets. Individual imagination becomes the architect.

And if you can design a home in your mind—lay it out on a set of plans and build it—you can do the same thing with much of your life. Virtual reality's underlying message is that the computer is only a tool, if more sophisticated than a hammer and saw. One form of virtual reality has always been available to design our futures. The software is your inner vision, waiting to be booted up. We see more with our minds than our eyes.

SOME SIGHTED PEOPLE ARE BLIND

Leaders must remain faithful to their dreams even when others doubt. The most insightful people can sometimes be blind to a great vision, especially if it represents a great challenge to the status quo. Even the great Mark Twain had trouble discerning good visions from bad ones. Despite his intellect, he fell prey to more than one wobbly and unscrupulous business scheme, which cost him lots of money.

One afternoon Twain was visited by yet another man in search of investors—an inventor who carried a strange-looking contraption under his arm. Eagerly and convincingly, the man explained his invention to the writer, who listened politely but in the end said he had to turn his visitor down; he'd been burned too many times.

"But I'm not asking you to invest a fortune," the visitor pleaded. "You can have as large a share as you want for $500." Still Mark Twain shook his head. He was unwilling to take the risk on an invention that made no sense to him. As the inventor started away with his machine, the writer called out to him. "What did you say your name was?" "Bell," the man replied, a trace of dejection in his voice, "Alexander Bell."

Other visions have brought their owners worse than rejection. Harland Manchester's *Gadget the World* tells of an inventor's trial for fraud in Federal Court in New York. The prosecutor used every opportunity to scorn the man and his invention, a glass gadget that resembled a small light bulb. With sarcasm dripping from his voice, he told the jury that the defendant had sold gullible investors on the preposterous claim that his worthless device would transmit the human voice across the Atlantic Ocean. The prosecutor urged prison terms for the man and his partners. Although two were convicted, the lucky defendant got off with a stern lecture from the judge. In time, Lee De Forest had even better luck convincing others of the benefits of his glass bulb. It was the audion tube that laid the foundation for the multibillion-dollar electronics industry.

SEEING FROM WITHIN

One of my most inspiring relationships is with Jim Stovall, founder of the narrative television network, a cable network for the blind. Jim lost his eyesight several years ago, but he has never lost his vision, his determination, or his stride. He creates programs that people can enjoy and profit from by using their inner vision.

Stovall is also one of the most gifted, dynamic public speakers on the national circuit. Not long ago, he captivated me with his ability to walk unassisted around the stage and down the steps in front, looking directly at each face in the front row. After questioning them, he was able to remember exactly where each was seated so he could walk back directly in front of that individual and personalize his remarks. The audience was spellbound.

Jim likes to relate an experience as a world-class weight lifter. During his team's travels for international competition, he was impressed by a young Japanese named Yoshimoto Ishay. For any given weight, lifters have three minutes to perform, during which they can try three times. But before Yoshimoto would attempt even a first lift, he'd stand immobile before the bar for nearly the full three minutes. Sometimes he waited so long that the buzzer sounded and he was disqualified. "Hey, what are you waiting for?" Stovall once asked him. "Don't you know you're going to miss the lift if you don't get with it?" Young Yoshimoto smiled, Stovall reported. "In Japan we always lift weights inside before we lift them outside," he explained. "First, we see ourselves achieving in a mental picture. So I always concentrate on that, and if I can't see myself lifting the weight, I don't try."

Stovall remembered his Asian friend's words when he was competing for the national title. His hands were hurting and swollen. He had only one lift left, and if he failed, he'd not only lose at that weight but also drop from selection for the top ten. Following Yoshimoto's advice, he saw himself lifting the 500 pounds. He even saw the gold medal around his neck. He put his hands on the bar, lifted, and extended. When he put down the weight, three white lights came on and he was the new national heavy-weight champion! It was a great moment for Stovall, even greater because he'd succeeded despite almost total blindness. But he had seen what he had to on the inside.[2]

Now totally blind, Jim Stovall moves and behaves in ways that seem to belie his affliction. Most importantly, he still sees clearly in his mind. He is a living example of how little we in the sighted world use our imaginations.

AMERICA'S BEAUTIFUL LANDSCAPE

Stovall reminded us of the Secretary of the Interior's new campaign to attract foreign tourists to America. The video promotion features an emotionally charged rendition of "America the Beautiful" over breathtaking panoramas of our national landscape. "Oh beautiful for spacious skies, for amber waves of grain; for purple mountains' majesty, above the fruited plain . . ." Combined with the magnificent vistas, this song of vision fills many eyes with tears of pride and exhilaration. The person chosen to sing it was Ray Charles, ironically, who has never seen the sky, the mountains, or the plains—which is the point of my message. Jim Stovall, Ray Charles, Stevie Wonder, John Milton, Helen Keller, and thousands of others are or were visionaries, creating from within.

By the end of this decade, it may be possible for totally blind people to see too. They will use a neural-prosthetic device employing a television camera attached to electrodes one third the circumference of a human hair, implanted in the visual cortex in the back of the brain. It would look something like Geordi's visor on *Star Trek: The Next Generation*. Similar auditory implants are being developed to restore hearing to the deaf, and electronic bypasses are being designed to restore motor functions for those with spinal cord injuries. The human mind has incredible potential for designing almost anything it can imagine and transmitting the blueprints anywhere in the world. The empires of the future are the empires of the mind.

THE DAY JACK NICKLAUS FORGOT

Actually, we needn't hold our breath waiting to use interactive virtual reality; its power is already available in our homes and offices—even on the golf course. One Sunday afternoon in June, I was at the Rancho Santa Fe Golf Club, near my home, celebrating one of the milestone birthdays you'd just as soon forget. It happened to be the final day of the classic Memorial tournament. I had just blown out my birthday candles—which, I'm sorry to confess, took several puffs—when I heard the crowd roar. In one of the most spectacular finishes of a major PGA tournament, Paul Azinger had chipped out of a difficult lie in a sand trap on the final hole to beat his friend Payne Stewart to the purse. Jack Nicklaus then interviewed Azinger on national television. "You know, Paul," complimented Nicklaus, "you and I could have stood in that trap all day and thrown golf balls at the flag—and not one of them would have gone in the hole." Azinger replied modestly that he'd actually imagined the ball going in, although he couldn't actually see the hole from where he was playing the ball.

I hope I'm not one to toot my own horn, any more than Azinger. But I'll report here that I nearly dropped a forkful of cake when Azinger quoted me to Nicklaus. "Denis Waitley's book," he said, "advised that 'You should imagine the mind to be a quart jar and always make certain it's full of positive thoughts—like intentions of hitting winning shots. While many are thinking what can go wrong with the shot, winners are thinking what can go right. The winner's mind is so focused on the desired result, there can be no room for negatives.' "

"With the round I had today," Nicklaus chuckled, "maybe I should have read that book." Azinger admonished him with a smile. "Jack, the author was writing about *you*. I was reading about how *you* think and play. Waitley was only quoting you!"

So even role models sometimes forget that the imagination is the most powerful mental force. Paul Azinger now uses that power for a challenge much greater than golf tournaments. He has been applying the best of medical science, together with his own vision and courage, to win a personal war against the enemy that interrupted his career at the very top, shortly after I saw him win the Memorial tournament on my birthday. Beating cancer is the new mission for his vision.

THE ORGANIZATIONAL MISSION

Organizations must have a vision of what they are, what they stand for, what they hope to accomplish, and how they will go about it. If the vision is compelling and well communicated, people will be motivated to make it a reality. Organizational and individual goals will be established as increments toward full realization over time.

If a vision is too large for an organization, perhaps it should expand to accommodate it. If a vision is too large for individuals, maybe *they* should expand, tearing down self-set limits. Although some visions are simply unrealistic, many are stifled by inflexible organizational structures or self-made personal barriers.

Some organizational structures are built on goals that are no longer appropriate. Yet those structures' very existence and nature—and their staffing by people who have built their careers on the outdated goals and methods—often generate massive resistance to change. Continually reinforcing adherence to the status quo, those structures strongly discourage risk.

Thus, the structure determines the purpose, which is putting the horse before the cart. Unless those organizations refine their visions or adapt to market conditions, the prognosis for their success—even their continued existence—is not good.

One of the clearest marks of leaders with constructive visions is an appreciation of the benefits of others' opinions. Dissenting views are taken as information that might be incorporated into the vision, not as personal attacks. Serious consideration of other points of view is essential to a healthy organization—which thinks of itself as an extended team of player-managers with the same goal, its leaders out there playing together with everyone else. Encouraged to contribute to strategic decisions, all players have opportunities for growth and development, and share in the rewards. Most important, they know that they—not the winning record—are the team's most valuable asset.

In a series of books entitled *Smart Moves,* Sam Deep and Lyle Sussman list ten steps for helping to envision the greater mission and to be motivated to achieve it. Not surprisingly, most of the steps involve creating, communicating, and clarifying individual visions.

1. Guide your efforts by an ambitious, inspiring, and well-conceived vision. Be able to see what your unit will look like tomorrow and have a plan for getting there. A vision is your mental dress rehearsal for success.
2. Share your vision and its rationale—your dreams, motivations, and reasons—with other employees. A) Include employees in creating the vision by involving them in strategic planning and encouraging them to make their own statements that support

the larger mission. B) Communicate your vision as vividly as possible so that employees can see, taste, and touch it. C) Don't tell people what to do, tell them what your needs are. Let them help decide how to meet those needs, at the same time using them to fill out your vision.

3. For each team member, generate expectations for helping achieve the vision. Draw up a specific list for each person.

4. Hire people capable of fulfilling your vision. (Perhaps management's greatest shortcoming is in hiring people incapable of sharing—and of expecting to be part of—the larger vision.)

5. Make your expectations known early, clearly, and often. Put them in writing before hiring someone.

6. Negotiate to get what you want from employees. Ask yourself how you can inspire them to *want* to fulfill team expectations.

7. Delegate responsibility that will encourage team members to reach for the top.

8. Listen to them unconditionally.

9. Give them the enthusiasm, initiative, commitment, energy, loyalty, dependability, honesty, thoroughness, caring, and competence that you expect them to give you.

10. Give them constant feedback on how well they're meeting your expectations.[3]

Your Personal Mission

Most successful companies, institutions, and organizations have mission statements. Most individuals don't. As the CEO of your own life in the knowledge era, you need a laserlike focus in your vision. You need a mission and a mission statement describing how you want to live, not just what you want to own; defining the person you want to become, not just the title you want to see on your door; outlining the knowledge you'll receive, not just the degree you'll earn or your next promotion or even your ultimate career.

I began the process this way:

"To be aware of the uniqueness of my associates, clients, friends, and family and to treat that uniqueness with loving concern. To encourage them to develop an 'I can, I will' attitude. To help them go a step above what they or even others might normally expect, and not be surprised when they take that step.

"I was created to lead myself and others to understand win-win relationships and how to use them to improve the lives of all persons with whom I come in contact. I am here to learn as much as I can, to experience as much as I can, to give as much as I can, to serve my fellow men and women as much as I can, and to love my family as much as I can—as honestly, joyfully, and long as I possibly can."

You can frame your mission statement starting with your core values, working outward to your material desires and financial needs—guided by another paradoxical proverb:

> *You must understand that seeing is believing, but also know*
> *that believing is seeing.*

Recognizing the formative influence on our lives of repeated observing, imitating, fantasizing, and verbalizing is critical. Our value systems are largely formed with no conscious awareness of the input on our part. Much daily information goes in "harmlessly, almost unnoticed," so that we can't understand the basis for many of our decisions—and only wonder about them later, often when those decisions have proved themselves harmful.

What if we could mentally switch to an interactive channel in which our minds became cameras instead of receivers, and we became producers instead of viewers? What if we scripted, cast, rehearsed, and broadcast our own programs—and made a CD-ROM disk for future broadcasts? Some of us—the achievers of our dreams—indeed do that every day and night. Consider these early fantasies:

> *His love of woodworking and violin music began in*
> *childhood.*
> —Antonio Stradivari

> *As a child in England, he spent hours creating cardboard sets*
> *for his puppet shows to entertain the family.*
> —Andrew Lloyd Webber

> *At fourteen, visiting state capitals during summer vacation,*
> *she pondered a career in lawmaking.*
> —Sandra Day O'Connor

Cut from his basketball team as a youngster, he still dreamed of playing.
—Michael Jordan

Swimming to gain strength in his two broken arms, the teenager changed dreams from astronaut to aquanaut.
—Jacques Cousteau

The young boy was fascinated with anatomical diagrams in the **World Book.**
—Jonas Salk

At twenty-one, she lived in a one-room flat over her father's grocery store and dreamed of public service.
—Margaret Thatcher

A high-school term paper was on being a cook and owning a restaurant.
—Dave Thomas (founder of Wendy's)

This college dropout had ideas about information access.
—Bill Gates

From our earliest years, we're exposed to role models, mentors, and leaders. Watching and listening, we acquire at least some of their beliefs and behavior patterns. Finally, we adopt them as our own, becoming what we've been most exposed to.

For now, ask yourself these questions:

1. What do I really imagine for my future?
2. Is it my vision or someone else's?
3. If it's someone else's mission, do I share it?
4. Can I imagine myself in a position of top leadership, with a life full of inner and outer excellence?

Life is not a rehearsal or a virtual reality game. What you simulate, you will generate. How you speak is what you will seek. What you say will determine your day. What you visualize will materialize.

ACTION EXERCISES FOR INNER VISION

Here are some action exercises for developing your imaginative powers:

Use Your Six Senses.

Wherever you are, appreciate the power of your senses. Be more curious and aware about everything in your environment, taking in as many sights, sounds, smells, textures, and tastes as you can.

Form Mental Images.

When you are listening to someone talk in business and social situations, try to form a mental image of the situation being described. Allow the words to form images, feelings, and sensations.

Become a Better Speaker.

Use words rich in visual imagery. Describe events and plans in more descriptive detail and with more enthusiasm. If you do, you'll enjoy a side benefit of becoming a better conversationalist and better public speaker.

Improve Your Recall Abilities.

Sit comfortably in a chair, relax for a few seconds, then deliberately look at the objects in the room around you. Now close your eyes and try to recall as many of those objects as you can. You'll be surprised at how many you miss. Continue this exercise as often as you can. Try to remember surrounding objects' color, shape, texture, and size. The key is to recall by image, not names.

Get in Touch.

Close your eyes and hold an object in your hand, feeling it as you move it from one hand to the other. Trace the shape with your fingers, at the same time picturing it in your mind.

Listen and Learn.

Buy a book on tape, narrated by actors and actresses and with sound effects. Put yourself in the plot as you listen. Next buy a book read by a narrator and add your own sounds, sights, and settings. Also listen to drama programs on radio. (Believe it or not, there are still a few around.)

Watch Television with Your Eyes Closed.

This is the best way to exercise your imagination with that medium, which almost never engages our thinking processes. This will improve with the building of the information superhighway. Meanwhile, however, television provides too many images with little opportunity for interaction or stimulation of our own powers of imagination.

Write Your Thoughts Down on a Regular Basis.

Always carry a notebook or other bound book with you. In your free time—for example, in and out of airport waiting areas—fill it with brainstorming ideas and other personal thoughts. At the same time, make mental notes of the people and places you see.

Learn to Draw.

Drawing develops your creative powers. Start simply, drawing things you know, such as stick figures and circles. If you have access to a multimedia computer, you can explore the fascinating electronic world of illustration and free drawing. As you feel more confident, make your drawings as complex and as intricate as you can, including visual details of shadow, shape, and texture.

Continue to Read.

You probably read newspapers, magazines, and thrillers. Don't stop with that! Find new fiction and nonfiction—genuine literature—by an author whose plotting skills, style, and vocabulary you admire. Observing the creative imagery of other talented people adds fuel to our own creative drives.

CREATIVITY AND RISK IN THE WORKPLACE

More and more organizations expect creativity and innovation—therefore also risk—from their employees. If you're not making a few costly mistakes, you're not making enough decisions or trying enough new ideas. This is not to say that some executives don't prefer stable operations with gradual changes and minimal risks. But the clear general trend as the business environment grows more competitive is toward creativity's increasing importance.

Industries can't reasonably expect to survive without building provisions for change, innovation, and risk into their systems and goals. This means flexible lines of communication and new criteria for judging performance. The trend-setting organizations are open to new ideas and committed to giving their employees latitude to make decisions. No less than obsolete technology, conformity is increasingly recognized as a burden. As we'll see in later chapters, these shifts in corporate priorities perceptions are causing major changes in management styles and, in our daily lives, our perception of our purpose.

SEVEN

❖

SELF-LEADERSHIP AND ATTITUDE: YOUR SELF-FULFILLING PROPHECY

———————— ❖ ————————

1 ❖ Would you classify yourself generally as optimistic or pessimistic?

2 ❖ Do you expect excellence from yourself and others?

3 ❖ Do you set an example of health and wellness in your lifestyle?

———————— ❖ ————————

N<small>OT LONG AGO</small>, S<small>OUTHWEST</small> A<small>IRLINES</small> <small>WAS NAMED ONE OF THE COUN</small>-try's ten best places to work. At this writing, it has the airline industry's highest rate of employee retention. Satisfaction levels are so high that employee turnover is less than 5 percent per year at some locations. Customer satisfaction is also very high, even though Southwest doesn't assign seats, serve meals, or integrate its reservation system with other airlines. What's going on here?

CEO Herbert Kelleher, who likes to mingle with employees and customers aboard planes, on tarmacs and in terminals, believes that employees with the right attitude are critically important. So important, in fact, that the hiring process takes on what he calls a "patina of spirituality." "Anyone who looks at things solely in terms of factors that can easily be quantified," Kelleher elaborates, "is missing the heart of business, which is the right people."[1]

Back in 1991, Xerox analyzed 480,000 customers for their satisfaction with the company's products and service. It found that *very* satisfied customers were six times more likely than the merely satisfied to buy more Xerox equipment. That information was so startling that it led Xerox to extend its efforts to create what it calls "apostles"—a term coined by Scott D. Cook, the CEO of the Intuit Corporation, a software company. Apostles are customers so satisfied that they convert friends and associates to a product or service. Xerox's goal was to achieve 100 percent apostles within two years by upgrading service levels and guaranteeing customer satisfaction.

THE SOUL OF THE CORPORATION

Change and competition are finally driving corporate America to its senses—forcing it to realize that there's more to business than just TQM (Total Quality Management), reengineering, the information highway, organization, pro forma projections, and just-in-time manufacturing. If anything puts America back on top in the world economic market, it will be the critical missing link of core values—the so-called "soul of the corporation."

One of managers' biggest mistakes is hiring employees who have less than positive attitudes—and who can't help reflecting their indifference or cynicism in the quality of their work. To compound the problem, some of those managers use wrong motivational techniques to try to increase productivity from pessimistic employees. The result is a downward spiral.

Some time ago, Billy Graham invited me to speak at a rally of some thirty thousand people. Before the event, Dr. Graham relaxed, as he often does, in a small trailer behind the arena. We shook hands. "So, Denis," he said, his penetrating eyes boring into mine. "How many lives have you changed in your career?" I blinked but smiled back. "I believe I've changed one that I know of, Dr. Graham. My own." "Me too," he replied, eyes now twinkling. "I believe the only life I've changed is mine. But I keep on trying to become a positive influence for others because I believe in what I say and I believe in what I'm doing—don't you?"

I nodded. My work, I said, is based on a deep core-belief system; my very soul is in it. He reminded me that when we talk about faith and belief, we must refer to what he calls the greatest book ever written and the greatest Teacher of the ages on the subject. He summed it up by saying, "Go your way—and as you have believed, so it will be done unto you."

THE TWO FACES OF FAITH

That simple statement cuts both ways, like a two-edged sword. Belief is the key that can unlock the right door for everyone, the means for getting rid of the lock that imprisons people, keeping them from ever knowing success. It is a power everyone has but few consciously use. No individual possesses more of it than any other. Therefore, the question isn't whether we have faith, it's whether we use it correctly. Belief as a positive force is the promise of realizing things hoped for and unseen. As a negative force, it is the premonition of our deepest fears and unseen darkness. There's no such thing as an absence of faith; it's always one kind or another—optimism, or cynicism and despair.

WHY BAD NEWS SELLS

My favorite news commentator is Paul Harvey, with whom I've been privileged to share many platforms. Paul observed in a recent article that much of the modern media features bad guys who seem to win. The well-behaved, healthy, and happily married won't be showcased on television, he wrote, because they tend to make watchers subconsciously feel sorry for themselves. The tabloid readership is intrigued by a successful person only when he or she is divorced, stricken with illness, or loses a fortune. Every hospital always has patients enough worse off to make us feel comparably fortunate.

Harvey calls this the "we're glad we weren't the victim of the day" syndrome. The plane crash we weren't in, the beautiful actress who had a mastectomy, the star athlete fallen from his pedestal, the public official in trouble—such stories will dominate the headlines as long as the fire that burns them warms the rest of us. But Harvey sounds an even more compelling warning about the effects of bad news. He believes it tends to sour us on a way of life that is the envy of the rest of the world. Much social rebellion, he suggests, may be a reflection of cynicism caused by the media's exaggerated focus on what's wrong rather what we could be doing right. We're inculcating the opposite of leadership. The younger generation is receiving a model for losing rather than for winning.

"Americans aren't so ugly, so cruel, so corrupt, so licentious as the headlines imply," Harvey says. And now, like a breeze off a clover patch, comes a new Princeton Research Survey study of two thousand heads of households—revealing that American family values are alive and doing fairly well. Ninety percent of those polled do not steal, 86 percent are married, 84 percent don't cheat on their spouses, 88 percent don't spread lies about others. . . . When we hear that almost 50 percent of American marriages end in divorce, we should know that the high percentage of repeaters leads to misinterpretation of that number. Clearly, the sensationalist focus on a small aberrational segment of our population is being forced on the rest of us—who live relatively mundane lives, trying to be successful and to maintain a positive attitude.[2]

THE MIND/BODY RELATIONSHIP

Much has been written for centuries about the self-fulfilling prophecy. A self-fulfilling prophecy is a statement that is neither true nor false but that may become true if believed. Our discussion of virtual reality and the imagination reminded us that the mind can't distinguish between things real and things vividly imagined—which is why faith and belief are so important. Studies of the brain conducted during the past several decades show that science and religion are very closely allied. Although we have much to learn about the brain and the central nervous system, we already know of the inextricable relationship between psyche and soma: mind and body. Thoughts and images have an unmistakable, measurable physical reaction. To put it another way, what the mind harbors the body manifests in some way.

The paradoxical proverb that applies is:

> *You must fulfill your expectations, but they may not be what you want.*

For example, when our fears and worries turn into anxiety, we suffer distress. Distress activates our endocrine system, changing the production of hormones and antibodies. Our immune system becomes less active; our resistance levels are lowered; we become more vulnerable to bacteria, viruses, and other ever-present hazards. I've long said that ulcers aren't what you eat, they're what's eating you. There is evidence that some forms of asthma are psychosomatic—more related to a smothering relationship with a doting parent ("smother love") than to outside allergens. In some cases, pictures of goldenrod were enough to bring on attacks of hay fever. In many cases, what we expect to happen, what we believe will happen, *makes* it happen.

The powerful loneliness and hurt associated with what we call a broken heart can indeed lead to heart problems. There is also an apparent link between bottled-up emotions and the growth of some cancerous tumors. Some splitting headaches might be precipitated by being pulled in opposite directions. A rigid personality and suppressed rage have been identified as factors in some cases of arthritis.

Faith is a house of many beliefs and it's time we put the house in order. How does your lifestyle—your expectations and your forecasting—affect your own health and well-being?

ENDORPHINS AND THE NATURAL HIGH

My research on how the mind and body work together began nearly twenty years ago in Sarasota, Florida. I served as president of the International Society for Advanced Education, a nonprofit foundation established by health scientists to study preventive medicine. The society sponsored continuing medical education seminars in cooperation with the medical schools of Harvard, Johns Hopkins, and other universities.

Some of the seminars aired the research of Dr. Avram Goldstein, director of Stanford University's Addiction Research Foundation. Dr. Goldstein and his associates suspected our brains use substances similar to morphine and heroin. In 1971, they had located receptor areas in the brain that act as locks, for which only the suspected, still unknown substances would fit like keys. Along with other researchers who were working independently, Goldstein discovered these "keys" were indeed present in the brain—in the form of natural hormones. Several were identified, including enkephylin, endorphin, beta-endorphin, and dynorphin, all of which serve as natural pain relievers, stronger than morphine—beta-endorphin fifty times and dynorphin ninety times more powerful.

Scientists knew that hormones play an important role in regulating some of our biological processes. Adrenaline enables us to "fight or flee" in the face of danger, and to get "up" for physical performances. Insulin regulates blood sugar levels. These later discoveries show that our bodies manufacture morphinelike hormones to block pain and give us a natural high.

Two of the endorphin hormones were found by Dr. Roger Guillemin of the Salk Institute in La Jolla, where I once worked. Further work on hormones would win Dr. Guillemin a Nobel Prize in medicine. In one test using endorphin he supplied, Japanese researchers injected minute amounts of the hormone into fourteen men and women suffering intense pain from cancer. The single injection gave them all relief from their pain for up to three days. In another experiment, fourteen expectant mothers given endorphin during labor all reported immediate and lasting relief and delivered normal babies. By the end of the 1970s, a University of California research team had made an interesting discovery that seemed to confirm the earlier findings about endorphins.

WHAT'S YOUR PLACEBO?

No doubt you're familiar with the placebo effect. (Placebo literally means "I shall please.") Placebos are inert substances given to some volunteers in a given study while other volunteers are treated with experimental drugs—whose effect is tested by measuring the difference in response to the powerless placebo and to the drug. Some of a group of volunteers who had just had their wisdom teeth extracted were given morphine to alleviate their pain; the others swallowed a placebo they believed to be morphine. Many of the placebo recipients said they experienced dramatic relief from their pain. However, when a drug that blocks the effects of the endorphin was given them, the pain returned almost immediately. The test confirmed something very important: When a patient believes he or she has been given a pain reliever, the brain releases chemicals to substantiate that belief. In short, the placebo effect is an act of faith.

Very recent studies have determined that the placebo effect is much more powerful than previously imagined. So be careful what you believe and pretend— it may come to pass.

THE OPPORTUNITY IN HEMINGWAY'S PROBLEM

One of the most desirable attitudes of a prospective employee, leader, or manager is an ability to see challenges as opportunities, setbacks as temporary inconveniences. This positive attitude also welcomes change as friendly, and is not upset by surprises, even negative surprises. How we approach challenges and problems is a crucial aspect of our decision-making process, whether in business or in our personal lives.

In the 1920s, when Ernest Hemingway was working hard to perfect his craft, he lost a suitcase containing all his manuscripts—many stories he'd laboriously polished to jewellike perfection—which he'd been planning to publish as a book. The devastated Hemingway couldn't conceive of redoing his work. He could think only of the months he'd devoted to his arduous writing—and for nothing, he was now convinced. But when he lamented his loss to the poet Ezra Pound, Pound called it a stroke of luck. Pound assured Hemingway that when he rewrote the stories, he would forget the weak parts; only the best material would reappear. Instead of framing the event in disappointment, Pound cast it in the light of opportunity. Hemingway did rewrite the stories—and the rest, as they say, is history: He became one of the major figures in American literature.

FAILURE AVOIDANCE

In companies and environments in which criticism, pessimism, cynicism, and motivation by fear prevail, a condition develops that I see all too often in business. Fear of failure leads to avoiding failure at all costs.

The trouble with failure avoidance is that it's simultaneously avoidance of success, which depends on taking risks. Innovation and creativity are impossible when employees are afraid because they're penalized for failure. The first play of Charles Lamb, a celebrated British essayist and critic, was hissed off the stage. Seated in the audience, Lamb was so afraid of being identified as the author that he hissed too. Tennessee Williams's first play was booed so loudly that the producers came forward and apologized to the audience.

Early experience usually teaches that failure is to be avoided at all costs. This begins in childhood, when we encounter the first "No!" It grows like a weed when we are criticized by our parents and other family members, by our teachers, and by our peers. It leads to associating ourselves with our mistakes, to a self-image of clumsiness and awkwardness.

Our world of put-downs does little to relieve this—a world in which the media magnifies problems and celebrity status, but where entrepreneurial business success is often viewed as the product of manipulative selfishness. Many people seek security from that noise by riding quietly with the system, not rocking the boat. Despite biographies, documentaries, and other programs about rags-to-riches success, most people, unable to imagine it for themselves, develop a habit of looking back at past problems—which is failure reinforcement—and of imagining similar performances in the future, which is failure forecasting. They either set their sights too high, reinforcing their fears and ensuring failure, or low enough to avoid failure with a sure thing. Their inner dialogue usually falls within the two extremes. "Stand by. Things are going too well, something will spoil it." Or, "I knew this was too good to be true. With my luck, it was bound to go sour."

Fear of failure can become a built-in motivation. Leaders like to succeed and feel good about themselves; fearful people, focused on failure avoidance so as not to feel worse about themselves, refuse to try. External factors can also boost fear of failure. If, for example, half a division must be laid off, factory or office workers who have long performed well may be seized by the diminishing, damaging fear.

IMPROVE OR ELSE!

I recently presented an employee productivity program to a large division of a Fortune 500 company manufacturing integrated circuit boards in competition with the Japanese. After my talk about leadership lessons, the huge facility's general manager mounted the stage and gave his two thousand workers what he thought was a parting motivational message. "What we must have from all of you is a 17 percent increase in quality production in six months, or we're faced with closing down the plant. Have a good weekend."

His words had the predictable effect. The leaders and achievers increased their performance by about 20 percent. But many nonachievers found more secure jobs and quit within weeks—and the plant did shut down after about six months. This was more confirmation that genuine leaders focus on the benefits of success, while those chiefly motivated by fear concentrate on failure's painful consequences.

Some bosses and managers argue that employees motivated by fear work as hard or even harder than those with positive motivations. They are deluding themselves. Fear motivation is as obsolete as communism because it simply doesn't work as an effective leadership tool.

Psychological research proves that people who fear failure are more likely to fail in assignments of medium difficulty—those with approximately equal chances of success or failure—than those without such fears. This is true even when the failure-avoiders are better qualified for particular assignments than their more positively motivated colleagues. Anxiety about failure doesn't merely diminish performance. It also stifles the motivation to succeed in the first place.

LEARNED HELPLESSNESS

Learned helplessness is a belief that we're at the mercy of external forces and no longer in control of what is happening to us. Behaviorists emphasize that this feeling is indeed learned. Martin Seligman, a psychologist at the University of Pennsylvania and author of the bestselling *Learned Optimism,* has made a very detailed study of learned helplessness—and confirms it's a trait we acquire, not inherit at birth.

Some years ago, I held a seminar for an NFL Super Bowl champion team that was trying to repeat a near-perfect season. A clinical hypnotist also on the program demonstrated how easy it is to learn helplessness. He put a burly fullback into a state of relaxation, then placed a three-ounce paperweight on the locker room floor, suggesting it weighed five hundred pounds. Then he asked the mighty fullback, who could ordinarily bench press a stocked freezer, to pick it up. "If it weighs five hundred pounds," the player replied, "I don't think I can lift it." But he tried. He strained and puffed. His face turned purple, the veins on his arms distended—but he couldn't budge the little glass cube. We all suspected this was a comedy act the two had worked up for laughs. But when the fullback's biceps were monitored with biofeedback instruments, they indicated that he was pulling up with a force that would have lifted a four-hundred-pound barbell from the floor. Why did he fail with the three-ounce paperweight? The same instruments measuring his triceps indicated that they were pushing down to keep the paperweight where he "knew" it belonged—pushing down, it was established, with more force than he was using to try to lift it.

The larger explanation was that the powerful man's mind forced him to work against himself so that he could confirm his picture of an immovable object on the floor. Thus, an idea he accepted made him his own worst enemy. How often we hypnotize ourselves or our employees or children into believing we're helpless victims of external circumstance when actually that's what we've *chosen* to believe. If you ever feel you're trying your hardest but getting nowhere, take a moment to ask yourself whether you really believe you can succeed. If you're not truly convinced of the possibility, make a conscious effort to clear your mind of learned helplessness. Think of the fullback who had the physical ability to toss the little paperweight through the Superdome roof when he wasn't fighting himself.

THE RATCHET EFFECT

One of the best ways to overcome learned helplessness and to help employees and others become positively motivated is to break down long-term goals into smaller, nearer ones so that a high expected probability of success can be maintained. We would choke on a steak if we tried to swallow it all in one go, but bite-size pieces give us several kinds of longer-lasting delight. It's easier to keep moving toward an initial, more reachable goal—and also easier to correct our course if we miss. Attaining smaller goals helps us believe we can achieve our larger ones, increasing our perception of success for even the most complex designs.

Sports and industrial psychologists have studied goal-setting carefully. Working with our Olympic athletes over many years, my colleagues and I learned to emphasize that the decathlon, for example, was a series of ten subgoals; that marathon races had a series of subgoals, with benchmarks along their routes. Almost every gold medal winner in sports and business forms an aerial view of his or her race as a whole, then uses smaller goals as progress guides and positive motivational reinforcements. Goals must be specific and vivid in order to be meaningful, with real pulling power. Although the human mind, the most marvelous computer ever created, can consider nebulous general thoughts, the more specific the input, the more detailed the image for generating motivational force.

THE VOODOO OF PESSIMISM

I share with many audiences a true story about a man named Nick. (A reenactment of this story on film is available through American Media in Des Moines, Iowa.) Nick, a strong, healthy railroad yardman, got along well with his fellow workers and was consistently reliable on the job. However, he was a deep pessimist who invariably feared the worst. One summer day, the train crews were told they could quit an hour early in honor of the foreman's birthday. When the other workmen left the site, Nick, the notorious worrier, was accidentally locked in an isolated refrigerated boxcar that was in the yard for repairs.

He panicked. He shouted and banged until his voice went hoarse and his fists were bloody. The noises, if anyone heard them, were assumed to be coming from a nearby playground or from other trains backing in and out of the yard.

Nick reckoned the temperature in the car was zero degrees. "If I can't get out," he thought, "I'll freeze to death." He found a cardboard box. Shivering uncontrollably, he scrawled a message to his wife and family. "So cold, body's getting numb. If I could just go to sleep. These may be my last words."

The next morning, the crew slid open the boxcar's heavy doors and found Nick's body. An autopsy revealed that every physical sign indicated he had frozen to death. But the car's refrigeration unit was inoperative. The temperature inside was about 61 degrees and there was plenty of fresh air. Nick's fear had become a self-fulfilling prophecy.[3]

LEE TREVINO'S POWER OF SUGGESTION

Once the brain has locked on to an idea, escaping it is almost impossible. I once played in a foursome with Lee Trevino during the Andy Williams/San Diego Open Golf Tournament, which I helped originate in 1968 as a charity benefit for the Salk Institute. Just before our group teed off, Lee did a little psych job on us. "Do you fellows breathe in or out during your backswing?" he inquired with seeming innocence. Preparing to tee off, I tried to put the devilishly disruptive question out of my mind—but ended thinking about it, or trying *not* to think about it, so insistently that I sliced my drive into the gallery of three thousand Lee Trevino groupies. Only his money golfer's wink betrayed his ploy. We never found my ball.

The lesson is not to anticipate setbacks—not to think about them—even if you acknowledge the possibility that some are inevitable. If you do think about them, they'll overwhelm you. Keep your eyes on the ball and your mind on the goal.

CONCENTRATE ON THE REAL THING

The FBI trains its agents to spot counterfeit bills by using real ones. The agents study, study, study—but only genuine money. They steep themselves in the characteristics of authentic one-, five-, ten-, twenty-, fifty-, and hundred-dollar bills until their appraisal of them becomes virtually instinctive—at which point they also instantly recognize counterfeit bills when they encounter them. With minds uncluttered with counterfeiters' common mistakes—what might be wrong, what's usually omitted—they know what they're looking for. To specialists in the real thing, imitations seem glaringly obvious. And if you allow yourself to think about all that could go wrong or the penalties of failure, you're far more likely to hobble your performance with those penalties. Continually tell yourself what to do, not what *not* to do.

Here are some action ideas that will help you avoid negative motivation by framing your own expectations in a healthy, positive way:

1. Visualize, think of, and speak well of your health. Don't dwell on your ailments or they'll reward you by visiting more often and staying longer. Focus on your own well-being and that of your close ones.
2. Read and listen to the news and reports of professional growth, but resist the temptation to pollute your mind with the sordid details of others' tragedies. Getting hooked on tabloid exposés will make you jaded and cynical.

3. Select more friends and associates who are optimists and highly motivated leaders. Mutual attraction should be less in the sharing of problems than in sharing solutions and goals.

4. Find a positive lesson and a positive reason for all your personal relationships. Accentuate the blessings and knowledge gained from each.

5. Learn to unhook your prejudices, especially in the new multicultural working environments. Make it a point to be more open and friendly with someone you may not have been comfortable associating with in your previous mind-set.

6. Learn to stay relaxed and friendly no matter how much pressure you're under. Be constructively helpful instead of unhelpfully critical.

7. Make a list of your current wants and desires and jot down the benefits you will get when you achieve them. Consult this list often during the day and before retiring at night.

8. When dealing with your associates and subordinates, don't criticize failures in front of others. Correct mistakes only in private, and allow more latitude by looking at them, whenever possible, as conceivable innovations. Open criticism of others' mistakes will make them failure avoiders who will stop innovating and experimenting.

9. Instead of comparing yourself to others, set your own standards for achievement. Accept yourself as you are, but keep upgrading your goals, skills, and desires so they're challenging and prompt real commitment and effort to achieve.

10. Above all, put your wishes and goals in positive terms. Live to greet success, not to avoid failure.

EIGHT

SELF-LEADERSHIP AND PASSION: YOUR PURPOSE IN ACTION

1 ◆ *Is your career driven by a mission?*

2 ◆ *Why did you select your current profession?*

3 ◆ *If it weren't for economic considerations and your current responsibilities, how would you spend your time?*

Lisa, OUR YOUNGEST DAUGHTER, RECENTLY EARNED HER MASTER'S DE-gree to start a career as a high school English teacher. I doubt she was more excited about her graduation than her parents were. As we entered the stadium for the commencement services, it dawned on me that after putting seven children through college and graduate studies, I'd finally be able to fund my retirement plan.

It was very hot in the concrete arena. A midday sun beat squarely in our faces. I suspected that the exercises would be long and merciless. As the graduates filed in, I was amused to see slogans taped to their tasseled caps. "Will work for food!" "Get my room ready, Mom!" Our daughter's read, "Thanks, Mom and Pop." Some wore bathing suits beneath their gowns. Some blew bubbles with a pipe and soap. Most were ecstatic about finally leaving school, visibly impatient for that night's parties and for freedom and the chance to earn.

OLMOS "STOOD AND DELIVERED"

As the warm-up speakers droned on about politically correct issues, I wondered whether any time would remain for the main speaker. In fact, his address lasted barely ten minutes, which may have set a national record for brevity. (Winston Churchill holds the international record: thirty seconds to repeat "Never give up!" nine times.) That main speaker was Edward James Olmos, the actor-activist who played Jaime Escalante in an inspiring movie about inner-city students called *Stand and Deliver.* Olmos stood up, removed his cap, and regarded the graduates. "So we're ready to party?" he asked. "Yeah, let's party!" they answered in unison. "I know, thank God it's Friday," he resumed. "But commencement means to begin, not finish. You've had a four-year sabbatical from life, and now you're ready to go out there and earn. You're only beginning Real World 101 in your education.

"One more thing before we leave," he continued. "Please never, ever work for money. Please don't just get a job. A job is something that many of you had while you worked your way through college. A job is something you do for money. But a career is something you do because you must do it. You want to do it, you love doing it, you're excited when you do it. And you'd do it even if you were paid nothing beyond food and the basics. You'd do it because it's your life."

What he was saying, which I have tried to recall and interpret in my own words is that many of you will go out and try to get the highest-paying job possible, regardless of the industry, regardless of the opportunity, regardless of the service or product the company may provide. If you chase money, it may catch you—and if it catches you, you'll forever be its slave. By letting money pursue you but never catch you, you'll always be its master. By always doing what you love, loving what you do, delivering more than you promise, you'll always be underpaid—which is how it always should be.

For if you're paid more than you're worth, you may be restructured, reengineered, replaced, fired, declared obsolete, disposed of. Overpaid people are overdrawn in their knowledge bank account. People who are *underpaid* for the level and quality of the service they provide are always in demand and always ahead of the money in their knowledge and contribution. So money and opportunity are always chasing them. This is what I got out of the commencement speech that day.

Olmos concluded with a charged voice and moist eyes. Chase your passion, not your pension! Be inspired to learn as much as you can, to know as much as you can, to gain skills as much as you can, to find a cause that benefits humankind—and you'll be sought after for your quality of service and dedication to excellence. This passion will make you oblivious to quitting time and to the length of your workday. You'll awake every morning with the passion of pursuit, but not the pursuit of money. . . . Those who do more than they're paid for are always sought for their services. Their name and work outlive them, and always command the highest price. Chase your passion, not your pension.

The graduates were stunned. Many cried with joy. I was speechless, which is rare indeed. Olmos was no actor speaking for an honorarium. He was all passion, pure and simple. "Maybe we should have taught that in a class," I heard a faculty member say. "Chase your passion, not your pension!"

The paradoxical proverb is:

You must get money to chase you, but never let it catch you.

MOTIVE IN ACTION

Motivation is a contraction of *motive* and *action.* An inner force that compels behavior, it comes from within, not from any external circumstance. You know where you're going because you have a compelling image inside, not a travel poster on the wall, a financial statement with a big bonus, or a slogan in the hall. The performance of many externally motivated individuals begins declining as soon as they win contests of one sort or another. I've personally witnessed this among Super Bowl champions and World Cup teams that lose the incentive to maintain their excellence after winning the cup, the honors, and the cash.

ARCHIE BUNKER LIVES AT OUR HOUSE

I remember admonishing our six birth children that their adopted sister, who came from very disadvantaged circumstances in Mexico, seemed to be succeeding more rapidly than several of them who had had a very substantial socioeconomic head start. My birth children thought for just a moment before replying. "I guess she's doing better, Dad, because we have your genes. Besides, you treated her more like a customer and us more like employees."

Lately, I've stopped lecturing my children and started listening more carefully to *their* desires and motivations. I'm also more aware of my friends' and associates' inner passions and desires. For we are all children who grew up with our individual childhood dreams—then tried or didn't try to attain them, felt hope, joy, frustration, and devastation along the way.

THE INNER DRIVE

If you're really committed to peak performance and leadership, you must motivate yourself from within. Studies of achievers show that inner drives for excellence and independence are far more powerful than desire for wealth, status, or recognition.

COMPETITION REDEFINED FOR THE KNOWLEDGE ERA

David Sarnoff, the founder of NBC, said that competition brings out the best in products and sometimes the worst in people. Although a competitive nature can help push individuals toward outstanding performance, it can also hold them back from enjoying the success that's been attained.

In this age of self-directed management teams, we must all be a member of a team rather than independent leaders. It's difficult for a highly competitive person to share success and the credit for it. And others, in turn, hesitate to share a mission with an extremely aggressive competitor whom they know is hell-bent to get ahead of them rather than helping them achieve their goals. I'm not trying to argue that it's inherently wrong for individuals to be highly competitive or to want to win in their industry. Or that it's wrong for an airline or burger chain or rent-a-car franchise to compete with the others. Hardly! It's enough to remember the Communist countries to appreciate how necessary competition is for providing goods and services of any quality. Competition itself is not the culprit. The real culprits are insatiable drives for status and power, at least a little of which is in all of us.

The Latin root of compete is *competere:* "to come together, agree, be suitable, belong, compete for." Nothing there suggests a need for a killer instinct. We've added that little feature by coming to believe that excellence can be achieved only at the expense of others. In true competition, a person or group wins for having done a superior job that, for example, moves them to a high level of management. But the right approach to competition should make everyone better off for having run the race.

An inner drive for excellence motivates you always to be the best you possibly can in whatever you do. Leaders and managers should take special note here. They must be careful in their use of external motivators—money, perks, prestigious offices and titles—in trying to inspire their team members and employees. Enduring motivation must always come ultimately from within the individual.

HIRE PEOPLE WHO HAVE EMPOWERED THEMSELVES

That's why empowerment and vision are so crucial to team performance and quality. *Their* power and *their* vision, not those of the leader, must compel team members. Interviewing potential members, you should look for internally motivated individuals who hold their work important for its own sake, who love their field or their industry, who seek the exhilaration of testing their limits and contributing to the world. Be wary if they show more interest in your compensation package than in their contribution package.

Behavioral scientists have found that independent desire for excellence is the most telling predictor of significant achievement. In other words, the success of our efforts depends less on the efforts themselves than on our motives. The most successful companies, like the most successful men and women in almost all fields, achieved their greatness out of a desire to express what they felt *had* to be expressed. Often it was a desire to use their skills to their utmost in order to solve a problem. This is not to say that many of them did not also earn a great deal of money and prestige. William Shakespeare, Thomas Edison, Estee Lauder, Walt Disney, Sam Walton, and Bill Gates all became wealthy. But far more than thoughts of profit, the key to their success was inspiration and inner drive by creating or providing excellence in a product or a service. All were motivated by the desire to produce the very best, to express the very best that was in them.

If you thought passion was out of fashion, the truth is the opposite. "Now is a great time to start a new venture," *Fortune* magazine flatly declared in 1994. The lessons of an article entitled "Lessons from America's Fastest-Growing Companies" are that fierce enthusiasm and faith in people who themselves exude the same enthusiasm are critical to self-assertion, perseverance, and expansion. David Birch, president of an economic research company named Cognetics, calls some of the smaller fastest-growing companies "gazelles" for their ability to leap ahead. Grow Biz International, a chain of almost six hundred franchised stores that sell new and used computers, sporting equipment, musical instruments, and children's clothing, is one of the leading gazelles. As many as 90 percent of its franchise owners are former middle managers who lost their jobs when their corporations reengineered and downsized. But they too, full of new passion, are doing well again.[1]

SETTLE FOR THE INNER APPLAUSE

The late Ray Kroc, a former neighbor who founded McDonald's Corporation when he was in his fifties, stressed the importance of people doing a good job for the inner satisfaction, not just for the money. Ray said most people find it difficult to associate applause with their work when they can't hear literal applause—but the important applause should come from within. It is the faster heartbeat, the pride and satisfaction of accomplishment.

Kroc told the University of Southern California's Business School that the first thing a business executive needs is love of an idea. If you don't love your concept, drop it. If you prostitute yourself at an early age by taking a job where the money is, you'll be working for money all your life. Loving their work is particularly important for younger people. If they lose that love early, they may never grow to anywhere near their potential for self-actualization.

LOVE IT OR LEAVE IT

In *Megatraits,* Dr. Doris Lee McCoy, a colleague of mine who studies leaders, reported that the chief cause of lost motivation is a career unsuited to the loser's talents. Too many people choose their work for convenience, then merely put in their hours before they can go home to what they really enjoy. Leaders do it differently. First, they seek careers that are most rewarding and interesting in terms of their potential. Second, they accept that they may have to go through several job changes, testing and discovering new talents in the process—until they find the career in which they can develop their talents to the maximum.

What does that mean for you and me? It means we should remember our benchmarking in Chapter 3. We should carefully access the fields and disciplines that are most enjoyable and in which we're most talented. This is where you'll do your best and feel most rewarded.

If money is your chief object in choosing a career, you'll be likely to abandon it when you can make more at something else. Eventually, you'll find yourself wondering what you're doing, maybe even who you really are. Without the inner motivation to stay on a particular path, your journey will be arduous. Your motivation will further weaken whenever the external financial reward seems remote or out of sight.

LOOKING FOR NIRVANA

What's it like to spend an entire life wandering from one path to another, always looking for an easier way to strike gold and never achieving a goal worthy of your passion or potential? I meet many such people. If they're in sales, they move from company to company, industry to industry, product to product. They're very hard to keep in your Rolodex because they are either coming or going, starting a new business of their own—and when that fails, joining a new diet company that promises you can lose all the weight you want by wearing a patch on your arm. In short, they go from one Roman candle to another, from one exciting opportunity to the next disappointment. Money is a destination, not the journey. It should be only part of the transportation system, like fuel for your car.

MISSION OVER TEDIUM

When I was growing up during World War II, parachutes were made by the thousands. It was a tedious job. Workers hunched over a sewing machine eight to ten hours a day, stitching endless lengths of fabric that seemed no more than formless heaps. But every morning, those workers were told that their every stitch was an essential part of a life-saving operation. They were asked to remember that one of their parachutes—*any* one of them—might be used by their husband, brother, or son. All would be used by *someone's* loved ones. Although the work was hard and the hours long, the men and women on the home front were buoyed by the importance of their contribution.

The same should apply to all occupations at all times. The passion of knowing what you want to do and where you want to go puts you halfway down the road to the empire in your mind. But only a tiny percentage of Americans think about those crucial considerations. Most people, it's been said, spend more time preparing for a family outing than setting specific goals for their lives.

LEARNING HOW TO CARE

In the summer of 1993, the rivers of the Midwest—the Mississippi, Missouri, and others—surged over levees into communities and farmlands. During this worst flooding in regional history, heroic volunteers worked to near exhaustion filling sandbags around the clock. In one instance, they were joined by a group of convicts from a boot-camp prison program in Greene County, Illinois. The convicts had been sent to help with sandbags for shoring up a levee. If it failed, the little town of Inota on the Iowa-Illinois border faced destruction.

The criminals worked with furious passion and energy. They refused to sleep. They wouldn't leave the sandbag brigades even to eat. Still, the levee gave way and the town, with its two hundred houses, was lost. Now the convicts wept openly in frustration and compassion. Why had they suddenly become good samaritans? Because after dealing in drugs, violence, and destruction, they had a positive purpose in life, perhaps for the first time. They had a mission to save a town. Observing people who cared for each other working as one for the same goal, they began to care.

GENERATION "X" AS IN eXCELLENT

Purpose is the engine that powers our lives. The fuel it burns to move us forward is the passion of a mission. When Mark Twain was asked the reason for his success, his reply reflected this understanding: "I was born excited," he said. A leader can't kindle a fire in others' hearts until it's burning in his or her own. That's what the following three people have done while still in their twenties—young men and women of a generation we often call Generation X.

Rent-a-Wreck

Chris and her husband, Jason, own two of Rent-a-Wreck's most profitable franchises. Their business in Palm Springs, California, went so well that they opened a large cellular phone and car service store. Initially Chris and Jason knew nothing about running a business. When their first customer asked the price of a mid-sized car, Chris put him on hold, called Hertz for its price, and shaved it by a few dollars. Now the young couple have paid off their loans, bought another franchise in San Diego, and swelled their fleet from twelve to nearly one hundred cars. Chris and Jason are not in the stands while the real players are sweating it out on the field. This dynamic couple knows where they want to go and are *doing* it: meeting their goals and tapping into the diamond mine of their own potential.[2]

Just "Do It" James

James is a musician who founded Rebuild/Rejoice, a Los Angeles gospel choir that brings together Korean and black youths, something he knew was necessary after the terrible Los Angeles riots in 1992. Unhappy with an office job, James sang backup for two years for blues singer Maxine Otis. Then, while getting an MBA at UCLA, James received a $3,000 grant from the Los Angeles Art Fund to start his choir. His record label, called Do It, already has gospel choir recordings to its credit, and from all appearances that's just the beginning. "My friends look at me like I'm some freak of nature," says James, "but they're just afraid of doing their own thing. That's what I have to do."

James is meeting a social and spiritual need in an inner-city context that cries out for healing and mutual respect. He discovered that he could break away in his own back yard.[3]

Beating the Odds

Kimberly, another person in her twenties who ignored the odds, was an indifferent student who never went to college. At twenty-one, she married a truck driver, became a secretary, and later was made director of an asbestos-removal holding company. But Kimberly was fascinated by computers and decided to go into business with a partner. They founded JVC Technologies, Inc., a Wayne, Pennsylvania, computer networking organization. Kimberly was then a divorced mother with a young child.

They started very small. At first, they were barely able to cover expenses. But as I write this, JVC Technologies is projecting double-digit millions in annual revenues and Kimberly is drawing a six-figure salary. Having finally discovered her passion—computer networking—she decided to go for it despite her wobbly educational background and the heavy odds.[4]

Ralph Gomory, president of the Alfred P. Sloan Foundation, warns that you can't win by comparing yourself to where you were last year: Your competitors are also learning and progressing. To catch up, you must actually go faster than the leader—which means devoting some of your leisure hours to reading books, magazines, and reports when others are watching television. It means using your own money, if necessary, for a self-improvement program. It means getting out of the office to talk to workers on the factory floor, to salespeople on the road, and to the customers, whom you must never take for granted.

THE PASSION LEASE ON LIFE

Passion in your purpose will help you take control of your life, and also give you one other advantage that is not widely recognized: ten more years of life, on average. Pursuit of a goal wears out very few people. But they rust out by the hundreds of thousands when their pursuit of happiness turns into a geriatric park.

On the *Today* show some time ago, Willard Scott interviewed a Mr. Smith, who was celebrating his 102nd birthday. Mr. Smith had brought along his potted plants, which he proudly referred to as his "upstarts" during the brief conversation. Willard became a little frustrated. Time was running out, and Mr. Smith's fond attention went only to his chrysanthemums and orchids.

"But Mr. Smith, we'd all like to know to what you attribute *your* long life," said Willard, trying to direct him to what he believed was the main point. Mr. Smith, not the least senile, continued showing off his flowers. He touched them, sprayed them with water, and gazed at them lovingly—while the clock ticked on at $100,000 per minute. "This little lovely won't bloom for another two years," he chuckled. Willard made a final attempt to discover his formula for longevity. "What's your secret for living so long and staying so alive?"

The old man replied with a question of his own: "Who would take care of these beautiful flowers?" Willard Scott sighed. The director cut away to a commercial. I hoped the viewers had gotten Mr. Smith's very profound point. He might never see some of his flowers in full bloom, but he had just given millions the secret of longevity: have a purpose that will outlive you and pursue it with a passion.

You must look within for value, but must look beyond for perspective.

DREAMS OUT OF ASHES

Most start-up companies begin with a compelling idea for a product or service, as James C. Collins reminded us in an insightful article in *Inc.* magazine of July 1993. And many of us once yearned to do something extraordinary. Maybe you too have a burning desire to do something great, to take a big risk and make your dreams come true—but you're not yet sure about precisely what to do. You have core values but you don't know what form they will take; you lack an idea suitable for the market. Take heart, because you're not alone.

In 1945, a young inventor named Masaru Ibuka decided to start a company in the ruins of defeated, demoralized Japan. Masaru rented a room in a bombed-out Tokyo department store. He started with seven employees and $1,600 in personal savings. "The little group sat in conference in the depressing surroundings of the burned-out department store," remembered Akio Morita, who joined them shortly thereafter. "For weeks they tried to figure out what kind of business the new company should enter." That was the birth of Sony Corporation.[5]

Hewlett-Packard started under similar circumstances. Bill Hewlett and Dave Packard had no specific idea to pursue when they founded their company in the late 1930s. Their goal was relatively vague—something like "going into the electronic engineering field." They developed a bowling foul-line indicator, a clock drive for telescopes, and a widget to make urinals flush automatically. While Hewlett-Packard is not famous for its urinal flushers, its name is on a wide range of high-tech electronic equipment and computer-oriented products, including the printer that produced the outline for this book.

And remember Paul Galvin, who started out repairing and later manufacturing battery eliminators for Sears radios—humble beginnings that eventually gave us Motorola. And Jay Willard Marriott, who wanted to build a successful business into a first-class institution. The young Mormon missionary started his company—later to become the Marriott Corporation—with an A&W Root Beer stand in Washington, D.C. Many businesses started with just an idea, which may have been no more than the core passion of the principals.

Here are some questions to stimulate your thinking while you look for your core passion:

1. What product or service can you offer that isn't now being offered?
2. How can you position yourself in a way that's different from how you're doing it right now?
3. Where's the niche that hasn't been developed?
4. How can you add value to the service or product you now produce?
5. Where is the market inefficiency?
6. What would make the process or procedure more convenient?
7. How can you do this less expensively?
8. What would people pay for what isn't now available?
9. What would my customer or client group want if it were available?
10. What do you most enjoy doing and want to do more of?
11. How can you make a living from doing what you consider fun, challenging, and never boring?
12. What trends will change your colleagues' and competitors' current assumptions about your field?
13. What's next for that small service corporation with the one employee: You, Inc.?

PUT YOUR SIGNATURE ON YOUR CAREER

No one could answer these questions better than Antonio Stradivari, an Italian violin maker who lived from 1644 to 1737. Stradivari died at the age of ninety-three, at a time when the average life expectancy was a little over thirty-five years. He taught himself his trade. His tools were primitive, and he usually worked alone until late in life, when his sons joined him. Stradivari had a passion. He put the best of himself into every violin and viola. When he was finished and was certain that his craftsmanship measured up to his personal standards, he signed his name on the instrument.

Nearly three hundred years later, his violins sell for hundreds of thousands and even millions of dollars, and Stradivarius is a synonym for quality throughout the world. But far from every man or woman with uncommon standards of excellence become celebrities. At this very moment, thousands or tens of thousands are working unknown and unsung in industry, the arts, and the sciences. The public has never heard of them and probably never will; yet they refuse to turn out shoddy work. They are in the minority, but that's where they've always been—playing for a gallery of one, for their own inner applause. Remember, people who consistently do things well set their own standards and make themselves measure up. In so doing, they:

- Give the best of themselves to benefit others, making their work a source of joy and satisfaction while they experience deep self-respect from being uncommon contributors.
- Build a kind of security that lasts a lifetime or beyond, because respect for quality always abides and will always command the highest price. If you accept nothing but excellence from yourself and feel entitled to put your name on your work, both will endure. The bitterness of poor quality lingers on long after the sweetness of low price.

Chase your passion, not your pension!

NINE

❖

SELF-LEADERSHIP AND POWER: YOUR INVISIBLE FORCE

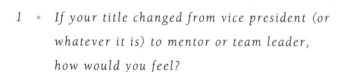

1 ❖ *If your title changed from vice president (or whatever it is) to mentor or team leader, how would you feel?*

2 ❖ *Is being nurturing and sensitive compatible with bottom-line leadership?*

3 ❖ *How easy is it for you to give up power, once you get it?*

THERE'S A NEW POWER TRAIN ON THE INFORMATION SUPERHIGHWAY. IF you run a business, lead a team, or are otherwise trying to remain competitive in the changing world, you'll be stranded if you miss it.

THE GLOBAL POWER TRAIN

Global competition is powered by information access. Information access is powered by technology. Technology is powered by capital investment. Capital investment is powered by profits. Profits are powered by revenues. Revenues are powered by volume and repeat sales. Volume and repeat sales are powered by customer loyalty. Customer loyalty is powered by customer satisfaction. Customer satisfaction is powered by value. Value is powered by employee productivity. Employee productivity is powered by employee loyalty. Employee loyalty is powered by employee satisfaction. Employee satisfaction is powered by the working environment. The working environment is powered by management stewardship. Management stewardship is powered by invisible leadership. . . .

And invisible leadership is exercising the vision to change the traditional role from commander to coach, from manager to mentor, from director to delegator—from one who demands respect to one who facilitates self-respect.

THE INVISIBLE LEADER

Effective leadership can no longer be exercised from a power position atop a command-and-control hierarchy. It must be redirected to independent relationships with shared visions, goals, and responsibilities.

Instant availability of most information to everyone is a key cause of the gigantic economic, political, and technological upheavals taking place throughout the world. Even diplomatic and foreign policy developments now become known around the globe as soon as they arise, thanks to CNN. The dramatic transformations caused by knowledge portability and global competition leave no time to pass orders down a chain of command. Leaders must empower others to react quickly. Either we work synergistically in teams or we fall disastrously behind.

One major consequence of the free flow of information is the growing awareness among the world's poorer peoples of the disparity between their lifestyles and those in the industrialized countries. Among the poor, including those recently oppressed by communism and prisoners of surviving dictatorships, there's a new hunger for individual empowerment. Vietnam, for example, is becoming a thriving free economy. "The Americans didn't destroy Hanoi," declared a Vietnamese foreign official recently. "We destroyed it ourselves—with a romantic view of socialism and rent control!"

The knowledge revolution has also spawned mass migration, not only westward in Europe from the former Eastern Bloc countries, but also from North Africa and the sub-Sahara countries. It continues relentlessly in North America—from Latin America, Asia, and the Middle East. The migration is partly driven by the declining importance of raw materials, replaced as the strategic resources by information, education, and know-how. McDonald's and Coca-Cola don't transport meat, bread, syrup, or containers, but knowledge, in the form of secret formulas and organizational techniques.

The sweeping changes have sharpened the focus even further on both customers and employees. With less margin for error and lower profit margins, corporations must place the right people in the key positions to get more productivity from downsized, already overworked staffs. Sheer survival requires them to inspire teamwork, creativity, and innovation—which is why human capital has become the most important resource.

Nothing can substitute for job satisfaction, the prime motivator of employee loyalty and performance. Often employees lowest on a company's pay scale provide its end product or service to the customers. The game's over unless they please the customer and help generate repeat business. And the customer expectations that drive the marketplace will be higher tomorrow, and even higher next year.

This chapter draws from "Reassigning Responsibility," an excellent article by Peter Block in *Sky* magazine of February 1994. Here are some of Block's central concepts.[1]

This is the age not of Aquarius but of celebrity. We pump up the star news anchor, the star football coach, the star everybody, and fly the image far above others on his or her team or company. That's evidently important for advertising and publicity, but the near-blinding spotlight on star leaders usually leaves in the dark those who actually assemble the outboard motor, check the motherboard, confirm the airline reservation, and deliver the envelope for the messenger service. And *they're* the people, the troops in the field of producing goods and services, who must change in order to make reengineering and other reform efforts a reality.

Are they changing, these modern hewers of wood and drawers of water? Not always, even in companies officially devoted to all the latest management trends and techniques. A study sponsored by the Association for Quality and Participation revealed that while more than 70 percent of the top thousand U.S. companies had employee involvement programs, they affected less than 15 percent of their employees, most of these being upper and middle management. And, as we've stressed, the attitudes of employees—their enthusiasm, sense of personal commitment, sense of satisfaction—is crucial to success.

In many cases, we'd do better to convert that spotlight on the company "name," or star, into a warm, diffused light that would shine into every corner, giving everyone the recognition and sense of value he or she needs to become a full participant in the knowledge era. The massive publicity focused on leader-celebrities often has the unintended effect of diminishing a sense of participation and responsibility on the part of those who need it most, for all our sakes. This is why another paradoxical proverb applies:

You must participate in person, but lead invisibly.

Effective leadership in the knowledge era must promote initiative and responsibility, which simply can't be done by wagging fingers and presuming to know what's best for others. All the old effort to exert supremacy, display self-importance, and maintain control only smothers the needed new qualities in our workers, and the acclamation of stars can do this too. Our leaders must call us to a mission and inspire us to get there, but be very careful not to try to hold on to outmoded power, which fosters dependence instead of independence and subverts a sense of community and responsibility.

Peter Block suggests that an alternative to traditional leadership might be stewardship—not a perfect concept, but a lead to exploring fundamental change in organizations seeking a competitive edge in the new era. Business stewardship is feeling deeply accountable for a company's future without trying to control others or saddle them with codes of behavior. Shifting the spotlight to the people actually doing the daily work, stewardship focuses on individual and team responsibility and sense of ownership or commitment. The idea is to center the change effort around those who serve customers, treating them pretty much like franchise owners. Workers are offered the training previously designed for managers. Work teams are empowered to find the means and to take the controls for creating and maintaining a productive environment for themselves. This process is transforming leaders so they exercise relationship power rather than position power.[2]

Since the 1950s, the cost of manufactured goods has more or less steadily decreased in real terms, while their quality, variety, and accumulation of attractive features have increased dramatically. This trend too will surely continue into the 21st century, probably accelerating as better design and materials improve and speed manufacturing processes and the capabilities of the service industries. The worldwide competition is certain to grow even more intense.

Those who meet it will do so by identifying and taking advantage of changes in technology, production, distribution, and organization. They will do this quickly, beating their competitors in reaction times.

Infused with entrepreneurial spirit, growth companies of the future will operate with newer facilities and lower unit costs. Unrestricted by bureaucratic attitudes or bureaucratic structures, they will be highly flexible. Very soon, new global market leaders will emerge, having come seemingly from nowhere—which again underlines the obsolescence of the old hierarchical model.

Sunrise Medical, Inc., designs, manufactures, and markets medical products used in institutional and home-care settings to address the recovery, rehabilitation, and respiratory needs of the patient. Based in Carlsbad, California, the multinational firm has increased its sales by 22 percent compounded for the last ten years. Net income rose by 31 percent compounded during the same period. The company has had seven consecutive record years, twenty-three consecutive record quarters—so its founder and leader would seem to know what he's talking about.

He is Richard Chandler, chairman and chief executive officer of Sunrise Medical, Inc. I followed him on the speaker's platform at a local chapter meeting of the Young Presidents' Organization (YPO) in Southern California. Everyone in the audience was taking notes, and I was impressed that he was willing to share his leadership philosophy with other company presidents on the Pursuit of Excellence program he has initiated throughout his company.

Chandler believes that company success depends on everyone from the shop floor up being a leader-entrepreneur.[3] To meet the competition of well-designed, high-quality products from home and abroad, we must steadily improve our products and service—and everything else, he warns, is fluff. He details a succession of paradigm shifts that compel us to change our leadership style. First, the shifts in product design and technology: We've had electronics miniaturization, distributed data processing (PCs and work stations), cable broadcasting, noninvasive surgery, and cellular communications that generate competition from everywhere in the world.

In manufacturing processes, we've come from frozen-food processing to plastic injection molding to continuous-roll steel production to an international standard of 32-millimeter production, which means that a variety of configurations of assembled products are available because the basic parts will be milled to that standard. And there are the

Japanese innovations, especially "just-in-time" manufacturing, that have drastically changed assembly-line production, eliminating inventory stockpiles and inefficient work flow.

Retail shopping patterns have changed no less dramatically. We have drive-through restaurants and banks. Sales are soaring at shopping centers, megamalls, and mail-order houses. Television shopping combines mail-order and cable channels. We have CD-ROM catalogs and we'll soon have interactive computers that will further facilitate shopping from home. Soon we'll go directly to the Nordstrom channel and the Spiegel channel; meanwhile, a host of other retailers are producing new kinds of shows for existing channels.

In organization, we've moved from the old military-industrial model of hierarchies to profit-center structures and franchising. And we have employee empowerment, self-directed management teams, and a new emphasis on training and education.

Richard Chandler believes that hubris—in this context, a tendency to ignore everything not invented by the company or in the country—keeps American leaders from reacting more aggressively to these enormous paradigm shifts.[4] I hear the same diagnosis on my Asian travels. The business leaders I meet in Japan, Taiwan, and Singapore, in all the emerging economies, including China's free economic zones, say that our greatest business problem is arrogance. Our kind of arrogance, they say, is a reluctance to accept that innovations may come from elsewhere because our myopic view has been that America has always been the leader.

THE LEADER'S TRAP

The sprawling structure of our larger companies also slows reaction time. Management's attention is often diverted to government lobbying, financial dealings, and bureaucratic imperatives rather than being focused on the basic elements of the entrepreneurial challenge: filling the customers' needs with quality products and services! Like heavily armored battleships that are hard to turn in the water, big companies find it difficult to respond to the global market's breakneck changes. Chandler calls this the Leader's Trap.

The Leader's Trap is dug largely to protect the Golden Goose. The

Golden Goose is our historical way of doing things—whatever best-selling products or services are producing our profits for the moment. But the dogged protection of immediate profits often causes us to ignore long-range paradigm shifts and concentrate instead on implementing marginal improvements.

The appeal of trying to maintain profitability by continually and regularly making small functional improvements is very great. It's easy to understand why this approach still reigns in much of corporate America. That's an entirely logical, rational response to profit maximization in the short term—but it's absolutely disastrous in the long run. The incremental improvements that convince us we're moving things ahead can obscure the direction of that movement, often straight into the Leader's Trap.

ESCAPING THE TRAP

Especially in the hard work of adapting to momentous change—of pulling people from their accustomed and, in that sense, comfortable patterns—companies must tap into basic human motivations. Immediate profit can no longer be the goal of company incentive programs. They must also give awards for time-saving, customer service, and other new performance-oriented criteria. Individuals and teams must be recognized and appreciation given to people devoted to process or service improvement, even if these efforts haven't yet produced profitable results.

Although awards are nothing new in business, they're much more important than is generally recognized, especially when the award-winners are chosen by their peers. We've seen (in Chapter 5) that a sense of belonging, sometimes called the affiliation drive, is the first of the four legs of self-esteem. Another leg is a sense of individual identity—and carefully structured award programs can do much to enhance both. They should be bolstered with conscious programs for team building, departmental cooperation and competition, and company social events at which everyone is truly treated like family. Creativity is bolstered by ensuring that all ideas offered through the company suggestion system are acted on—at least preliminarily, with acknowledgment and explanation of what to expect further—within two weeks. Of course no employee who submits a suggestion should ever be made to look foolish or criticized for a "stupid idea." There's no such thing as a stupid suggestion but there *is* such a thing as stifling potentially valuable suggestions with insensitive reactions.

Another job attribute employees value deeply is autonomy: the opportunity to show their worth and develop their excellence by being given responsibility. Empowerment is the latest term for this management technique. Self-directed teams—teams that hire, evaluate, and discipline their own members, set their own goals, divide up their tasks, and take responsibility for their collective results—can become self-contained profit centers of a kind. The autonomy and empowerment must be supported by continuous training and education, perhaps the most critical aspect of the new corporate culture needed to meet the knowledge era's challenges.

YOUR CULTURE, MY CULTURE

Culture is the sum of social patterns characteristic of a group, from a coffee klatsch to an entire country. A firm's culture is formed by its history and by interpretations of, or myths about, that history; by management behavior, policies, and procedures; by formal and informal rules; by the lines and forms of company-wide communications; by reward structures; by the nature and tone of instructions and of group meetings; and by a hundred other determinants, down to the use of first or second names and the cleanliness of the rest rooms. If management doesn't mold the corporate culture, it will be done by whispers, rumor, innuendo, cynicism, griping, factional attacks, and all kinds of petty—or substantial—score-settling. If it is negative, word-of-mouth can be insidious for an organization. But if positive, it can be a powerful influence for the good on behavior.

Corporate culture affects every function. Whatever business you're in, it's multifaceted and all-encompassing—and almost impervious to change by a single-issue campaign. New leadership must be across-the-board and all-inclusive: a coordinated approach based on a genuine commitment to meet the information revolution head-on.

First among the knowledge era's essential requisites is intensive associate training. Other vital requirements are:

- Total Quality Management (TQM);
- a proven-in-action suggestion and recognition program;
- just-in-time manufacturing for inventory and production savings;
- continuous reinvestment in technology and in new plants and/or new equipment;
- productivity improvement programs;
- a program for rapid response in customer service.

Chandler suggests a test to measure cultural transformation. Is the company benchmarking with leading companies in its field? Is there a formal quality program? Is customer service performance measured regularly? Are formal training programs constantly upgrading employee skills? Are asset management measures steadily improving? Does an effective suggestion system stimulate associate/employee creativity? Are supervisors decreasing and self-directed teams increasing in number? Does the new company culture operate in all phases of daily life at work and at all company functions?

BEYOND COMPETITION

Individuals have their cultures, too. Whatever your job, whether you're an hourly worker or an executive with a bright white collar, you're the product of your personal culture—and if you don't consciously work at changing your personal culture to meet the demands of the knowledge era, you relinquish responsibility for that to the informed or ignorant opinion of friends, the water-fountain gossip, and the often baneful influence of the media, including the tabloids.

Richard Chandler believes CEOs have the key responsibility for transforming their corporate cultures. I believe that as the CEOs of our own lives, only we can make individual changes—changes urgently necessary, as we've seen, to cope with the massive technological and business transformations. The first step toward shaping your personal culture is launching a consciously planned excellence program to empower yourself and those who work with you. Many of the other corporate requisites also apply—such as corporate benchmarking, for example. Are individual managers and employees benchmarking with leaders in their own and other fields? Only you can reengineer You, Inc. By using examples of the best practices available to help renew yourself continuously, you'll be going beyond the competition.

So while the corporate CEO must provide the inspiration and vision for cultural change, he can complete it only by stepping aside and leading invisibly rather than telling others what to do and how to do it. This whole new approach to leadership, rooted in sharing power so that others can take responsibility, leads to an upward spiral of accelerated personal and corporate growth.[5]

THE HARRIS CORPORATION

A couple of years ago I spoke at a recognition meeting of the Electronic Systems Sector of Harris Corporation, a major government contractor who has diversified successfully into nondefense products and services. Meeting near their corporate facilities in Melbourne, Florida, we reviewed one of their management achievements, which was winning the gold medal for excellence in self-directed team activity during a nationally recognized, Olympic-type competition.

Teams at every level throughout Harris's divisions and in support groups have consistently produced results that have positioned them to win programs, manage and control costs, enter new business areas, and creatively approach the challenge of prospering in the current volatile business climate. The best practices of their most effective teams were compiled and disseminated throughout the organization. Core concepts were drawn from the book *Teamwork: What Must Go Right/ What Can Go Wrong* by Larson and LaFasto.

Here are some of the best practices of Harris Corporation's top teams:

The first requirement is a clear and elevating mission to establish unambiguous, measurable goals, which the leadership constantly reinforces.

The second is a results-driven structure for organizing plans and scheduling and documenting team progress. A results-driven structure is vitally important because in the transition from position power to relationship power, employees are assigned to teams—and my research throughout America shows that one of the problems of teams is that some people hide in them. In other words, some team members seek safety in numbers. Without guidelines and documentation of progress that shows everyone his or her responsibility for the organization's success, such teams may embrace mediocrity. Giving power to the people can decrease rather than increase productivity.

The third requirement is team competence, which usually increases when members embody a blend of skills and desire. Not everyone burns to contribute to his or her organization, but when everyone must play on a team, mixing skills and desires tends to produce better results. That's why I team rookies with veterans, outgoing extroverts with introverts, people who interface easily with people less gifted in communication skills.

The next concern is building team identity, unity, and dedication—which is one reason why sporting teams and marching bands wear uniforms and display their colors on vibrant banners. But winning also depends on team spirit during the actual game and the actual work, which is the next consideration. Blame-fixing is very widespread in our society of increasing irresponsibility, and the "not me" generation rules the airwaves. However, in any good team relationship in which empowered members care about results, the focus must be on problem-solving, which is fostered by conscious efforts to maintain a collaborative climate.

Standards of excellence must be established, preferably by the team members themselves. As can happen on teams without a results-driven structure, lack of the highest standards may leave teams with something less as their goal.

Management's visible presence during team activity is highly desirable—not so much for supervision as for a sign of participation and support. Setting up a team and then disappearing is not the answer, as another paradoxical proverb makes clear:

> **You must participate in the activity, but be invisible as the leader.**

Management also ensures that external recognition is properly given—by a method that recognizes and features every member's individual contributions in addition to the team results. This is called "sticking out while fitting in." And, of course, management establishes guidelines for principled leadership. One of the ways to make a genuine team is to select members who are equipped and trained in leadership skills, have strong communication skills (which we'll examine below), and are capable of sustaining the principles of responsibility and integrity.[6]

SARA LEE

So far, relatively very few American corporations (not to mention foreign corporations) of any size are managed by women. But those few include some of the best-run, best-"cultured" companies I know. The Sara Lee Corporation is among them. Rather than wait for women to climb slowly up the rungs of power, often against well-known resistance—what might be called the trickle-up approach—the Sara Lee Corporation began placing them in high-level jobs during the 1980s, and watched the needed cultural changes trickle down. "The more women are in top management jobs, the more women are attracted to them," says Gary Crom, senior vice president of human resources. "Suddenly women lower in the company had solid proof they could make it to the top."

Judy Sprieser, president and CEO of Sara Lee's Bakery Division, likes to tour her plants. "Invariably," she says, "a woman on the line will pull me aside and say, 'We're so excited you're up there.' " When executives want to hire more female managers, they can turn to their top women, who often have wide networks of qualified candidates. According to *The Wall Street Journal,* Sara Lee has one of the highest percentages of women—36.2 percent, to be precise—in the consumer, noncyclical industry group. These changes required a solid commitment from Chairman of the Board John Bryan, a former civil rights activist who became Sara Lee's CEO.[7]

For the year 2000, Sara Lee's target is to have 20 percent of the company's fifty-five division presidents be female—up from 11 percent in 1993—and 30 percent of its top 500 managers be women, up from 17 percent. "We're the largest company in the world named for a woman, a distinction we're proud of," says Bryan. "It gives us a little bit of responsibility to be ahead of the curve on women's issues."

In a world of cultural diversity, accelerating technological change, increasing competition, and interdependent ecology, the idea of the warrior as leader is becoming obsolete. I love dipping into the *Tao Te Ching,* which was written in the 5th century B.C. by Lao Tzu. The ancient insights of China's most popular book of wisdom are wonderfully relevant today. Lao Tzu observed that leaders were popularly seen as powerful warriors who used their might. He referred to that as the *yang,* or leadership's masculine aspect. But actually, he said, leaders must act more like healers, maintaining an open, receptive, and nourishing demeanor. That is leadership's feminine, or *yin,* aspect. The yin is like water, the yang like rock. Water, which always yields, seems less strong than rock—yet it will wear away rock, which is too rigid to yield. The wise leader knows that yielding overcomes resistance, and that gentleness can melt rigid defenses.[8]

My friend Pat Riley, the legendary NBA coach, creates an atmosphere in which his team members flourish—both freeing and inspiring them to use their best talents. In my opinion, coaches like Pat and former UCLA basketball legend, John Wooden—who is the winningest college basketball coach ever—set a standard for leaders in every field. They don't rant or rave. They never intimidate. They teach excellence and inspire confidence. They want to win and have a game plan, but adjust it as the situation requires—and they step aside and let their players play without fear of tongue-lashings on the bench or in the locker room. With all respect to the legendary Bobby Knight of Indiana University, he's not riding the wave of the future. Knight *is* a brilliant coach despite his temper, and it's sad that many younger coaches mimic his antics without learning the game as he knows it— superbly. Still, Knight's management style went out with the Berlin Wall.

During most of the 20th century, no more than lip service has been paid to the idea that real power comes from empowering others. But that idea has prepared the soil for growth and harvest in the 21st century, when executives rooted in the old military style of leadership will be hard pressed to find a following. Even now, the CEOs of our best-run companies believe that the more power leaders have, the less they should use. The reasons most cited in the recent rash of firings among the CEOs of Fortune 500 companies include abrasive personalities, autocratic management style, lack of vision and flexibility, lack of people skills, and remoteness from customers and employees.

Power multiplies only when it is shared. More than 50 percent of the present American work force is women—who will comprise more than 62 percent of those entering the work force in the next decade. In particular, more women than men will enter the highly skilled, highly educated professions during the next decade. The work force will also age—from an average age of forty now to forty-five as we enter the 21st century.[9]

With current birth and immigration rates, one of every four Americans will be Hispanic, black, Asian, or Middle Eastern by the turn of the century. Less than thirty years from now, those categories taken together will be the majority, which is to say they will make up more than half the American population, and European Americans will be just one group in a thoroughly integrated nation. So if you're a young white male, start contemplating your new status as a minority. You'll quite possibly manage people much older than yourself, and *your* supervisor may well be a woman. Without a doubt, you'll be working in a multicultural environment, which can offer a rich experience for personal growth. But it would be wise to unhook any lingering prejudice you might have, lest you feel its effects going full circle and coming back at you.

THE SOON-TO-BE-SHATTERED GLASS

The glass ceiling is far from fully shattered in business, the professions, and politics—but it will be. When it is (and why not anticipate that day in your actions?), women and men will enter into a genuine partnership of understanding so that they can work side by side with equal opportunities for achievement and fulfillment. The two points of view, to the extent that the genders *do* have different points of view, will blend into a new attitude of give and take, an outlook of "strong but gentle."

In this large country, it goes without saying that there are many exceptions to every rule—in this case, to all generalizations about the sexes and their inherent natures. Still, I'm convinced that there *are* overall differences that hold true in a general way for large numbers of people—and one of them is that most women listen more openly and fully than do men. Women listen between the lines, capturing body language together with the actual words.

Not long ago, an aggressive promoter pitched me a piece of a real estate project that promised a 40 percent return on my investment. He thrust the financial projections at me and handed me a pen. "Just sign here, Denis, and you'll be rich." I looked again at the tempting figures, which I had seen before. I took his pen. I had nothing at all against being rich. But I prudently glanced at my wife before I signed. She was silently shaking her head and motioning me to join her in another room.

I excused myself and followed her out of the promoter's hearing range. "What's wrong?" I asked. "The numbers make sense. His outfit did show a 40 percent return over the past three years." "What's wrong is that man's vibes," my wife replied. "I don't trust him. He doesn't look you in the eye when he talks. His heels are all worn down and that diamond ring of his is awful. Besides, he's too eager to close. Remember the gold-mining project you invested in? Same type—and he left the country after he got our money. I think we should pass because if it looks too good to be true, it is."

We *did* pass and the investors lost their money. My wife and I are partners. Sometimes I open her eyes, but she often sees what I miss—and does it with her intuition.

Another difference—despite the many exceptions inevitable in such a large sample—is that women *are* more intuitive, possibly by nature. They ask more questions to draw others out. They are better at forming groups because they more easily subordinate their egos for the common good. They're better at understanding customer needs. They are naturally better communicators, perhaps because their communication skills mature earlier than men's, almost always in their teens. The only reason more men occupy the higher positions in the communication arts and in university communications departments is because of the previous male domination throughout society.

Men would do well to emulate women's leadership strengths. They'd profit in the largest sense by listening more before presenting; by opening up and yielding more often, rather than forcing; by facilitating others rather than moving quickly to assert themselves; by empowering rather than trying to overpower.

It's no surprise that men are generally more assertive than women. For centuries, Western men (like the men of most other civilizations) believed, as they were raised to believe, that the outer world was *their* arena. They took the risks there, while women ran things in the more protected homes. Of course, there were many exceptions to this rule too. But generalizing to make a point, men need to listen and nurture others more, as women need to assert and risk more. And both sexes should view those qualities as neither masculine nor feminine.

It's probably inevitable that as women *are* slowly becoming more assertive and risk-oriented, they are acquiring some traits and habits previously considered male. Twenty years ago, the incidence of lung cancer in women was minuscule; now the terrible affliction is on a steep upward curve and has already become a leading cause of death in women. Heart disease, which used to be far more prevalent in men—although that was partly because women were less carefully diagnosed—is also rising rapidly among women. There is little doubt that the assumption of what used to be exclusively male roles is related to the appearance of these new "epidemics" in women. Naturally, it's sad to see a small percentage of the most visible women taking on some of the least pleasant traits formerly associated almost solely with men: chauvinism, win-at-any-cost aggressiveness, and other behavior patterns that can only be losing, as I see them, in an age that demands the new style of leadership. But these are essentially rites of passage. Liberation has released far more positive than negative qualities—and will continue to do so because equality of opportunity is an idea whose time has come. Generally speaking, the media focuses far more attention on the handful of disagreeable examples than on the mighty contribution to enlightened business practices by a still small but increasing corps of women executives.

As president of Tenneco's Natural Gas Marketing Subsidiary, Rebecca McDonald is the youngest woman senior executive in the industry. Recently interviewed about how she was managing in these chaotic times, she said that several years ago, when natural gas was moving from a regulated to a market-driven industry, diversified Tenneco was hemorrhaging with unexpected losses. "Corporate arrogance was our culture," she recalled. "We were saying, 'Here are the services we think our customers want, but we never asked them.' The hierarchies suppressed new ideas and made us very risk-averse. To date," she says, "it's a blank page."

Rebecca McDonald has some attractive ideas on the role women can play in the new environment. "You hear a lot of talk about change in the way we teach little girls," she says, "because they're taught to listen and accommodate while little boys are taught to win at all costs. I wonder if really we shouldn't rethink the way we're teaching boys. The rigidity that comes with expecting to win at all costs doesn't necessarily play to the new skill sets for corporate America."

The new management skills include dealing with less than clearly defined needs, issues, and market forces. "Women have a higher tolerance for ambiguity," McDonald continues, "because they've always been responsible for attending to the emotional needs of others, which are very fluid. Women learn to read between the lines and come up with creative solutions for accommodating people." McDonald is far from suggesting the touchy-feely approach. The bottom line remains results. What she *is* suggesting is that women may be good at getting results because they've long been trained and are especially suited for today's demands on management: listening, communicating, getting to the root of the problem.[10]

Executives like Rebecca McDonald are setting standards in business. Remarkably effective, clear-sighted women are doing the same in other vocations: In the administration of justice, for example, they include Janet Reno, the first female attorney general of the United States, and Sandra Day O'Connor and Ruth Bader Ginsburg, gender-pioneering justices of the United States Supreme Court. Women are helping rethink and restructure our leadership and management styles in virtually every field. I'm not the slightest bit embarrassed to state that more women than men are among my most inspiring personal role models. They've helped me to become much more nurturing—which, as with the other most essential human characteristics, is gender-free because it makes women more feminine and men more masculine.

Here are seven essential tips for building a winning team:

1. Just as the United States has the Constitution and Bill of Rights, every group assembled to accomplish a goal needs a clearly defined vision—which must be communicated consistently and repeatedly. Leaders set that vision and help team or organization members define their mission. Profits are seen as a way of keeping score, not the vision itself, which must touch on major societal concerns and inspire individuals to put group needs before their own. At Federal Express, the vision is people, service, profits. At Quality Inns, the vision is "to pursue excellence and become the most recognized, respected, and admired lodging chain in the world."

2. In simpler times, when success depended less on team members responding quickly and creatively to opportunities that come and go in the blink of an eye, the egotistical boss could better survive. Now lead-

ers must empower others so that they can make those responses. "Sublimate your own ego," said Fred Smith, chairman of Federal Express, when we asked him to specify the most important ingredient for team building. "If you don't have the discipline to do that, or if you have an ego that has to be stroked all the time, you're not going to build an effective team."[11] Failed automaker John DeLorean specified arrogance and ego as the causes of his downfall, admitting that his chief concern was not to let "this car with my name on it go down."[12]

Many of today's best leaders take pains to see themselves as others see them. Carl Jung observed, "Where love reigns, there is no will to power."[13]

3. Leaders respond to the needs of others. Most leaders used to demand respect for themselves; the new leader cares much more about creating opportunities for people to respect themselves. To feel that respect—to be given meaningful work and asked to perform it without being bossed—is increasingly the goal of contemporary American workers. It includes a wish to be seen as a whole person with needs beyond the organization. And within the organization, a sense of belonging to a winning team is a great incentive, as is a share in the profits based on productivity.

4. Leaders delegate authority. The most important determinant of job satisfaction is work autonomy. A University of Michigan study established that employees now value the opportunity to make their own decisions and to influence what happens on the job even more than the amount of their pay. Give them ownership in this sense and they'll give you their best.

5. Leaders encourage experimentation and tolerate mistakes. Toyota has achieved close to "zero defects" quality in its production of automobiles—perhaps the most enviable quality record in any manufacturing industry. Management's job there is largely to walk around factory floors, observing and questioning. Key Toyota questions are, "What can I do for you today? How can I make your job easier and what can you tell me about it that we should change so you can do it better?" Toyota employees are rarely criticized for mistakes. Employee suggestions are truly wanted, and management understands that people will not speak up in an atmosphere of anxiety or fear.[14]

This *does* work in America too, when it's given the chance. "We let people take chances," says Fred Smith of Federal Express, "and we don't punish them when they fail. It cost us in the beginning in terms of peak efficiency, but we've saved a million times over because people feel free to speak their minds and be innovative. If you don't tolerate experimentation, you avoid two things: failure and success."[15]

6. Leaders attract people who complement their own skills. "Always hire someone as smart or smarter than you are," advises Mo Seigel, founder of Celestial Seasonings, the herbal tea company. "Take plenty of time to screen your key people. Check their references carefully. Give them behavioral assessment tests. Find out what they're really good at."[16]

7. Leaders inspire and motivate every member of their team. The late Sam Walton of Walmart and his mentor, James Cash Penney, built their merchandising empires largely by treating everyone in their organizations as associates and having an incentive plan—which included pay for performance plans, bonuses, profit sharing, stock ownership plans, and cash for good ideas—for them all. Personal recognition is an extremely effective motivator, especially if given regularly rather than only at an annual awards program. (J. C. Penney called his employees "associates" because he knew that if they were his associates and he empowered them, they would make him rich.) Remember the derivation of the word "tip" (to insure performance) for ensuring good work. Paying value to your people is an attitude, not a performance. Don't wait until the end of the year—do it *now*.

The enormous, dizzying changes of our new era have made the old saying that the future is no longer what it used to be truer than ever. As customers are given an ever-wider choice of goods and services, as their access to information and options soars, they are becoming more demanding—and meeting their demands requires a new kind of leadership: strong because it is flexible, fluid, and adaptive.

You must yield authority but gain strength in the process.

ITT AND THE WAY IT WAS

Our old competitive corporate culture was epitomized by CEOs like Harold Geneen, who took over ITT several decades ago when it was floundering. Geneen partitioned ITT into divisions and had them compete fiercely with each other. The most vivid expression of his management style came at a huge conference table, equipped with microphones for the 150 people it could accommodate. This was the battlefield site of the monthly reports by division managers.

They were subjected to a ruthless interrogation intended to root out any weakness or uncertainty. Geneen, whose memory was prodigious, often led the questioning himself, tearing weak presentations to shreds. More than one manager was reduced to tears under the grueling pressure.

As Robert Sobel noted in *The Rise and Fall of the Conglomerate Kings,* Geneen was the master of certain bottom-line techniques—based on measuring corporate management in terms of balance sheet results—of the sixties, seventies, and early eighties. His system of management by competition—and anxiety!—paid off handsomely as ITT prospered and climbed. Widely praised, Geneen was used for case studies at the Harvard Business School. But soon after he left ITT, the business media reported more about ITT's management blunders than its earlier success—and with good reason. The departure of the dominating figure revealed a leadership vacuum. His stress-ridden division managers, long driven chiefly not to be seen as losers, were more motivated to avoid failure than to achieve excellence, let alone exercise their independent judgment.[17]

Geneen's replacement, Rand V. Araskog, had to struggle long and hard to heal the company's internal wounds and repair its public image. "The lanky Mr. Araskog is rightly described as a mild-mannered man in contrast to Mr. Geneen, who had the reputation of an overbearing autocrat, who ruled through intimidation," wrote *The New York Times* on July 1, 1984, five years after Harold Geneen's departure.

The Times went on to note:

> To the relief of many employees, Mr. Araskog has done away with such Geneen trademarks as the huge corporate meetings in which employees were dressed down in front of the group. It's less based on star magnetism and more on back to basics. To the outsider, the culture used to be one of working eighteen hours a day and having an answer to every question. It almost appeared as if internal competition was as important, if not more important, than business achievement.[18]

"Managers like Geneen are guided by an ethic of competition, of winning the game," Terrence Deal and Allan Kennedy summed up in *Corporate Cultures.* "Heroes, by contrast, are driven by an ethic of creation. They inspire employees by distributing a sense of responsibility throughout the organization. There is more tolerance for risk taking, thus innovation. Everybody performs with tangible goals in sight that are tied back to their own personal views of excellence and desires for achievement."[19]

Competition is of course inevitable and necessary in athletics, business, and life as a whole. It is desirable when employed in ways that encourage people to push to greater heights. But the larger objective is to develop inborn potential for achieving a goal or purpose that makes the achiever happy by fulfilling his or her inner desire for personal excellence. This is the ethic you should instill in your family and organization, and how you should frame leadership for yourself and for when you lead others.

It is the competition that escalates into a free-for-all—an increasingly frequent aberration in sporting events—that pushes us astray, competition deriving from the notion that the ultimate goal is becoming Number One rather than discovering and achieving the best we can do. That kind of competitiveness, usually linked to a drive for power and domination—and to fear of failure—is rooted in a desire to defeat others. And concentration on others diverts us from developing our own potential. We become outer-directed instead of inner-inspired. The ultimate motivation may be the same—the need for self-esteem, the powerful, innate desire to be satisfied with one's self—but the genuine realization lies not in victory, only in the higher territory of self-actualization.

No Creation Without Communication

Even the most enlightened conception of leadership can't work without constructive communication—but how to achieve that?

Not by technique alone. We must constantly ask ourselves if we are operating with the old win-lose approach of position power rather than the new win-win approach of relationship power. Is our interest in others only for what they can do for us? Are we in this or that relationship primarily to satisfy *our* needs? Do we give as little as possible in return for a reward we envision?

The best communication techniques in the world won't fool most people for very long. Still, if your understanding of the substance of relationships is solid, learning new techniques for management communications can make a very significant difference.

Tom Peters's Managing by Wandering Around (MBWA) has won deserved attention, but the concept isn't yet widely practiced. "Many senior managers," suggests Joseph F. McKenna, "take their cue not from Tom Peters and his ilk, but from Greta Garbo's 'I want to be alone.'" After recent interviews of executives and consultants, McKenna found that they advise a third way, or at least a way not limited to wandering around. To communicate with subordinates, they advise, do it directly.[20]

McKenna's interviewees urged managers and executives to spend as much time as possible communicating directly with people at all levels, inside and outside their organizations. In particular, they recommended sharing bottom-line information. One company now doing that is Convex Computer Corporation. "Each quarter, after our quarterly financial data has been publicly announced, the manufacturing managers meet with employees to review the numbers and explain the implications of each," reports Shari Navarette, a manufacturing engineer at Convex. "They share names of new customers and information on how those customers are using our products. They discuss the implications of company decisions and seek honest feedback and questions."[21]

Implementing a quality program? It won't get far without clear and certifiably *received* communication. "Message communicated is message received is a fundamental maxim of quality organizational communication," warned Alan Zaremba recently. "That is, in order to improve communication, a manager must adopt the posture that a message sent to a subordinate or colleague has *not* [italics added] been communicated unless that message has been received."[22] And we might add, received does not mean understood.

"What effect does communication have on a TQM (total quality management) process?" asks E. James Coates. Wide experience in industry shows that his seemingly self-evident answer is often ignored:

"TQM will fail when the improvement process is not understood by those who must use it."[23] In other words, it's no good—can never work—if those who devise and/or inaugurate plans don't "tell all" to all who are supposedly affected.

Empowered teams require a new communication style. "In a traditional work group, you want compliance," says Dr. Jean Lebedun. "In an empowered group, you want initiative. Directional communication (announcing decisions, issuing orders) inhibits team input. If the team leader or supervisor is still using 'boss' language, the team gets the message that they're being told what to do." Lebedun recommends that managers of empowered teams learn to ask open-ended questions and develop the skill of truly listening to the answers.[24]

To "debureaucratize" your company, create an informal "shadow" organization that tackles some of the issues entrusted to the formal one and serves as a problem solving test laboratory. Kenneth Johnston recommends a network of "teams with names like steering committee, task force, action teams, etc." "Without a shadow organization," Johnston explains, "the bureaucracy in the existing organization will, in spite of good intentions, unwittingly sabotage and ultimately destroy the change effort, and it may take years to discover that the change effort has failed."[25]

Leaders need both advocacy and inquiry skills. Michael P. Thompson of Brigham Young University suggests that most Western organizations inherit their communication styles from a tradition of argumentation and debate. "The core communication skills are the skills of advocacy. [But] another set of communicative skills is usually required before a proposal or a position even exists. These skills are rooted not in the ability to advocate a position but to create one. These are inquiry skills."[26]

To create a learning organization, widen your communication channels. Tom Kramlinger recommends committing organizations to the following assumptions: "Everyone can be a source of useful ideas. The people closest to the problem usually have the best ideas. Learning flows up as well as down in the organization. Nothing is sacred except the governing vision and values. The process of open dialogue improves ideas. The more information people can access, the better. New ideas are valuable. A mistake is simply an opportunity to learn."[27]

Build a company-wide clipping service, perhaps modeled after the one operated at Co-op Building Consultants in Texas. Its incoming magazines and other documents are routed to appropriate employees at all levels throughout the company. Those employees read the material and clip articles for upper management, which keeps the former better informed while decreasing the paper load of the latter, who no longer must peruse the full material themselves.[28]

COMMUNICATION AND THE LOST ART

Letter-writing is all but a lost art, but to some extent it has been replaced by telephone, facsimile, and other modern means of communication. Listening is a lost art, which must be rediscovered. Few people truly listen to others, usually because they're too busy thinking about what they want to say next. In business transactions, clear communication is often colored by power plays, one-upmanship, and attempts to impress rather than to express. In our work as well as our personal lives, how we listen is at least as important as how we talk. Genuine listening to what others want would allow more sales to be made, more deals to be closed, greater productivity to be gained. Although it's not always necessary or possible to satisfy those wants, understanding them is the glue of a relationship.

Not paying value by listening is a way of saying, "You're not important to me." The results are reduced productivity (I don't count here, so why should I even try?), employee turnover (Who wants to work in a place where I don't feel valued?), absenteeism (I'm just a cog in the wheel, only noticed when I make a mistake), retaliation (They only listen when the griping gets loud enough), lost sales (They don't seem to understand what I need), and dangling deals (I can't get through to them; it's like talking to a brick wall). Genuine listening can cure a remarkable range of supposedly intractable problems.

ADVICE FROM THE STAGE

"Acting is reacting," a great theater director once declared. "It's done with the ears, not the mouth." Contrary to popular belief, listening— at least quality listening—is an active, not passive, activity. Perhaps you're clever enough to win attention with brilliant observations or witty remarks—but if you want to get people truly interested in you, talk about what's important to them. The most common mistake in communicating is talking about me, myself, and I. What do *I* want to sell? *My* present needs are . . . I'd like this job because *I* . . . Instead of these turnoffs, turn your attention to the other person's needs. How can you help *him* or *her* or *their* organization?

Then listen. It's rightly been said that you can make more friends in twenty minutes by showing interest in people than you can in twenty weeks by showing how interesting you are.

Here are a dozen tips for better communication:

1. Introduce yourself up front. Lead with your own name, in person or on the telephone. Few things are more distracting in a conversation than wondering who you're talking to.

2. Develop a good, firm handshake—women as well as men. Take the initiative; extend your hand first.

3. Remembering a stranger's name is one of the clearest tributes you can pay him or her. Pay attention during introductions and repeat the name immediately, as in "David Johnson" or "Kay Johnson, I'm glad to know you." If you didn't quite catch the name, apologize and say so; then write it down or ask for a business card. The other person will much appreciate genuine interest in this "detail."

4. Make eye contact during conversation. A direct look in the other person's eye communicates your confidence in what you're saying, your genuine interest in the other person's observations.

5. Resolve to make the other person happy for having talked with you. Say something pleasant about him or her. Ask questions about his or her interests. Help draw that other person out and he or she *will* be glad for the conversation with you.

6. Talk positively. A positive outlook is contagious. You'll find people eager to associate with you if you share your enjoyment of your work, your day, your life, your reading, or other interests. By the same token, avoid complaining or griping even when you feel you have cause. Negativism drags people down. They have their own troubles; don't burden them with yours unless they may be directly involved with a solution.

7. Learn discretion. Not everything you are told is intended for repetition to others. Give people the assurance that they can trust you with their confidences.

8. Be service- rather than self-oriented. People can sense genuine interest in their concerns, and are drawn to those who express it. Conversely, people become uneasy when they sense someone has only his or her own interests at heart.

9. Make the other person feel important by giving him or her your full attention, especially when he or she is relating a job problem or experience. Keeping the other person's interest in your foreground will win you respect for intelligence and compassion.

10. Make sure you fully understand what the other person has said. Misunderstandings and misinterpretations cause more job headaches than anything else. To be certain you grasp the other person's meaning, repeat what they've said in your own words and ask if you've understood correctly. He or she will much appreciate your concern.

11. Be prompt for meetings and appointments. Late arrival is another way of saying, "This is not important to me." If circumstances beyond your control cause you to keep others waiting, telephone with an honest explanation and an estimate of your arrival time. That will win respect for your consideration instead of consternation for your tardiness.

12. Empathize with others. Try to view the world as others see it and become more sensitive and open to their differences and needs. And try seeing yourself as others see you. How would I like working for me? How would I like my performance if I were my supervisor? You'll become a far more effective communicator when you understand how you're coming across to others.

The central secret of good communication is bringing the other person over to your side by satisfying one of every person's most fundamental emotional needs: Make him or her feel valued. With rare exceptions, people who feel valued—who are allowed to feel important in the sense that they are recognized—answer with openness, cooperation, and reciprocated respect.

Try to become an active listener in every encounter, appreciating that listeners learn a great deal while talkers learn nothing. Listen openly and carefully, even when you disagree with what's being said— even when the talkers seem dull or ignorant, for they too have their story. Ask questions without imposing. Draw people out by getting them to talk about themselves, and try to find qualities for which you can praise them sincerely. Don't assume what their reaction will be, or try to read people's minds. Be confident in meeting strangers, knowing that no matter how secure other people may seem, almost everyone harbors a little fear of rejection or exploitation.

The late Dr. Hans Selye, a distinguished pioneer in the study of stress—and a favorite friend and mentor of mine—condensed his life philosophy into four words: "Earn your neighbor's love." A consistent effort to win others' respect and gratitude will fill your home and office with happiness. The more we modify our win-lose approach, the more acceptance we gain; the more acceptance we have, the safer we feel and the less stress we experience. Much more than trying to accumulate money and power, leaders in the new era acquire good will by helping their associates, customers, neighbors, and loved ones to win.

> *The child: "What can you do for me?" The adolescent: "I want to do it alone." The adult: "Let's do it together." The leader: "What can I do for you?"*

As adolescents, we attempt, sometimes ingeniously, to maintain a dependent child's self-centered privileges while demanding to do our own thing on our own terms. Although we supposedly put that behind us when we become adults, most of us live much of our adult lives at an emotional level that ranges from childish to adolescent. The chief symptom is preoccupation with immediate gratification.

Giving up position power is so difficult because, to some extent, it seems like a part of our nature to want it. But that doesn't mean that it's healthy for us in the long run or for society at any time. We must teach ourselves to "do the unnatural through self-discipline," as M. Scott Peck put it. Peck is convinced that what most distinguishes us as humans, at least as *adult* humans, is "our capacity to do the unnatural, to transcend and hence transform our own nature."[29]

TEN

SELF-LEADERSHIP AND KNOWLEDGE: YOUR INFORMED TOUCH

---

1 ◆ *How "user-friendly" are you with advanced computer and communications technology?*

2 ◆ *Are you more high tech or "high touch"?*

3 ◆ *What do you think of the idea that employee satisfaction ultimately determines bottom-line profits?*

Y OU'RE A BUSINESSPERSON WITH NO COMPUTER OR COMPUTERIZED CASH register, let alone a modem. No fax machine, no voice mail or answering machine, no access to overnight delivery. You work—laboriously —on an IBM Selectric, making changes with frustrating correction tape and whiteout, and retyping entire pages when the corrections become too messy. All the documents on which your business depends take three to five days for delivery because there's no alternative to the U.S. Postal Service. . . .

Unless you're a small, local enterprise in a remote corner of the country, you're probably no longer in business. Yet that's how major firms operated as recently as the early 1980s.

I was fascinated by the revelations in an article entitled "The Superhighway and You" by Jordan E. Ayanis (in *Mind Play,* June 1994).[1]

Less than a decade ago, many of us fought the threat of having to use a personal computer. People also resisted installing an answering machine, insisting that no self-respecting person would talk to a machine. They said they had no need of a fax machine either. And overnight delivery? Too expensive! What's the rush? Why waste the money?

Now people are similarly hesitant about the information superhighway. Either they say they don't know what it is or they don't need it—

or both! But midway into the 21st century's first decade (that is, a mere ten years from now), you'll wonder how you lived without the electronic thoroughfare cutting through so much of the underbrush of routine that eats your time now.

Those who embrace the new information technology *today* will of course have a crucial head start. But precisely what *is* that new technology? Some say it's Internet, a vast computer linkage that allows people to send electronic mail (E-mail) and files throughout the world in an instant. Others believe it's an electronic network that will link phone, television, and computer systems together. Actually, it's both of these and far more, a combination of all available information media, including computer, telephone, data networks, cable television, satellites, fiber optics, and software.

THE MERGER OF MERGERS

These seemingly separate technologies are slowly—in some cases rapidly—being molded into integrated services. Platoons of foresighted people are already using them. The current reengineering of American corporations, including radical downsizing and rightsizing in many industries, is eliminating many managerial jobs, especially at the middle levels. However, a significant portion of these former corporate players, including many who lost out to the computer and who otherwise felt gravely threatened by it, are forming small enterprises to which the big corporations are increasingly turning for on-line communications.

These new entrepreneurs are providing services for collections of businesses from their nearby homes or small offices. Teleconferencing is rapidly being accepted as a convenient, accessible, and relatively inexpensive alternative to increasingly expensive business travel. To get on-line with hundreds of stores throughout the country, you now must journey no farther than your local Kinko's store. The mathematicians and engineers who named the computer in English chose a word suggesting that its main purpose is in their fields. The French term—*ordinateur,* a machine that organizes—is more descriptive.

PLEASE PLUG IN

Marshall McLuhan remarked perceptively that lots of things happened in the 20th century, most of which plugged into walls. All the devices we plug in—computers, telephones, fax machines, radios, television sets, VCRs, and even kitchen appliances—are emerging into a unified information machine. Very soon, a single device will perform all their functions and more. Together with our appliances, our credit cards, medical records, automobile registrations, driver's licenses, etc. will be hooked together. Some scientists envision a small card on which our entire medical history will be electronically encoded. To ensure it's always available in case of a traffic accident, it has been suggested that it also serve as our car key. Insert it into a dashboard slot and it will adjust the seat, steering wheel, and rearview mirror to our personal ergonomics.

All such technology will become as commonplace as a bank card for cash machines. I'd guess that early in this century, a few traveling salesmen got a jump on their competitors by using automobiles instead of trains. Freed from rail routes and schedules, they began servicing small towns that had been "off the loop" until they had the flexibility to reach them. The same will happen during the next, crucial few years, until the technology becomes pervasive—and some innovators are already leaping ahead into the stunning new possibilities.

EMPIRES OF THE MIND

Thus one main reason for the title of this book. Until the knowledge era, empires were controlled by a small number of people with enormous wealth or political power. But power and wealth will now rest on knowledge and information, which are becoming—and this can't be repeated too often—the most important form of capital. Fortunes are made from this alone. In 1988, the rights to the *Official Airline Guide* sold for more money than most airlines were worth at the time.

The information superhighway will soon become the modern equivalent of Gutenberg's first presses. We're on the threshold of the greatest exchange of knowledge and ideas in history. Who will own and control that intellectual property? How will it be paid for? How will the information transactions be monitored and secured? That's still not certain, but one thing is: Few will be able to afford any price at all unless they join the initiated who can read the information—information absolutely vital to success and even survival—as transmitted in its new, electronic form.

The new system's heart is the tiny microprocessor, which teamed with ingenious software and laser optics to inaugurate the information age. This technology facilitates more control over time as well as information itself. That facilitates more control of your life, giving you greater freedom. Answering machines and voice mail systems may annoy you, but refusing to use them multiplies the number of calls you must make until the person on the other end answers.

Information technology needn't mean information overload. In fact, it can give you more control over the information you receive. You can't fend off the junk that packs your mailbox, each piece of which you must handle if only to give it the toss. With E-mail, your computer can electronically filter out what you tell it to. Customized newspapers are also available. ("Give me, in headlines, everything published in the world every day about my company. Also give me everything on baboons, moon flights, the Seattle Mariners, and a rap group called Gang Starr.") Some filtering systems can even give you the enjoyment of perusing a newspaper or of browsing in a bookstore by opting for a specified amount of randomness.

Where and how to buy the hardware and software that's appropriate for you and your growth? Find a guru. The most important criterion for choosing any item of information technology is to have easy access to a friendly someone who is very experienced in using it. Get an Internet address and check it daily. Your company may have access through its own E-mail system; if not, you can get on-line for a few dollars a month to a service like MCI Mail, CompuServe, America on Line, Prodigy, or the like. Several commercial on-line services have wonderful interfaces at modest monthly fees. And don't mess with difficult commands and codes. Would you want to stop and adjust your carburetor every time you drove onto an interstate highway?

In the end, the information superhighway may become a great equalizer. Ever-cheaper information is of course a boon to big business, but the little guy will also reap many benefits—and some of these smaller businesses are already becoming giant-killers. Armed with ever more powerful computers and high-tech communications—which cost less and less, and can be installed in small, low-overhead offices—legions of individual entrepreneurs are seizing the advantage from bigger companies and also breaking chains of command. Inside the large companies themselves, technology is giving low-level workers power to make decisions that were long reserved for their managers, and also giving techies a leg up on the career ladder.

Thus digital technology is dramatically transforming businesses, their workers, and the suppliers and customers who trade with them. No change is more potentially liberating than organizational change. New electronic systems are breaking down old corporate barriers by allowing critical information—the kind that used to be management's exclusive purview—to be shared instantly across functional departments or product groups, even with workers on the factory floor! IBM salespeople now have data on product costs that until recently were higher management's closely guarded secret. In operations, manufacturers are using information technology to drastically shrink cycle times, reduce defects, and cut waste, while service firms are using electronic data exchange to streamline ordering and communication with suppliers and customers.

In staffing, new systems and processes have slashed employment levels and deleted entire management layers. The most advanced companies are using computers and communication devices to create "virtual offices"—which are far less costly than establishing real offices—in far-flung locations. For new products, inventive information-feedback loops, together with technology's huge help in design applications, are collapsing development times. Companies now electronically feed customer and marketing comments to product development teams, which quickly rejuvenate product lines, often targeting specific consumers. In customer relations—which is no longer simply an order-entry job—department representatives are tapping into company-wide data bases to solve callers' demands, from simple changes of address to billing adjustments, in a fraction of the time previously required.

Recent research by John Huey supports the prediction that our working lives will soon be more profoundly transformed than anything we can imagine, and nothing can stop the process. "The microprocessor has been around for more than twenty years but its power has been increasing exponentially and it's now become an essential, affordable, ubiquitous fixture in our lives."[2] Huey foresees that the new economy will be driven by the microchip just as forcefully as the old one was driven by the internal combustion engine—this spells good news for the U.S., still the world leader in developing microchip technologies, applying it, and exporting it.

During most of this decade, American industry has spent more on computers and communications equipment than on all other capital equipment combined: the total of all machinery needed for services, manufacturing, mining, agriculture, construction, and all the rest. And this trend is actually speeding up in response to ever-greater technological innovation. Chip capability—raw computing power—doubles every eighteen months.

This explains why computing power recently considered awesome now seems trivial as silicon intelligence worms its irresistible way into cars, cellular phones, microwave ovens, pagers, stereos, children's toys, watches—everywhere. As we mentioned earlier, when you throw away the greeting card that wished you a Happy Birthday as you opened it, you're casually discarding more computer processing power than existed in the entire world before 1950. Your camcorder wields more processing power than the IBM 360, the then stupendous machine that launched the mainframe age.

The next step in computer technology is clearly identifiable. Simply put, the computer will be used as much for communication as computation. Steve Jobs, Apple co-founder and one of the personal computer's fathers, is emphatic about the significance of this evolution. "If you knew what was going to happen in advance every day, you could do amazing things," he says. "You could become insanely wealthy, influence the political process, and so on."[3] Even if no one will ever be certain about what will happen in advance, Jobs's point about information is critical. Actually, most people don't yet know enough about what happened *yesterday* in their fields, which is why many businesses are discovering the great advantage of finding that out as soon as possible—the advantage of beating their competitors in collecting, examining, and contemplating information.

The business world recently realized how much could be accomplished if a way were found to allow computers to communicate effectively with one another. That explains the current boom in networking, groupware, and E-mail; the swarm of new companies trying to build businesses on Internet; the rapid growth of such computer-consulting giants as EDS and Andersen Consulting, which help clients integrate their computers. It also explains IBM's repositioning as a solutions company.

CEO Robert Allen's view of the nature of the company he heads may surprise people unacquainted with the drift of the new technology. "AT&T is fundamentally a networking company," Allen says. "We bring people, information, and services together, all in the name of time-based competitive advantage. What's shifting is the minds of our large customers. They want all their computer capacity integrated into networks so they can get real-time information from their customers and then make faster, better-informed operating decisions. It's exciting because so much business is going to be enhanced by this move to networks."[4]

Bill Gates, Microsoft's founder and president, is convinced that this huge access to information will trickle down to the consumer. "In another ten years," he predicts, "most decisions—hiring a part-time worker for your home, buying a consumer product, choosing a lawyer—will be made on a much more informed basis because of electronic communication." As so often, Gates sees the larger picture and puts his finger on the momentous, if not yet fully appreciated, changes there. It changes the nature of competition, he said, because "in a networked world, I can ignore geographical limits to my shopping."[5]

COMING TOGETHER

The popular phrase *digital convergence* hints at the direction of the new developments. In the new economy, an electronic bond will pull most industries, professions, and trades closer together in at least one aspect. Digitizing work products into the zeros and ones of computer language spawns revolutionary ways of conceptualizing that work. A gathering of thinkers in automaking, banking, medicine, retailing, art, film, publishing, and aerospace will no doubt find that this common computer language sparks their conversation. This, in turn, will surely prompt new ideas for tackling challenges in the respective industries.

Some believe the changes will go even further. Consultant William Bridges recently predicted that the "job" itself may disappear. In the future, Bridges predicts, work may be "assigned" by market-driven projects in postjob organizations.[6] That is to say, greatly enhanced ability to assess market needs, then communicate and respond to them, may open the way to direct interaction between the buyers and sellers, consumers and suppliers—replacing the old kind of work within a corporation that gathers the information and passes it to you in the form of commands.

No doubt the disappearance of the job, in its traditional form, will be well in the future, if it comes at all. But the new technology is working its radical transformations this very minute, perhaps most dramatically of all, by arming individuals and small groups—those with the foresight and skills to operate that technology—to think and act for themselves. "The nineties are not a good time to work in the large organization," says Paul Saffo of a California think tank called the Institute for the Future. Saffo notes that the average size of the effective organization is plummeting. "The organization of General Motors in the sixties was a complex analog of a mainframe computer. In this new era, the model organization mirrors our network information structure. It's a web, not a hierarchy."[7] The big difference is this: In a hierarchy, your title or position determines your power; in a web, it's what and who you know. As we saw in the previous chapter, your relationships are crucial.

Future senior managers will guide their artists, artisans, and scientists more like conductors leading an orchestra than colonels commanding infantry brigades. The leader's most important function will be to inspire by articulating a clear vision of values, strategies, and objectives, and to know enough about the business to be the risk manager of risk managers.

HISTORY REPEATS, WITH A BIGGER PIVOT

When the Industrial Revolution began in the mid-18th century, no one could have predicted the immense economic, social, and lifestyle changes that would follow the transformation from a stable agricultural and commercial society to one in which large-scale factories, with far greater specialization, produced vastly more equipment and goods. Until then, the vast majority of people lived meagerly on and from the land, using hand tools and, among the more prosperous, the power of farm animals. The introduction of the new industrial technology, chiefly the use of steam and the machine, truly revolutionized life, not least in the sudden, spectacular growth of cities and the migration there from fields and pastures.

It's precisely because we've had the experience of the Industrial Revolution's upheavals that we *can* predict the nature and scope of the present revolution, at least in outline. We have recently entered one of the great historic pivotal points that will forever change the way all society will work. A brave new world is here. It is driven by technologies whose inventiveness and power would earlier have seemed the fantasy of science-fiction addicts. The opportunities are boundless, but the penalty for failing to recognize the implications of the pivot point will be severe. If you're not on-line, you may soon be in a kind of bread line.

THE GREAT GOAL OF BALANCE

But technology isn't *everything*. On the contrary, the new technologies—especially since they're coming at a time when the world is much advanced in human rights and well versed in consumerism—can have little economic or social value unless they're combined with, or grounded in, understanding of human ways and needs. To put it another way, the new technologies can't succeed in business or society as a whole unless greater, not less, attention is given to people.

Since the publication of the visionary *Reengineering the Corporation* by Michael Hammer and James Champy in 1993, *reengineering* has become the American economic community's newest buzzword and call to action. So far, the enthusiasm for it shows no signs of slacking. A survey of 1,200 American corporations by a newsletter called "Systems Reengineering Economics" established that spending on reengineering will increase by nearly 20 percent a year from 1994 to 1997, by which time it will reach more than $52 billion, three quarters of which will be for information systems.[8] But information about what? As with technology, reengineering without a firm grasp of purpose—which must ultimately reside in *people*—can have little value.

As exciting and promising as the theory of reengineering is, its practice has been far less than satisfying. One expert who predicted in 1992 that nearly two thirds of reengineering efforts would fail sees no reason now to revise his pessimistic estimate. Far from being a critic of the concept, that expert happens to be Michael Hammer, co-author of *Reengineering the Corporation.*

Needless to say, reengineering is not supposed to waste money on miscarried efforts. On the contrary, its goal, in case anyone didn't know or suspect it, is to trim costs and maximize profits. But with so many reengineering projects failing to accomplish that, why do executives continue spending greater and greater amounts on them? One answer is analysis paralysis, or the lemminglike attitude of many corporations. Having invested a great deal of money in the effort, the temptation is to spend just a little more to make the effort work. "It works like this," wrote Bruce Caldwell recently. "If you make a mistake, spend some more money and try again." That was the kind of thinking, Caldwell noted dryly, that kept the Vietnamese War going and going.[9]

Michael Hammer himself believes that most reengineering flops are caused by companies' failure to understand the true nature of the process and less than total commitment to carrying it out. Investigation of fifty companies that claimed to be reengineering showed him that 42 percent of them were not actually trying to radically redesign their business processes but only tweaking things here and there in a search for incremental improvements to ongoing operations. Hammer's attitude was reflected in his *Harvard Business Review* article that originally started the buzz. Its title was "Reengineering Work: Don't Automate, Obliterate."

Elaborating on the failures, Hammer states that three major causes are responsible: People "don't know what they're talking about, they don't have committed executive leadership—reengineering absolutely requires passionate top-down leadership—or they don't know how to go about it. They improvise, and reengineering isn't something you can make up as you go along." Failure can cost loss of credibility on top of vast amounts of money. Corporate cynicism naturally grows when you've announced you're going high tech and then fail.

Philip Andrews, a principal of EDS Management Consulting Service, which is headquartered in Dallas, says that there are "a thousand reengineering trap doors," and most companies fall through at least one of them.[10] Lynne Markus, associate professor of information science at California's Claremont Graduate School, feels that reengineering is the wrong metaphor. It implies a mechanical view of the organization, green eyeshades within, and a get-out-there-and-sharpen-your-pencil attitude rooted in scientific principles. "Instead," says Markus, "reengineering is driven by lots of blood, sweat, and tears."[11]

Peter Scott-Morgan, associate director of Arthur Little and author of *The Unwritten Rules of the Game* (McGraw-Hill, 1994), argues that if managers don't master the unwritten rules of the reengineering process—"such as make the boss happy, protect turf, and avoid association with failure"—reform seeds a company's destruction. Scott-Morgan cites teamwork as a common example. "Although almost every CEO preaches teamwork," he told *Informationweek* in 1994, the most telling rewards—such as respect and career advancement—too often "require you to stand out as an individual." Teams won't work, he continued, unless reengineered companies change their reward systems to match the new roles individuals are asked to play. Without that change, each team member will try to make certain that, as Scott-Morgan put it, when top management looks at a team, "they'll see *me* [italics added]."[12]

Another common pitfall of reengineering is misidentifying the company's business. That may sound far-fetched—but not to Philip Andrews of EDS, mentioned above. Andrews tells of a recent meeting with the executive managers of a major aerospace company. When experience prompted him to ask the company president to identify his business, the president bristled. That question, the senior executive objected, was an insult to his highly seasoned managers, many of whom had thirty years' experience with the company. But Andrews persisted. He asked the seven executives present to describe their business in a single sentence. When they handed back their seven sheets of paper, all had different answers.[13]

THE ROAD TO WHERE?

All this means that getting on the information highway may be an expensive road to oblivion unless you know exactly what your mission is, what your objectives are, and who you're targeting for your market and customers. Yes, you must ride the highway or you'll die in your

Model T beside the old country road. But it's not much good trying to get on without being very certain you're in the right vehicle going at the right speed.

Which brings us back to the human element—what I'll call the primacy of people. Some managements that attempt to reengineer put their companies off course with a belief that their first priority must be to install high-tech information systems. As they see it, this is doing first things first in the difficult adaptation to the new global competition. In fact, however, the most important reengineering may have more to do with people than systems—or, to put it another way, the transformation may have to be more cultural than technological. Millions of dollars have been wasted on costly MIS (management information systems) and hardware before discovering that human capital needs must precede high-tech needs.

I'm not suggesting that new systems, in particular information systems, are anything less than utterly essential. It would be fatal to believe that by being a warm, high-touch, customer-focused firm or individual, you can avoid the investment in technology that offers access to the global information network. I won't apologize for repeating that if you're not on-line, you may be on some form of a bread line. It may amuse you or please you that your grade-school children tend to be far more comfortable and skillful than you, their parents, with the computer and with Internet. But if you want to be frightened, visit Asia. It seems that almost everyone there has a cellular phone—so many that in some countries, they must be checked like a coat when entering a restaurant. More to the point, nearly all schoolchildren in the developing Asian nations—at least, so far, in the major cities—are becoming truly computer literate. This is so central a determinant of who will succeed in the future that to fall behind is like being sentenced to travel via clipper ships in the age of steam.

I'm trying to argue as forcefully as I can that successful firms must be on the cutting edge of technological *and* human skills; sooner or later, you're likely to go under without *both*. Heaven help you if you're a techie who believes that being high-tech is enough to put you in touch with the world; that electronic wizardry alone will somehow provide the necessary customer satisfaction. That will get you run right over on the information superhighway. The Asian countries clearly recognize the need to blend touch with technology. Increasingly thinking like techies, they behave—perhaps as Asian cultures have long taught them to—like grateful, devoted stewards who'll go to any lengths to make you their customer for life. So here's one of the most important paradoxical paradigms:

> **You must think like a high-tech research firm, but must act**
> **like a high-touch service firm.**

I maintain that becoming high tech without learning to be high touch won't be much help in the ultimate battle for excellence and customer appreciation. I'm also convinced that in America, at least, there is a direct correlation between how firms view the role of technology *within* their organizations and how they apply it externally, in their dealings with their customers. Internally, the most farsighted corporate reengineers clearly see the importance of the primacy of people. As Bruce Caldwell pointed out, words such as *creativity, holistic,* and *organism* often crop up in their speech.[14] (Holism is a theory that living nature should be seen in terms of interacting wholes that are more than the sum of elementary matter.) Even the management consulting–services unit of EDS, long dedicated to paramilitary organizational structure, has embraced the holistic view of organizational transformation.

But America has a long way to go before she will manage to reengineer some of the basic attitudes that underlie our views in society as well as in business. In the previous chapter, I mentioned a certain view of American business widely entertained throughout much of Asia. Recently, I asked a group of leading Asian chief executives for a one-word definition of America's greatest leadership problem. They answered in unison: *arrogance.* When I asked them for a one-word solution, roughly half said *example,* and the other half offered *accommodation.*

I don't think the Asians or anyone else have a perfectly objective view of America, nor can they offer the solution to our problems. Nor do I believe most Americans are in fact arrogant by nature—except, perhaps, in the sense of being generally very ignorant of other cultures and, therefore, strongly inclined to dismiss the experience of others on the assumption (not historically accurate; it has only been true for part of the 20th century) that America has always been the leader. But there *is* something to this view of us as arrogant, never mind that much of it derives from misinterpretation of American directness of speech and the tendency to be personal, in contrast to Asian nuance and *indirectness*, sometimes seen as delicacy. And I believe that that something relates to essential questions of how to reengineer, how to use the information superhighway, how to combine touch and tech.

Let's start with an example of what remains to be done, and how an understanding of the primacy of people can help do it. Some of our large hotel chains are very good at providing standard rooms at reasonable prices. They have, of course, installed extensive computer networks to help manage reservations and a wide variety of operational tasks. They have even instituted Total Quality Management and empowerment programs—without, however, instilling the essential message in the staff who *actually serve the customers.* Those team members—the clerks, receptionists, bellmen, waiters—are key. Guests rarely interact with the managers of the hotels in which they stay, let alone with the top executives at management headquarters. However, they are in frequent, if brief, contact with the men and women who handle their luggage, register them at the check-in desk, and deliver their room-service orders—and who do the most to form their impression of the establishment. Many of those "lower" employees still don't get the point about service because it hasn't been made to them with sufficient reason and urgency. They don't feel responsible. They haven't been included, let alone empowered.

A consultant friend was recently asked to spend a few days with a client in Cincinnati, where the client offered to put him up at the Hyatt Hotel. He and his wife decided to combine the trip with a further one to Baltimore to deliver some furniture for their daughter's new apartment. They rented a van, packed it with the furniture, and drove to Cincinnati, where a Hyatt valet parked it for them.

The following afternoon, they presented their claim check to the valet parking counter and waited. They waited and waited. Finally a member of the staff appeared. "Are you the people with the van?" he asked. "Hasn't anyone told you what happened?" No, no one had told them anything. It seemed a long time before he broke the suspense. "Someone in the garage didn't see our valet tag on it, so he had it towed. We're getting it back, but it'll take another half hour or so."

The staff member wasn't rude and certainly not arrogant, simply insensitive enough to appear uncaring. That was hardly a way to treat a guest who mattered to the hotel, or whom a hotel wanted to make *feel* that his business mattered. It wasn't hard to imagine an entirely different kind of explanation/apology—and from the manager, not a parking attendant; and the minute the mistake was discovered, at the convenience of the parking counter. But my friend could only shrug and suggest to his wife that they get a cup of coffee while waiting further. The employee disappeared, having said nothing more—that is, having missed his first opportunity for empowered decision. Still no expression of regret, no apology from him or a supervisor.

The van arrived after forty minutes or so. The towing—with front wheels lifted—had shifted all its contents to the rear. However, examination by the consultant and his wife revealed that nothing was seriously damaged. They prepared to leave. As they climbed into the van, the hotel employee again appeared, now clutching a sheet of paper. "Here's a new copy of your room charges," he said, apparently unaware that they had been charged to my friend's client. "See, we've deducted the $12.50 for the valet parking." "Thanks," said the consultant dryly. "And of course," said the employee, "we'll pay the full cost of the towing."

Contrast this with the Asian high-touch approach from five thousand miles away, via the information superhighway. For comparison, I could pick virtually any Asian hotel of any standing, but one that comes to mind is Taiwan's Ritz Hotel. To ensure that a recent stay there would be comfortable, it sent me a customer-focused questionnaire, several weeks in advance. Did I prefer a king, queen, or double bed? With firm, medium, or soft mattress? Down or regular pillows? Would I require a computer, a fax, a modem and/or a VCR? And what were my video preferences? (I selected *Wild Kingdom* reruns, Jacques Cousteau's *Undersea Adventure, National Geographic,* and some action movies for the kids, although we'd seen them all many times.) Did I want a smoking or nonsmoking room, on an upper or lower floor? Did I have a special need for quiet? For a fitness program? For diet requirements? What beverages would I like in my minibar? Nothing was left to chance.

After I'd faxed back the questionnaire, a welcome letter arrived. Gold-plated baggage tags were enclosed—with my name, my wife's name, and the names of our seven children correctly spelled. (The tags had no hotel logo, just our names.) I thought the gold plating was a little much until we landed at Taiwan's Chiang Kai-shek Airport and three Mercedes limousines pulled up in front of the baggage claim area. The driver of the first was in a tuxedo, complete with a top hat and cane. He jumped out, ran to the baggage carousel, spotted the gold-plated tags, and retrieved our bags. With a beam and a bow, he said, "Welcome to the Ritz Hotel, Denis and Susan Waitley and family."

Thus did the Ritz ensure that our first impression was of excellence—and that it happened from the moment we set foot in the country. Of course the driver had been trained, but wasn't that the point? In any case, he performed his welcome flawlessly—and it worked! Our baggage filled one of the limos. As he escorted our family of nine to the other two, I noticed him studying our children's faces, repeating their names as they climbed inside. Soon after we were on our way, he telephoned the hotel. One of my daughters had studied Mandarin in Beijing for six months. She whispered that the driver was notifying the hotel staff of our expected arrival time and specifying where each family member was seated in the two cars.

The general manager was at the door when we arrived. He greeted us all by our first and last names as we left the limos, then escorted us through the lobby to the elevators. I asked about checking in. The general manager smiled. They knew we were on the way, he said. They also knew we'd be tired from our travels and would want to go directly to our rooms to shower and relax. Therefore, he'd taken the liberty of registering us, using information from their computer.

Involuntarily, I remembered less happy experiences in American hotels. I can no longer count the number of times I've traveled for most of a day or night, arrived at a crowded lobby, and waited in line for fifteen or twenty minutes—only to be told that a convention had caused some unfortunate overbooking. But if I'd wait another half-hour or so, a shuttle would take me and others to an overflow hotel—which was no more than another half-hour away. At Taiwan's Ritz, the service was even better, if that was possible, when you were in your room. A conspicuous button marked SERVICE is installed next to your bed. When pushed, it brings a floor attendant to your door within sixty seconds. Shoes are shined, suits cleaned and pressed seven days a week, at any hour. Buttons are sewed on, luggage is repaired . . . the response to everything is, "Can do, no problem."

Within an hour of our arrival, every member of the staff called us by name. When we were about to leave for our return home, the maids appeared. "We're so sorry to see you go, Denis, Susan, Debbie, Dayna, Denis Jr., Darren, Kimberlyn, Lisa, and Graciela. Why are you leaving so soon? It seems like you just arrived." If their air of disappointment was slightly exaggerated, their personal attention had made our stay truly memorable. "We have to leave because I'm out of money from spending on your fine goods and services," I replied in mock exasperation. "But we'll be back." "That's good, please make it soon," said the maids. The bellmen also smiled. "It's been a pleasure having you as our guests, especially your daughters."

As we walked through the lobby, I took a final survey of the gleaming marble floors; rich, clean carpet; shining brass rails; immaculate rest rooms; oiled wood panels; sparkling windows and glass doors; crisp clean uniforms; white-gloved doorman. I remembered the speedy, courteous service in every instance, and the thoughtful anticipation of customer needs.

This is the economic battlefield of the 21st century in miniature. In mainland China's free economic zones, over 150,000,000 workers have been unleashed to produce high-quality goods for the world market. For the first time ever, those dedicated men and women can taste an opportunity for a higher standard of living, and they are rapidly acquiring skills. Their energy and ambition are helping expand China's gross national product by 10 percent a year. And standing in line behind them are a billion more Chinese eager for their turn to learn and earn. That's motivation!

As we noted, tiny Singapore has been the world's most productive country for more than a decade. Government-owned Singapore Airlines, rated the world's top airline in customer service, is also a training institute for top executives, who learn how flight attendants—the most skillful in the business—cater to passenger-customers. Proportionately speaking, Singapore's National Productivity Institute is as well attended on weekends as Disney World by Americans. While American parents treat their children to attention-relieving attractions, Singaporeans are inclined to show *their* children how to perform goal-achieving activities. They see recreation less as a major goal than as a side benefit to a productive life.

We also mentioned that Taiwan is the world's eighth richest nation, with a surplus of over $80 billion in its national treasury. That represents over $60,000 for every Taiwanese man, woman, and child, which is almost exactly every American's share of our national *deficit.* Unlike America, with its abundance of natural resources, Taiwan's chief resource is its people. This recognition is transforming Asia, starting with its schools. To take another example, Indonesia's 180,000,000 people are also eager to develop skills and improve their standard of living. Her motivated, trainable workers are producing high-quality products for several major German and Japanese firms, including Toyota.

I see the 21st century everywhere in Asia: in Malaysia, Taiwan, Korea, Vietnam, the Philippines, China, Hong Kong, and, of course, Japan. Asians' willingness to work very hard and very long to get what we have long taken for granted helps explain why the use of high technology is absolutely critical to our survival.

THE ASIAN WAITER SYNDROME

After our every sip of water in a Hong Kong restaurant, our glasses were refilled to the rim—as everywhere, if you'll excuse the pun, along the Pacific Rim. My family and I noticed that every waiter and waitress seemed like little radar stations, searching for where service would next be needed. A gentleman in the smoking section finished his meal and reached in a pocket. In seconds, five lit cigarette lighters were at his disposal.

Our young waiter, who was computer literate and totally bilingual, was working his way through college and planning to finish his study of finance at Stanford University. When he refilled our glasses yet again, we asked him why the service was so good. "Because there are hundreds of thousands waiting to take our jobs," he said. "If we don't refill your glasses every time, someone else is waiting to do it."

I wish every leader would read Lester Thurow's *Head to Head: The Coming Economic Battle Among Japan, Europe, and America.* Thurow offers a plan he believes American business must adopt today if it expects to compete abroad tomorrow. He predicts that Europe, not Asia, may become the 21st century's dominant economic force. In addition to the benefits of the Common Market and German manufacturing discipline, he says, European countries are already interdependent.

Forced to become team players, they are learning to subordinate "Me first" nationalism to a "Let's do it together" community approach.[15]

Thurow may be right, but my concern about America's competitors continues to focus on the rising expectations and rising skills of Asia. Despite its temporary current recession, Japan has shown the way to the developing nations. With a "can do, no problem" work ethic and cultural habits that foster more stability and synergy than is usual in the West, they are in a prime position to become leaders. In any case, the race for economic supremacy is hardly over; on the contrary, it has just begun.

I chose my kind of work in a hope that America may be the only society in history to stage a successful comeback: to return to the top after having rested on her laurels, having succumbed to complacency and been replaced as Number One in many areas. Other countries criticize us more and more loudly for being extremely short-sighted. Motivated, they say, by craving for immediate profit and gratification, we won't save for our future or invest in it.

It is of course true that excellence and high quality require heavy investment in better education, improved infrastructure, and superior technology. I don't apologize for stressing a truism in my seminars: that winners engage in positive activities promising long-term results and losers engage in short-term pleasure. You *do* get what you pay for in life, which is why the correlation between investment for the long-term future and the excellence you can attain is often very strong. We can't maintain our standard of living without investing in research and development of the industries and technologies that will manufacture the goods and improve the services of the future.

Manufacturing high-quality goods is impossible without an educated, highly motivated and trained work force—which, in turn, is impossible without investment. Investment is like shopping for value more than price: buying for long-term worth, not a fleeting ability to impress. Most custom-made suits are made of fine materials, and in classic, long-lasting styles. They also take more wear and tear because they're fitted to your body. Yes, they cost more, but look better after fifty dry cleanings than cheaper suits after two or three pressings. Real bargains usually require real investment.

Gold is expensive because it's indestructible even after centuries on the bottom of the ocean. Diamonds are expensive because they endure.

A knock-off "Rolex" watch I bought in Hong Kong for one of my sons turned his wrist green and stopped dead after three weeks. Why didn't I remind myself never to settle for less than the real thing, in service or manufacturing?

If you were buying a parachute for yourself, would you shop at a discount store? Think of any product or service you shop for as a parachute, and be diligent—consulting *Consumer Reports,* if possible—about failure rates and manufacturers' guarantees. If you needed a heart operation, you'd of course seek out a qualified, respected surgeon with a record of success. Look for the same level of quality in every purchase and every area of your life. When you need expert advice, go to an experienced, highly trained person with a proven track record. Check backgrounds; many so-called experts are charismatic salespeople with more style than substance. When you're buying equipment, buy the best you can afford—which will be a bargain in the end.

When developing a relationship, invest it with quality, time, energy, and creativity. Make your time with that person really count. In relationships too, success requires investment.

Answering these questions can help you improve the quality of your results:

1. How do I define quality?
2. How do I measure quality?
3. Am I prepared to invest time and money to obtain quality?
4. How much will it cost to do it right the first time?
5. How much will I lose by not doing it right the first time?
6. Am I trying to conceal poor service and poor quality with cosmetic actions?
7. Am I demanding quality from my vendors and suppliers?
8. Is everyone in my organization equally committed to quality?
9. What can I do to ensure that quality is in every associate's best interests?
10. What can I do today that will save time and reduce the number of steps necessary to solve my customers' problems and please them in the process?

Your answers to these questions may be as valuable as a reengineering program, a systems development, a procedural manual, or zero-defect manufacturing or service policies. What separates the winners from the also-rans in the new economy is that admirable quality displayed by a high percentage of immigrants: always doing more than is expected of you.

For a smooth drive instead of becoming road kill on the information highway, the paradoxical proverb can be repeated as a road sign:

> *You must think like a high-tech research firm, but act like a high-touch service firm.*

The customer is the ultimate employer—in a sense, the new emperor. That's an essential reality for the empire of your mind.

ELEVEN

SELF-LEADERSHIP AND SKILLS: YOUR WINNING (AND LOSING) HABITS

1 ◆ *What are your healthy, winning habits?*

2 ◆ *What habits would you like to replace?*

3 ◆ *Do you believe people can learn a new set of skills or habits if they have been "like they are" for a long time?*

Eagles could easily teach leadership to the less focused human species. When it's time to lay her eggs, the female eagle locates a perch high on a mountain, selects suitable materials, and assiduously prepares the nest. She works carefully and very hard, following mental blueprints of great functional quality. After the eaglets are born, she spends virtually all her time responding to their needs. She hunts for fish and small game to ensure that they are properly nourished—which is an eaglet's sole task, apart from sleeping and crying for *more* food.

Instinct tells the eagle that the day will soon come when her offspring must make their own way. Somehow she knows that feeding her eaglets will be followed by a second, absolutely critical task of teaching them to fly.

STIRRING THE NEST

When she senses the eaglets are ready, she puts them on alert by stirring up the nest. One morning, she returns from an outing without food. Moving to the edge of the nest, she uses her sharp beak to rip out big chunks, then drops them from the cliff. As the chunks fall hundreds or thousands of feet to the canyon floor, the eaglets watch and look at each other in astonishment. "I told you Mom had a strange look in her eye today!" the most talkative observes. The eagle continues for several hours ripping apart the sturdy nest she built with such care and skill. What had given the eaglets total security is now a most uncomfortable resting place.

COMFORTABLE NESTS BREED CO-DEPENDENTS

Human leaders must take care that their nests at home and workplaces are not so comfortable and all-providing as to eliminate challenge for the young. Keeping subordinates and children dependent on us too long clips their wings.

ROLE MODELING AND MENTORING

After stirring the nest, the eagle begins fluttering over her brood like a helicopter. Then, while the eaglets watch intently, she sits on the nest and thrusts her beak into the air. When a breeze blows up from the valley, ruffling her feathers, she balances herself until the wind begins to gust. Then the perfect role model hurls herself into it. Catching the front end of the breeze, she hovers above the eaglets. No other bird can do this: The hollow bones that enable eagles to fly higher than any other bird also allow them to hover. Meanwhile the eaglets, if not yet graduates in aerodynamics, learn that the wind is their helper for controlling flight.

Repeating her demonstration several times, the eagle flies to a vantage point out of the eaglets' sight. They hesitate a moment, some more than others. And then they begin to fly.

IF IT WALKS LIKE A DUCK, IT'S PROBABLY A DUCK.

If it looks like a duck, walks like a duck, and quacks like a duck, chances are it's a duck. If it hovers like an eagle, looks like an eagle, and flies like an eagle, chances are it's an eagle.

Your life, too, is governed by habit patterns. Layer upon layer, you establish your identity by what you observe, imitate, and learn—which is how you will behave. Seemingly insignificant repetitions, innocent cobwebs of watching and believing, turn into patterns, then unbreakable cables that will shackle or strengthen your life. One of those patterns manifests itself in the people from the audience who approach me after my speaking engagements. "I like what you said, Denis," goes a comment I hear again and again. "But gee, you don't know how bad it is for me. I didn't come from a good family. We had no money, I never got much of an education. So no wonder I got stuck with some bad habits. I just can't help it."

THE ENVIRONMENTAL UNIFORM

I understand them because I've been there. The frustration of people who feel their lives were predestined to remain out of control is very familiar to me.

"If you're not careful," went the warning of warnings that was imbedded into my youthful mind, "you'll end up a chip off the old block." My chain-smoking, heavy-drinking father died prematurely of lung cancer and liver disease. Being a slave to his habits robbed him of a chance to fulfill his personal life. He loved football. He would have been immensely proud to watch a grandson play alongside Herschel Walker on a championship Georgia team. A tear of joy would have wet his cheek had he lived to see his granddaughters become successful executives and educators while raising families of their own. His great-granddaughter and great-grandsons would have given him great happiness.

My father was a wonderful, caring man with great potential, but he died too soon—and penniless, frustrated, and sad, like Ali Hafed. He had very little money and no goals he believed he could achieve. He had no dreams for himself, only for his children. In that respect, he was an example of how not to live.

PAYING MR. GOODWRENCH

"You can pay me now or pay me later," Mr. Goodwrench, the television auto mechanic, reminds us. Sooner or later your good habits bear fruit and your bad habits summon failure. I loved my father. I think of him often and thank him for encouraging me to brush away his bad habits and develop the positive ones he encouraged me to consider from biographies of men and women who climbed from poverty to a life of service.

My father and mother struggled and argued. Finally, after years of being worn down by the negative habit patterns, they divorced. As a boy, I kneeled beside my bed, crying softly and praying. "Guide me never to drink, never to smoke, and never to get married." Fortunately, I was able to stick pretty much to my first two requests, but a wise God intervened, blessing me with a marriage too good to describe and with a family that's given me far more than any fame or fortune could.

BORN TO LOSE?

When I'm told that some people are born to win and some to lose—and that people can't change after they've grown up—I like to counter with the true story of a young man from San Francisco. As a teenager, Robert sold drugs night and day: That was, he thought, his only way to survive. He used, abused, and pushed heroin wherever he could and to whomever he could. He slept on empty sidewalks or in alleys with other street kids who also used and abused.

FOLLOWING IN MOTHER'S FOOTSTEPS

Robert's mother hadn't exactly raised him with the best of examples during his formative years. She was in and out of jail since he could remember. Her specialty was robbing banks, but her arrest record indicated she was less than expert at it. Robert found himself in and out of foster homes from the age of eight. He became a survivor who indeed survived rather than lived. With his mother as role model, he began packing a gun for holdups. He also knew how to use his knife: Many victims still carry its scars. While still a juvenile, Robert was arrested and charged with twenty-seven armed robberies.

HIS EMPIRE WAS SAN QUENTIN

How could Robert ever achieve any good, considering his sorry family history, the bad role models, the cobwebs of drugs and alcohol, and the seeming impossibility of thriving in such an environment? You can just hear people insisting he'd never make it. "He's a goner. On his way down the tubes like the rest of his type." He did have a goal: to serve time in a big-time prison. That dream came true when he was escorted into San Quentin Prison at the age of nineteen. "I'd lost touch with everything and had no belief in myself," he said later. "I had no hope, no trust in myself or anybody else. I wanted to go to prison so I could be somebody, but even in San Quentin, nothing was exciting. I'd already done it all."

CROSSING DELANCEY

"When I finally got out of prison, I thought about changing my life," Robert continued. "Then I got busted again for selling heroin to an undercover cop."[1] That was in 1987. But instead of perpetuating the vicious cycle of another prison term, another parole, and back to prison again, he was given one final chance to rehabilitate himself.

Today Robert is uncommonly well groomed. His suit would look good in any conference room, and he carries himself with a confidence that everyone—and most importantly, he himself—would have thought impossible. In the years since he was released on parole, Robert has learned eight construction trades, taken college courses in criminology, tutored other ex-convicts in geometry, and helped them earn their high school diplomas.

Robert is one of twelve thousand men and women with similar tragedy-to-triumph stories, one of the fortunate who became residents of San Francisco's Delancey Street Foundation. This alternative sentencing program for ex-cons has received worldwide acclaim for its no-nonsense approach to fixing broken lives, helping transform former criminals into responsible citizens.

MIMI SILBERT'S GENIUS

The force behind the foundation is Dr. Mimi Silbert, who began the program with the late John Maher. Mimi earned a joint doctorate in psychology and criminology at the University of California at Berkeley in the late 1960s. Since 1972, she has dedicated herself to maintaining and expanding Delancey Street, all of whose residents faced the alternative of near lifetimes in prison. "We're just as selective as Berkeley, Stanford, and Harvard," explained Silbert. "They take the top one or two percent. We take the same—from the bottom."[2]

Delancey Street, which is named for the mecca of down-and-outs on New York's Lower East Side, has no teaching staff. Senior residents ground new residents in the fundamentals they missed in their dysfunctional families: how to dress, eat, and speak properly. How to set a table, and how to keep things clean. Then the residents learn one of three marketable skills and earn the equivalent of a high school diploma. What Dr. Silbert says goes. Newcomers are given chores from the moment they set foot in the residencies; not to perform them is not to remain. Former drug addicts are handed brooms and told they're no longer addicts. Why? At that point, simply because no drugs are allowed inside. They are told in advance that breaking the rules is an automatic ticket back to prison.

FROM CONVICT TO CITIZEN, A DAY AT A TIME

Residents must cut their hair, dress as for business, even adopt a normal walking gait. Although many—perhaps most—retain the deep pain and suspicion of life on the streets, they are asked to act as if they were upstanding citizens, even CEOs. During his first eight months there, Robert believed in nothing Dr. Silbert or Delancey Street stood for. "There was no way I was going to trust anybody with my feelings. Nobody ever cared about me, so why should I care about anyone else? 'Get away from me' was all I wanted." But one day, he found himself shouting hysterically at a man who was going to leave the program, trying to get him to *listen* and stay. He failed, but the effort was highly significant. "You know what, Robert?" observed another resident. "You're starting to care." Realizing this was true, Robert fought back tears.

> *Habit with him was all the test of truth.*
> *It must be right, I've done it from my youth.*

George Crabbe's lines describe a universal condition. We all begin by believing that what we observe, often unwittingly and unconsciously, will work for us too. With no other teacher, we naturally imitate. We behave as if our way—even when it's self-destructive heresy of the highest order—represents the gospel truth. But nothing is right just because you've been doing it that way.

MISSION POSSIBLE

"You see, once you know it's *possible* to change, you can take the risk of starting again," said another resident. "Then the best part of life is the struggle!" Five hundred former drug addicts help run a fashionable restaurant, a printing shop, a moving business, Christmas tree sales, and more. Dr. Silbert also bought the abandoned Hilton Hotel in midtown Los Angeles, where five hundred more residents are now accommodated. Delancey Street facilities also operate in New York, New Mexico, North Carolina, and other states. The federal government, in obvious need of new techniques for its own criminal justice rehabilitation and welfare reform programs, is observing closely.

HABITS TAKE NO HOLIDAYS

Although few of us hit bottom as Robert did, the principles of exchanging new habits for old are the same. Whoever we are, we make our habits and then our habits make us—which happens so subtly that we remain unaware of the process. The bindings of our habits are too small to be felt until they become too strong to be broken. Like comfortable beds that are easy to get into but hard to get out of, our literally mindless routines master us unless we master them.

You must replace habits, but not try to break them.

"Two men looked out from prison bars," goes a line of another insightful poem. "One saw mud, the other stars." Robert learned the principles of leadership and habit formation the hard way. Finally tired of mud, he wanted to try stars.

YOU CAN CHANGE THE CORE, FROM THE OUTSIDE!

Delancey Street's lessons dramatically affected my understanding of behavior modification. Throughout my career, I believed that people always project to the outside what they feel on the inside—in other words, that your attitude determines your behavior. Again and again, I lectured—as you know by now—that you must feel value within you before you can enjoy genuine success in the external world. What I learned at Delancey Street, however, jolted me into realizing that some beliefs I'd taken as absolute truth were only opinion based on my too-narrow observation of certain situations—but not others.

What I learned, in short, is that some change must come from the outside. Practicing bad habits over a long period of time can so ingrain your attitudes, beliefs, and feelings that escape seems impossible. In such cases, you must exhibit change—*do* it, perform its outward manifestations—before you can learn to believe in it. Delancey Street shows beyond doubt that core values can be changed by learning and repeating new behavior patterns.

THE PAST IS NO LONGER PROLOGUE

This means that no matter what your past, how many times you've failed or been hurt or haven't reached your goals—no matter how long certain habits have controlled you—you can make a permanent turnaround if you change environments and routines.

For corporate America, this can be very good news. Establishing self-directed management teams opens the way to great individual and collective advancement. Think of what can be rubbed off and synergized between members when teams work together, coach each other, and establish their own internal standards of excellence. With management participating in monitoring performance, one plus one can equal three.

THE RULES OF CHANGE

Rule 1: No one can change you and you can't really change anyone else. *You* must admit your need, stop denying your problem, and accept responsibility for changing yourself.

For acceptance into Delancey Street's program, a written request must be made, clearly stating the reasons why the applicant needs the program and how committed he or she is to sticking with it.

Rule 2: Habits aren't broken but replaced—by layering new behavior patterns on top of the old ones. This usually takes at least a year or two.

To change a habit—including smoking, substance abuse, and other destructive practices—forget about the 30-day wonder cures, the 60-day diet delights and the get-fit, get-rich fads. And for achieving excellence and higher productivity, let alone just-in-time manufacturing and Total Quality Management, forget about 60- or 90-day, even 120-day programs. Internalizing permanent change takes a year or two at the minimum.

I don't know where motivational speakers got the idea that it takes twenty-one days to learn a new habit. It may take that long to remember the motions of a new skill, but after many years of you being you, it takes far longer to settle into a new habit pattern and stay there. One reason why Delancey Street's success rate is so high is that the participants must commit for a two-year minimum.

Don't expect immediate results from whatever program you install in your company, your institution, or your home. Give it a year and stick with it, knowing that your new ways can last a lifetime.

Rule 3: A daily routine adhered to over time will become second nature, like riding a bicycle. Negative behavior leads to a losing lifestyle, positive behavior to a winning lifestyle. Practice makes permanent in both cases.

This point is so obvious that it's often completely overlooked. If you do it right in drill, you'll do it right in life. Practice your mistakes on the driving range and you'll remain a high handicap golfer-duffer. Practice the correct swing for each club as demonstrated by a professional, and you may become a tournament player.

"If it walks like a duck," they say at Delancey Street, "eventually it becomes a duck. If it flies like an eagle, eventually it becomes an eagle." The residents get up, take a shower, make their beds, learn a skill, settle into a positive routine of physical and mental labor, and go to dinner in a jacket, suit, or dress. In short, they get into a winners' groove directed toward achievement.

If you want to become successful, begin by acting successful—and in the company of successful people. The greatest coaches and greatest leaders use the same basic techniques: explanation, demonstration, correction, and repetition. Winning and losing are themselves habit-forming.

Rule 4: Having changed a habit, stay away from the old destructive environment. Most criminals find themselves back in prison because they return to their old neighborhoods and gangs when released or paroled.

Dieters who reach their desired weight usually slip back into their former eating patterns because the new ones haven't been imbedded long enough to make them stronger than the temptations. Meanwhile, they should steer clear of buffets.

To remain optimistic and successful, you must avoid neighborhoods of pessimists and quick-fix pushers. To remain successful in business, you must be on a team of which each member takes responsibility for being a leader—and if you leave that team environment, you must not return to the old, cynical, pre–knowledge era company ways.

Recognizing your *good* habits is also essential, but for the moment, let's continue with overcoming the bad. My own bad habits include scheduling too many activities to be effective in all of them. Disorganized filing—sometimes in my computer filing too—makes me waste precious time finding research material. And I still don't balance my work with enough recreation and physical exercise.

Several years ago, I allowed myself to become very overcommitted and began arriving late for appointments, meetings, and social events. Friends and associates called me Waitley Come Lately. Then I chose new goals and made new affirmations: "I'm an on-time person." "I always arrive on time for meetings, appointments, and trips." "Because time is important to others, I respect and honor the commitments I make." After a few years of practice, I became known as First at the Gate Waitley. What I'd learned was to frame a goal statement that's the opposite of the bad habits I wanted to convert, then schedule activities in my planner that confirmed my goal. The new habit patterns followed.

WE BECOME WHAT WE WATCH

While our brains receive thousands of positive inputs daily, something makes most of us lock on more strongly to the negative ones. And those negative ones not only abound, they're *pushed,* and not only by the underworld. If you're still uncertain about the impact of the commercial media on your life, here's what the Children's Workshop concluded after substantial research: "If Madison Avenue believes it can teach children on Saturday morning to buy a certain brand of corn flakes, why are we so complacent about the anti-social messages?"

By high school graduation day, the average American student has seen 18,000 murders during 22,000 hours watching television—which happens to be twice as long as the time he or she spent in both grade school and high school classrooms. Television violence is dismayingly pervasive—and television of almost any kind offers only sensory stimulation. "The trouble with television," said Edward R. Murrow, one of the medium's handful of truly distinguished practitioners, "is that it is like a sword rusting in the scabbard during a battle for survival." And Murrow's comment came well before the steep decline of American television into vulgarity, sensationalism, the promotion of naked greed, and boundless violence. The very act of watching the cathode screen overwhelms the mind and the imagination. This may change somewhat when full interactive multimedia becomes available. Meanwhile, the process of gaping at a screen without opportunity to participate—to support, object, or debate—dulls the mind drastically when violence isn't perverting it.

SECONDHAND VIOLENCE, SECONDHAND SMOKE

Don't let network executives fool you with their protests about censorship. A task force on television and society appointed by the American Psychological Association found that the influence on viewers' attitudes and concepts is the same whether the television characters watched are real or fictional. I think secondhand violence and secondhand pornography are as damaging as secondhand smoke. If you're exposed, you're affected. Observation, repetition, and internalization equals habit.

GOOD HABITS CAN OVERRIDE BAD ONES

But the good news is that you can change your life by changing your habits. Psychologists have done scores of studies of how habits are formed. We can now track a habit from the time sensory nerves carry messages to our fertile brains from our organs for hearing, touching, seeing, tasting, and smelling. The brain uses this information to make decisions, then sends working orders through motor nerves to the body parts needed for action.

It should come as no surprise, then, that habits are formed after the body responds the same way twenty-five or thirty times to identical stimuli. But here's an interesting discovery: After a certain amount of this repetition, the message from the sensory nerves jumps directly to the conditioned motor nerves without a conscious decision by the brain. So while a mere twenty-five or thirty repeats can form a habit, I'm happy to report that the same number is involved in developing good habits, depending on input practice and supporting environment.

If twenty-five or thirty repeats can form a new habit, you may wonder why making it permanent requires at least a year of practice. The reason is that the old patterns remain underneath. If you slip back—even if you associate with them—a link immediately recalls and tries to reassert them.

Here are some action tips for habit formation:

1. Identify your bad habits. When, where, and why did you learn and develop them? Are you unconsciously imitating peers or negative role models? Do you use them to cover fear or feelings of inadequacy—emotions that would cause you to seek (false) comfort in tension-relieving instead of goal-achieving activities?

2. Learn what triggers your bad habits. Identifying your unwanted patterns makes replacing them easier, beginning with the triggers—which are often stress, criticism, guilt, or feelings of rejection. Identify the situations that cause you the most frustration and tension and plan ways to avoid or reduce them as much as possible.

3. List the benefits of a new habit that would replace the old. Self-esteem, improved health, longevity, improved relationships, more professional productivity and respect, better focus, enhanced promotion potential, accelerated financial security . . . each helps lead to your ultimate goal of lifelong improvement and growth.

4. Say farewell forever to excuses for mistakes and failures. Accept your imperfection when an old habit begs for attention. Instead of "There I go again," say, "Next time I'll be strong enough to do what's

right." Instead of thinking "I'm too tired," say, "I've got the energy to do this and more." Change "It's too late" to "As I get organized, I know I'll have time."

5. Visualize yourself in the new habit patterns of a positive new lifestyle. It takes many simulations and repetitions to spin new cobwebs on top of your old cables. If you want to give up smoking, intentionally sit in nonsmoking areas and request nonsmoking hotel rooms. A clean environment, with hands and teeth of normal, healthy color, will help you feel in control. And if you can keep the new habits going, fresher breath, cleaner-smelling clothes, furnishings, and a steadier heart will augment that control.

You deserve as much happiness and success as anyone. You're worth the price—which is effort, training, practice, and courage. You control your thoughts, and your thoughts control your habits.

And when you hear someone say, "I can't help it, it's just the way I am," remember Robert from San Francisco's Delancey Street, the former drug pusher, robber, convict, abuser, and loser who did a 180-degree turn. Cross your own Delancey Street, remembering that practice makes permanent. Your mind can't distinguish a vividly repeated simulation from a real experience. It stores as fact whatever you rehearse. The software drives the hardware—which is true for ducks, eagles, and humans.

TWELVE

❖

SELF-LEADERSHIP AND RESILIENCE: MISFORTUNE'S MASTER

❖

1 ❖ *How do you view failure?*

2 ❖ *What do you find most humorous about life?*

3 ❖ *How patient and persistent are you in pursuing your goals?*

❖

THE KNOWLEDGE ERA'S NEW LEADERS, MANY OF WHOM ARE IMMIGRANTS and women, are managing change by conceiving innovative organizations and novel ways to attract and motivate employees. They are learning to be proactive instead of reactive, and to appreciate the full importance of relationships and alliances. As we've seen, they share a passion for excellence and self-determination. As we'll now see, they have a healthy aptitude for risk and perseverance, and know how to gain strength from setback and failure.

"I remember thinking I was very comfortable financially," says David Pomije about the salad days before his computer mail-order company, Funco, sank into Chapter 11 bankruptcy. "Then the crystal chandelier hit the floor . . . I remember scraping up twenty-five dollars to buy a lawn mower at a garage sale . . . [and] trying to find enough money to buy groceries. You never forget that."[1]

But CEO Pomije also didn't forget the essentials of enterprise in our new age. He studied his company's financial reporting, management policies, distribution and marketing systems. He hired talent that complemented his own: skillful executives who knew what he didn't. In short, he used his setback to fashion a comeback, coming back wiser and more resilient. Now Funco, a chain of stores that buys and sells used, top-of-the-line video games, is among America's fastest growing firms.

In a world where change is the rule, entrepreneurial failure is normal, maybe even a prerequisite for success.

LIFE'S BATTING AVERAGE

Baseball's greatest hitter ever grew up near my neighborhood in San Diego. When Ted Williams slugged for the Boston Red Sox, my father and I kept a record of his daily batting average. And when I played Little League ball, my dad told me not to worry about striking out. In Williams's finest year, he reminded me, the champion failed at the plate nearly 60 percent of the time.

Football's greatest quarterbacks complete only six out of ten passes. The best basketball players make only half their shots. Even with satellite mapping and expert geologists, leading oil companies make strikes in only one out of ten wells. Actors and actresses auditioning for roles are turned down twenty-nine in thirty times. And stock market winners make money on only two out of five of their investments.

Since failure is a given in life, success takes more than leadership beliefs and solid behavioral patterns. It also takes an appropriate response to the inevitable, including an effective combination of risk-taking and perseverance.

MAINTAINING THE STATUS QUO

When I was doing research for *The Psychology of Winning,* my first major work, I came across a study of a South American tribe whose members had been dying prematurely for generations. The cause was a rare disease. Scientists finally discovered it was carried by an insect that lived in the walls of their adobe lodgings. The natives had a choice of several solutions. They could destroy the insects with a pesticide. They could tear down and rebuild their homes. They could move to where that species of insect didn't live. Or they could do nothing and continue to die young.

In the end, they chose the last alternative. And although that might sound incredible to us, I meet many people with a similar attitude toward achieving personal success. Knowing that certain changes would make that much more likely for them, they nevertheless take the path of least resistance: no change. For the temporary, often illusory comfort of staying as they are, they pay the terrible price of a life not truly lived.

> *There was a very cautious man*
> *who never laughed or cried.*
> *He never risked, he never lost,*
> *he never won nor tried.*
> *And when one day he passed away*
> *his insurance was denied,*
> *for since he never really lived,*
> *they claimed he never died![2]*

In other words, missed opportunities are the curse of potential. Just after the Great Depression, Americans, perhaps understandably at the time, took many steps intended to minimize risk. The government guaranteed much of our savings. Citizens bought billions of dollars worth of insurance. We sought lifetime employment and our unions fought for guaranteed annual cost-of-living increases to protect us from inflation. This security-blanket mentality has continued in recent decades as executives awarded themselves giant golden parachutes in case a merger or takeover took their plum jobs.

These measures had many benefits, but the drawbacks have also been heavy, even if less obvious. In our eagerness to avoid risk, we forgot its positive aspects. Many of us continue to overlook the fact that progress comes only when chances are taken. And the security we sought and continue to seek often produces boredom, mediocrity, apathy, and reduced opportunity.

We still hear much about security, especially from federal and state politicians. They propose programs to make our financial future secure, just as ever more locks and burglar alarms will supposedly do the same for our homes. We have a guaranteed minimum wage and some argue we should all have equal—at least *equalized*—health coverage. But total security is a myth except, perhaps, for those six feet under.

We may indeed ask our government for guaranteed benefits. But we must be aware that when a structure starts with a floor, walls and ceilings will follow. And herein lies another paradoxical proverb:

*You must risk in order to gain security, but you must never
seek security.*

When security becomes a major goal in life—when fulfillment and joy
are reduced to merely holding on, sustaining the status quo—the risk
remains heavy. It is then a risk of losing the prospects of real advancement, of not being able to ride the wave of change today and tomorrow.

IF YOU CAN'T STAND THE HEAT . . .

Although innovators are no longer burned at the stake for their new
ideas, leaders remain subject to walloping heat. They must deal with
the weight of the past and with resistance to change. To introduce improvements or new ideas is to upset the status quo. That causes fear in
the minds of people set in group-think—who might include members
of your profession, your company, and your inner circle.

Early in her career, my wife, Susan, worked as an audiologist in the
Memphis offices of John Shea and his brother Coyle, ear surgeons of
world repute. After graduating from Harvard Medical School and
fighting in the Korean War, John Shea completed his education in
Europe. There he encountered otosclerosis, a form of arthritis that attacks the sound-conducting bones of the middle ear.

John resolved to find a cure. Working eighteen-hour days, he de-
voured volume after volume of yellowed medical journals. He dis-
sected the ears of hundreds of cadavers in the basement autopsy
room of Vienna Hospital. The solution struck him one snowy Sunday evening while he was reading in his overcoat in Vienna University's unheated library. It was a procedure called stapedectomy,
which had been abandoned as ineffective after a brief trial in the
early 1900s.

John Shea thought he knew why the operation worked only
sporadically. In patients with otosclerosis, the tiny stapes bone becomes frozen in place, unable to vibrate or conduct sound. Stapedectomy as previously practiced was simply removing that bone, after
which the eardrum sometimes grew in such a way that it was able to
conduct sound—but often didn't. In a flash of insight, Shea saw the

solution: remaking the sound-conducting mechanism by creating an artificial stapes.

Returning to the United States, he experimented with dozens of materials and finally developed one made of Teflon. After successfully performing his new stapedectomy, the time came to face the heat of his profession. The thirty-one-year-old doctor prepared to present his findings at an international conference of ear surgeons. Just before he was to speak there, a friend of his late father took him aside. "Don't do it, John," the older doctor warned. "I beg you not to make this presentation. If you go out there with your idea, you'll disgrace yourself and your father. You'll ruin your reputation."

"There I was, trying to get started and to be respectful to this older man," Dr. Shea later reflected. "And he was telling me not to do what I'd worked so hard on. Finally I just said, 'Look, I'm sorry, I wish I could accommodate you, but I know I'm right. I've done the procedures and I owe it to these people and to myself. I have to tell about it.' "

Shea *did* tell about it—and was ostracized during the next two years. Although some of his colleagues saw the light, most rejected his new procedure out of hand. Later, as the operation gained wide acceptance, he became philosophical about facing the heat. "The people who oppose you most," he said, "are those who represent the establishment your innovation will overthrow. The people who criticized what I'd done were doing another operation called a fenestration, which created a window in another part of the ear. That operation was difficult. Only a small number of surgeons could do it well, and it gave only fair results. The stapedectomy threatened them. Their pride was involved because here was somebody coming along and making them look silly—and of course they were making a lot of money from it."[3]

Your changes or innovations may prompt dug-in resistance from members of your own profession, from your own organization, or from the media. The heat may even come from your family. Expect it—but don't let it stop you.

PROCRASTINATION DOESN'T MAKE PERFECT

Perfectionists are often great procrastinators. Having stalled until the last minute, they tear into a job with dust flying and complaints about insufficient time. Perfectionist-procrastinators are masters of the excuse that short notice kept them from doing the job they *could* have done.

But that's hardly the only variety of procrastination—which is one of my own favorite hiding places when I try to blame external conditions instead of myself for some difficulty. Mine comes with a gnawing feeling of being fatigued, always behind. I try to tell myself that I'm taking it easy and gathering my energies for a big new push, but procrastination differs markedly from genuine relaxation—which is truly needed. And it saves me no time or energy. On the contrary, it drains both, leaving me with self-doubt on top of the self-delusion.

We're all very busy. Every day we seem to have a giant to-do list of people to see, projects to complete, letters to read, letters to write. We have calls to answer and calls to make, then more calls to people who have called us and left messages.

Henri Nouwen's classic *Making All Things New* likens our lives to "overstuffed suitcases that are bursting at the seams." Feeling there is forever far too much to do, we say we're really under the gun this week. But working hard or even heroically to solve a problem is little to our credit if we created the problem in the first place. When most people refer to themselves as being under the gun, they want to believe, or *do* believe, that the pressures and problems are not of their own making. In most cases, however, the gun appeared after failure to attend to business in good time.

THE PROCRASTINATION INQUIRY

1. Do you put off tough jobs or avoid difficult assignments in a hope that something will change and you can escape the responsibility?
2. Do you put off important tasks by reorganizing your desk and cleaning your files—one or another form of sharpening your pencils?
3. Are you afraid of change, risk, or new situations?
4. When faced with a difficult or unpleasant situation, do you tend to get sick or even have accidents?
5. Have you ever delayed a task or performed it so badly that someone else had to take over?

6. Do you avoid confronting others even though you may have a valid complaint? Do you give up on a just cause or discard information that could really help another person?
7. Do you tend to blame "them" or "it" for your failures or for delay in reaching your goals?
8. Do you resort to criticism or sarcasm to escape difficult or tedious jobs?
9. Do you postpone medical/dental checkups because you're "too busy"?
10. Are you using only part of your potential in your work, claiming that it's too boring for your full energy?
11. Is your planner or software organizer chock full of unfulfilled targets?
12. Do your to-do lists remain filled with things that never get done?

One of the best escapes from the prison of procrastination is to take even the smallest step toward your goal. People usually procrastinate because of fear and lack of self-confidence—and, ironically, become even more afraid when under the gun. There are many ways to experiment and test new ground without risking the whole ball game on one play.

Two major fears that sire procrastination are fear of the unknown and fear of inferiority or looking foolish. A third fear—of success—is often overlooked. Many people, even many executives, fear success because it carries added responsibility that can seem too heavy to bear, such as setting an example of excellence that calls for additional effort and willingness to take risks. Playing it safe can seem more tempting than a need to step forward with determination to do it now and do it right.

Here are some ideas for moving from procrastination to proactivating.

1. Set your wake-up time a half hour earlier tomorrow and keep the clock at that setting. Use the extra time to think about the best way to spend your day.
2. Memorize and repeat this motto. "Action TNT: Today, Not

Tomorrow." Handle each piece of incoming mail only once. Block out specific times to initiate phone calls, personally take incoming phone calls, and to meet people in person.

3. When people tell you their problems, give solution-oriented feedback. Ask what's the next step, or what they would like to see happen.

4. Finish what you start. Concentrate all your energy and intensity without distraction on successfully completing your current major project.

5. Be constructively helpful instead of unhelpfully critical. Single out someone or something to praise instead of participating in group griping, grudge collecting, or pity parties.

6. Limit your television viewing to mostly educational or otherwise enlightening programs. Watch no more than one hour of television per day. Watch news programs on a need-to-know basis and don't go to sleep at night with the dulling input of the 11:00 P.M. headlines or sensational tabloids.

7. Make a list of five necessary but unpleasant projects you've been putting off, with a completion date for each project. Immediate action on unpleasant projects reduces stress and tension. It is very difficult to be active and depressed at the same time.

8. Seek out and converse with a successful role model and mentor. Learning from others' successes and setbacks will inevitably improve production of any kind. Truly listen; really find out how your role models do it right.

9. Understand that fear, as an acronym, is False Education Appearing Real, and that luck could mean Laboring Under Correct Knowledge. The more information you have on any subject—especially case histories—the less likely you'll be to put off your decisions.

10. Accept problems as inevitable offshoots of change and progress. With the ever more rapid pace of change in society and business, you will be overwhelmed unless you view change as normal and learn to look for its positive aspects—such as new opportunities and improvements—rather than bemoan the negative.

There is actually no such thing as a "future" decision; there are only present decisions that will affect the future. Procrastinators wait for just the right moment to decide. If *you* wait for the perfect moment, you become a security-seeker who is running in place, unwittingly digging yourself deeper into your rut. If you wait for every objection to be overcome, you'll attempt nothing. My personal motto is "Stop stewing and start doing."

No Train, No Gain

The key to dealing effectively with unusually stressful or challenging situations is careful, diligent advance preparation.

Thrusting the original astronauts into a completely new and foreign environment subjected them to an inordinate amount of stress—and it also made a good study of leadership and resiliency. Those men knew they had to assume full responsibility for their actions, that a single error of judgment in space would be critically dangerous and possibly fatal, and no one could cover for them. Despite the tremendous pressure, however, they reported little fear and stress during their flights.

They attributed their confidence to training that had prepared them to deal with any problem that could realistically be expected. That they made no mention of *unrealistic* expectations of problems is important. Leaders, like astronauts, give little thought to remote threats for which there can be no rational preparation. The astronauts concentrated their efforts on what they could control and what they had to do to prepare for it. All said they had felt more fear during their previous combat flying. Repeated exposure to stressful situations over time gradually moved them from courageous behavior toward a higher level of courage known as fearless behavior.

In a real way, you share the needs of the astronauts who undertook the first space travel when you face your future as a leader in the knowledge era. Earlier, we suggested that the fourth leg of self-esteem was self-efficacy, the exercise of competence and control. Self-efficacy means that your confidence grows with each achievement; self-efficacy also means that courage grows and spreads when it is nourished. Repeated experience of success breeding more success, combined with the knowledge that they were expertly trained, gave the astronauts increased confidence that their mission would succeed. That's what we all need.

No one has ever done precisely what you are now doing. No one has ever faced your future. Leaders understand that small successes today breed the confidence and courage to risk and persist tomorrow—and to be patient while watching for opportunities to establish their empires.

Here are some action steps for more perseverance:

1. Do high-priority work first. Most people spend most of their time on low-priority busywork because it requires no additional knowledge, skills, or imagination—or courage. In a word, it's easier.

2. Concentrate your time and energy on the 20 percent of your activities and concepts that have proven most productive in the past. Remember the 80/20 rule named after Vilfredo Pareto, the 19th-century economist: 80 percent of production volume usually comes from 20 percent of the producers. This means that you should focus your effort on the most productive people and ideas.

3. Don't worry if a change in your professional or personal life doesn't bear immediate fruit. In fact, anticipate a temporary drop in productivity and efficiency. Assimilating change takes time. Productivity will increase as familiarity and confidence rebuild; meanwhile, don't stew while it simmers.

4. If you fail the first time, try again. If you fail a second time, get more feedback about why. If you fail a third time, your sights might be too high for now. Bring your goals a little closer from the horizon.

5. Try to associate with people who have similar goals. Many of us join groups combating the same problems or habits, such as smoking and being overweight. Similarly, regular meetings with groups with the same values and dreams help bolster perseverance, and can also provide effective action ideas.

6. If you reach a dead end with a problem, change your scenery and mood. Solutions often come during a day of relaxing and reflecting at the ocean or in the country. This is landscaping, not escaping. Remember that when the left side of your brain, which deals with logic, slows down, the more creative right side remains available.

7. When you've gained general knowledge in a field or subject, con-

centrate on learning one aspect of it particularly well. Specialize successfully before you diversify. Doing one thing well until you have mastered it brings confidence and a reputation for excellence. Having mastered playing golf, Jack Nicklaus is now doing what he always wanted to do: designing golf courses.

8. Approach your problems with logic and honesty. Problems generally fall into two categories: those that are relatively easy to solve and those that have become emergencies, requiring urgent attention. Most people naturally want to deal with only the first category. A good way to gauge your balance is to ask whether you're spending your time on what's truly important to you and your family or whether you're always under the gun of deadlines.

9. Always expect the unexpected.

GETTING HIGH ON YOUR MISFORTUNES

Norman Vincent Peale, the inexhaustible positive thinker, was a friend and mentor for twenty years. Traveling with him regularly on the international circuit, I marveled at his enthusiasm and vitality. His wife was rarely far from his side, and she provided more than just supportive morale. Ruth Peale was a full, active partner in his professional as well as his personal life (just as Susan Waitley, who has her own professional life, is as much my partner as her responsibilities allow. We firmly believe that traveling together helps a family stay together—and Susan is a rich source of advice as well as the greatest possible comfort after my errors).

Dr. Peale's talks were truly inspiring. He liked to say that a person without problems was a person safely planted in a cemetery. If he himself went too long without a problem, he would lift his hands toward the sky and ask why. "Lord, don't you love me anymore? You haven't given me a challenge or setback for days. How about a nice, big, healthy problem just to let me know you really care?" His eyes twinkling, Norman would then assure his audiences that "God always heard my call and granted my request." I'm convinced that his approach to daily challenges kept him young and active for ninety-three years until his death on Christmas Eve of 1993.

One of the lessons embodied in Norman Vincent Peale's life is that even he struggled with discouragement. More than that, he gave up before reaching an important goal. When he was in his fifties, he wrote a book and sent it to a host of publishers. Regarding the stack of rejection notices in frustration one day, he threw the manuscript in the wastebasket.

Ruth Peale reached in to try to salvage it. "No," he said sternly. "We've wasted enough time on that. I forbid you to take that thing out of the wastebasket." The following day, she personally visited yet another publisher. Shown into his office, she handed him an oddly shaped parcel—much too big and bulky to be a manuscript. Unwrapping it, the publisher was startled to see a wastebasket. It contained the manuscript of *The Power of Positive Thinking*, one of the most influential books of the mid-20th century.

While following her husband's command—literally—Ruth Peale would not let him give up on his goal. For her persistence, the couple—and the world—has reaped the benefits of the scores of millions of copies of that classic book sold, together with several best-sellers that followed it. The telegram I sent Ruth after Norman's death said that he will always live within those who believe in looking at life's positive side and laughing at misfortune. She wrote back to say that Norman was probably giving a positive-thinking lecture to the angels.

> *Humor is falling downstairs if you do it in the act of telling someone else not to fall.*

Many extraordinary people like Dr. Peale, who have lived more than eighty years, retain a great sense of humor on top of their positive attitude. I think of Maurice Chevalier, Rose Kennedy, Lowell Thomas, Bob Hope, George Burns, Ronald Reagan. And we'll all be thinking of more and more such people because the number of centenarians living in the United States—more than 35,000 already—is increasing rapidly.

The Census Bureau reports that this is the nation's fastest-growing age group. When I celebrate my hundredth birthday in 2033, nearly a million Americans will do the same. In case anyone believes that *I* believe the number will significantly change if I'm not around for that celebration, I'll say that another way. In roughly 40 years, more than a million Americans will be 100 or more years old. Their common traits will be passion and the ability to laugh at their own misfortunes—which is another way of saying that they won't consider themselves the center of the universe. The excitement of being alive no matter what is the key. I'm amazed by the similarities in emotional qualities between centenarians—people over 100—and business and athletic leaders.

> *We are in the world to laugh. In purgatory or hell we shall no*
> *longer be able to do so, and in heaven it wouldn't be proper.*
>
> —Jules Renard

One long-ago Christmas Eve when my children were young, I climbed on my roof after midnight and tried to produce a noise that would sound like Santa's reindeer. Unfortunately Santa never yelled like I did when I fell off the roof into some oleander bushes. Recently, a puzzled young college student approached me after a speech at a large rally. "Are you really Denis Waitley?" he asked. "You're a lot older than you sound on your audiotapes." I explained that I was in a vocal cord fitness program to keep my voice youthful as my body withered away. Obviously, I'm in what's politely called middle age—but my ability to get into mix-ups is little diminished.

When I was the keynote speaker for a Congressional luncheon, I thought I dressed appropriately. But no doubt a certain penchant for ridiculous seriousness made me take it too formally, because a leading senator mistook me for the maître d'hôtel. He asked for four rolls, butter, and a napkin. I could think of nothing to do but go to the kitchen and fetch them for him. Later, we had a good laugh on me.

Not long ago, a day when I had a speaking engagement in Toronto dawned in a driving snowstorm that caused cancellation of the flights. But in my business, where the hall's been hired and large audiences are expecting you, there's no satisfactory excuse for not showing up for work. I chartered a small plane with a brave pilot. After risking our lives in the angry weather—and paying $5,000 for the "thrill"—I grabbed a cab from the airport. We slithered down the highway into the city, then to the hotel where I'd be speaking to a thousand conventioneers. Hurray! We were on time! There was just one problem: No convention was booked at the hotel. Actually, two problems: There was also no hotel. It had been torn down six months earlier, and our office somehow missed the crucial notice that the convention had been moved to Vancouver. The taxi driver considered this the biggest hoot of his life. "Shouldn't you call your wife before you fly home?" he asked between sips of hot chocolate back at the airport, where the plane was being refueled. "Maybe she moved too."

Laughter is one of the best antidotes for failure, and I'm never so happy with my sense of perspective as when I can laugh at my own goofs.

Among those whom I like or admire, I can find no common denominator. But among those whom I love, I can. All of them make me laugh.

—W. H. Auden

I much enjoy my friendship with Art Linkletter, who was born and raised in my hometown of San Diego and never lost the sense of humor that keeps him ageless. Octogenarian Art found the secret of youth: looking at life through the eyes of a child. On his speaking tours, he encourages us to laugh at ourselves and to find the child within each of us, because children get old when they grow up. Urging us never to do that, Art reminds us of our youth by recounting some of his beloved interviews with children during his years and years on radio and television. To me they're the essence of honest humor—because children themselves are so honest.

One of my favorite Linkletter stories is about a television interview of a grade school youth. What did his father do for a living? Art asked. The boy seized the microphone as if it were a baseball bat and he was the clean-up hitter. "My dad's a policeman," he announced proudly. "He catches burglars and crooks. Then he spread-eagles them and puts the cuffs on and takes them to the station and puts them in jail." "Wow!" replied Art. "I bet your mother worries about his work, doesn't she?"

"No," the youth assured. "My dad brings her lots of watches and jewelry and stuff. She doesn't mind his work at all."

Art gave another boy on one of his shows a hypothetical problem to solve. "Let's say you're an airline pilot flying to Hawaii," he began. "You've got two hundred and fifty passengers in the back of your plane, and your engines quit. What would you do if you were at the controls?" The boy thought for a moment before offering a solution. "I'd put on the fasten-seat-belt sign and then use my parachute." He was visibly proud of his answer until he heard loud laughter from the studio audience. He shoved his hands in his pockets and tears began to well in his eyes until Art, characteristically, came quickly and gently to his rescue. "That was a great answer, son. They weren't laughing at you, they were happy with what you said." But this didn't console the boy. "Yes," he added, "but I was coming right back to the plane. I was just going down to get some more gas."

Maintaining our sense of humor is a wonderful way to adapt to life's ups and downs. Let's keep the child within us alive and awake. When we can look at ourselves through young eyes—not take ourselves too seriously—we've learned the essence of adaptability, perseverance, patience, and even leadership. Since change is inevitable, we'll always have new challenges and new delights. Discovering the secret that the good old days are here and now, we can look forward to each day's surprises and promise.

Here are some action steps for maintaining your sense of humor through misfortune:

1. Examine your sense of humor to determine how it serves you. Is it mainly a warehouse for jokes or does it function, as it should, to help you perceive your own occasionally ludicrous traits and behaviors?

2. Acknowledge that you own your emotions and take responsibility for them. Instead of saying that someone *makes* you angry, recognize that only *you* can do that. When you express your anger or dissatisfaction, first remove yourself physically from a potentially hostile situation.

3. When you reprimand someone or express your unhappiness, try to do it after your hostility or distress has subsided. A normal speaking voice, without warlike body language, will get your feelings across best. When you're upset, try releasing your adrenalin in a physical exercise such as running, tennis, racquetball, or handball. Do speak your mind, but wait until you can be reasonable—until you can criticize without attacking.

4. Don't argue. There's no such thing as winning an argument, only winning an agreement.

5. View change as normal. Constantly evaluate your capacity for flexibility, for adaptability to change, and your receptiveness to new ideas and surprises.

6. Don't engage in all-or-nothing management. If things don't work out exactly as you planned, salvage what you can—don't be like a top team that loses an important game and considers the season a failure. Demanding unrealistic perfection from yourself or others will generate

continual discrediting of your performance. Nothing you do will fully measure up.

7. Let other people take responsibility for their own behavior. Don't engage in the game of self-blame or false guilt when close ones suffer setbacks. Even your own adult children are responsible for their own lives. Build adaptability into your home and workplace, encouraging courage and flexibility.

8. Learn to say no as if it meant yes. Yes, I'm already committed. Scheduling your time so that you can comfortably keep your commitments is an excellent way to release stress. Only you can place yourself under the gun. Being permanently there, which is characteristic of so-called Type A behavior, increases the risk of coronary and other stress-related diseases. Saying no in advance is far less painful than admitting you couldn't deliver later on.

9. Simplify your life. Get rid of the clutter and the nonproductive activities. Continue asking yourself at least once a week what you really want to spend your time on.

10. Engage in inspirational recreation. Get out the kites, grab the Frisbees, dust off the picnic basket. Share a project with children or friends, attend a local theater production, and choose movies and television shows that tend to warm your heart.

Some time ago my colleague, Gerhard Gschwandtner, who publishes the popular magazine *Personal Selling Power,* went to the Library of Congress for some research on success. He found 1,200 books in categories having to do with success—and 16 about losing or failure. Puzzled, he returned to the computer to search for "disappointment," which he rightly considered one of the most common human experiences.

He looked for material in English, German, and French. He found a single article—"The Management of Disappointment"—that had appeared in the *Harvard Business Review* way back in 1967. Gschwandtner traveled to Harvard University's Graduate School of Business Administration to meet its author, Dr. Abraham Zaleznik—who was surprised by the visit. In the many years since the article had appeared, no one had ever discussed it with him. Dr. Zaleznik, a well-known management consultant, now believed the reason was obvious. Disappointment is a downer.

Yet the issue of *Personal Selling Power* in which Gschwandtner featured Dr. Zaleznik talking about disappointment sold more copies than any previous issue of the magazine,[4] and the clamor for reprints lasted almost two years. So the subject is obviously not quite so "untouchable."

Some of Dr. Zaleznik's key thoughts about disappointment—specifically, his disappointment-trap concepts—that appeared in that issue include the following:

A superficial definition of disappointment is the feeling of not getting something wanted, but the phenomenon goes deeper. When what we want is very important and valuable to us, disappointment can become significant, even life-threatening: People unable to cope with their feelings of severe disappointment can end in suicide. Two of the most common misconceptions about disappointment—understandable misconceptions, since the world loves winners—are that it's a "bad" emotion and it should never be shown. Especially in America, we are taught to deny disappointment because it can't possibly have anything to do with success.

But the truth is that disappointment doesn't equal failure. Seen in a positive light, it can stimulate learning and growth. When you feel disappointed, you can either seek comfort or seek a solution. The best approach includes some of both. First step back, stop what you're doing, and try to obtain some comfort—but don't get trapped into staying comfortable. Having licked or otherwise healed your wounds, prepare for another effort based on a new solution to the problem. Going straight for the solution without being comforted can also be a trap—in workaholism, for example, putting in long hours that produce few results. Besides, it's healthier to confront and release your disappointment, together with any rage or anger that came with it.

To resolve disappointment Dr. Zaleznik suggests these steps:

1. Talk about your disappointment with someone intelligent and caring—and whom you can trust to keep your confidences.

2. Deal with how you really feel by writing down your feelings. Don't try to bottle up your anger if that's what you feel; let it spill out on paper.

3. Talk with people who have also known disappointment. Find out how they dealt with it and what they learned.

4. Read about gifted leaders who suffered setbacks. How did they handle them? What universal principles can you find to apply to your own situations? Since we all have different notions of success, our definitions of it will vary. In a way, failure is more universal—and developing attitudes for facing and dealing with it is more urgent.[5]

When we begin a new project, our confidence is often low because experience hasn't taught us we can succeed. This is true in teaching, leading, building a business, learning to ride a bicycle, skiing, flying a high-performance aircraft, closing a sale, being a parent—everything. I believe that success indeed breeds success, but not that failure must breed failure. Some say that failure should be avoided at all costs—but that cost itself is too high, since the only way to avoid failure at all costs is to sacrifice your chances for victory and success. In other words, to try nothing.

Some say too that failure is like toxic waste: Thinking about it pollutes and ultimately undermines the attitudes needed for success. I see failure more as fertilizer, to be used to enrich the soil of your mind, where the seeds of success must be planted. Turning failure into fertilizer is accomplished by using your errors and mistakes as learning, then dismissing them.

Failures and disappointments used only as corrective feedback can help get you back on target. Soon you'll forget the failures as such and focus on future success. And to be a self-leader in the knowledge era, never label lack of success as failure, because it's just part of the journey.

THIRTEEN

❖

SELF-LEADERSHIP AND LOVE: YOUR GREATEST GIFT

--- ❖ ---

1 ❖ *Do you consider yourself possessive in your close relationships?*

2 ❖ *How often do you experience feelings of jealousy?*

3 ❖ *Is your most important personal relationship based on filling mutual needs or sharing values?*

--- ❖ ---

I HOPE THAT USING A FAIRY TALE TO ILLUSTRATE MY CENTRAL THEMES—empowering, nurturing, facilitating, and setting one's self free to build win-win relationships in our era of radical change—won't be taken as an attempt to trivialize them. On the contrary, fairy tales often convey the most profound truths. In the case of the tale I want to cite now, the truths concern a subject that underlies all my themes: genuine love for other human beings.

If you saw the recent Disney film of *Beauty and the Beast,* I'm sure you were delighted by the artistry, music, and humor. But I want to examine the message. We'll have to discard the old, chauvinistic interpretation of male and female roles, which can't be relevant today. In real life, beauty is in the eye of the beholder and the beast of selfishness and insensitivity can reside in us all, regardless of our position or gender.

BEAUTY AND THE BEAST: THE TALE

Once upon a time in a faraway land, a young prince lived in a glorious castle. Although—or because—he had everything his heart desired, he was spoiled, selfish, and unkind. One winter's night, a haggard old beggar came to the castle and offered him a single rose in exchange for shelter from the bitter cold. Repulsed by her appearance, the sneering prince told her to go away and never bother him again.

Offering the rose once more, she warned him not to be deceived by appearances. When he turned her away again, the old woman's ugliness melted to reveal a beautiful enchantress. The awestruck prince quickly tried to apologize and gain her favor—but too late: She had seen there was no love in his heart. As punishment, she transformed him into a hideous beast, then cast a powerful spell on the castle and all who lived there.

Ashamed of his grotesque appearance, the Beast concealed himself inside his castle with a magic mirror as his only "window" to the world. The rose, also magic, would bloom until his twenty-first year. If he could learn to love another and earn the other's love in return before its last petal fell, the spell would be broken. If not, he was doomed to remain a prisoner forever.

As the years passed, he lost all hope and fell into despair. Even if he did find someone to love, who could ever return the love of a beast? How could he hold her there?

This concern about holding on is how many relationships are perceived, pursued, and destroyed. More than anything, the message of *Beauty and the Beast* is that love is an expression of the value we place on a person independent of his or her ability to meet our needs. Authentic love makes you want to set your partner free, not possess him or her. This dovetails with the yin and the yang model of life we mentioned when discussing the change from position power to relationship power. There, we focused on power and synergy in the interaction of male and female attributes, and how enlightened understanding is dramatically changing organizational leadership. Our focus here will be more on personal than business relationships, although one underlies the other.

In my own relationships, I like to think I'm more liberating than possessive, that I'm rarely captured by envy or jealousy, that I tend to give without worrying about what I might get in return. But I'm as far from perfect as everyone else. Sometimes I sense that my tendency to be a good samaritan nurturer comes from a need for approval. Trying to share my values out of love is one thing. Seeking approbation in order to neutralize the fear of abandonment that may have sprung from my childhood in a broken home is another—and I can't always be certain of my ultimate motive. How about you? Do you help others so they can fly free or in hope that they'll approve of you? Of course, human motives are almost always mixed, but the constant is that the best way to ensure you are loved by those important to you is to empower them to become as independent and valuable as they can be. The paradoxical proverb is:

You must strive to be lovable, but never seek to be loved.

When others sense you have their interests rather than only your own at heart, they begin to trust you. That foundation of all friendships and healthy marriages is also the key to customer service and satisfaction. You never just close a sale. What you do is open a long-term relationship based on mutual disclosure and mutual trust.

The lessons of *Beauty and the Beast* are fundamental to raising emotionally healthy children, enjoying a nurturing marriage, and gaining self-fulfillment. To understand the beastly prince and how he arrived at his sorry state, the story is best divided into four parts: the Spoiled Prince, the Belligerent Beast, the Empowerment Transition, and Love Returns.

THE SPOILED PRINCE

The spoiled, selfish prince had everything he wanted—an interesting condition because we parents, unfortunately, tend to spoil our own princes and princesses, either by overindulgence or by deprivation.

Childhood should be the time for shifting from primary selfishness to sharing, for learning to cope with deprivation and disappointment—and learning to overcome failure, since breaking a toy and forgetting a homework assignment are far less serious than breaking a marriage or forgetting to prepare for career advancement. But excessive deprivation, as is common in underprivileged families, leaves many children stuck in the stage of personal gratification. They lack resources for developing a sense of responsibility for others and a wish to care for them. And children needn't be poor to be underprivileged. The overindulged are also deprived, cheated out of learning how to cope.

Ironically, it can be more difficult for the wealthy to be effective parents. Children of lower-income families are often forced to learn competence and the need to provide for themselves. Rich parents can easily be tempted to use money or things as bribes to gain affection or establish control. Their children, in turn, sense that the mom and dad who can no longer do without their high standard of living are weak parents. It takes strength and discipline for the privileged to stop manipulating and being manipulated.

One of the media's more destructive myths is glorification of the child-centered home. Rather than revolving around children, the home should be based on the loving commitment of adults whose relationship provides a model. Child-centered homes promote selfishness and an unnaturally elevated sense of importance on the part of the princes and princesses, retarding development of open, loving relationships. Thus the vain prince looked down on the old woman who offered her rose in return for shelter.

The more we do for our children after the age when they're capable, the less they can do for themselves. The less they do for themselves, the more we rob them of the opportunity to gain self-respect. Without self-respect, the deprived ego roars like a beast for approval and service.

THE BELLIGERENT BEAST

The Belligerent Beast despises his own reflection in the mirror. Unless he can find someone to love and love him back, the mouse inside the monster is destined to remain in exile, forever talking to teapots, candelabra, and clocks.

When the young woman from the village offers to trade her freedom for her father's life, the Beast is all too willing to accept. He believes that if he can control his prisoner in the castle, she will gradually learn to accept him as her master. Fast running out of options and rose petals, he selfishly interprets this as love. Maybe the spell *will* be broken.

When the young woman resists his advances, the Belligerent Beast goes on a rampage—which can be a symbol for our current society. Attempting to blame others for our troubles, trying to manipulate others to get what we want, we become dependent on others and often resort to violence in a vain attempt to solve our problems and relieve our frustration.

Attacking those who disagree with their beliefs, the selfish and insecure try to prove they're right with might. Have-nots release their resentment by attacking the haves, demanding their fair share. Haves exhibit disdain of the have-nots who can't control their rage. This vicious, no-win cycle will continue until human beings, who must have a sense of consideration and responsibility for others' well-being, stop roaring and start listening.

THE EMPOWERMENT TRANSITION

Which is what happens to the Beast: Considering his captive's well-being at last, he begins treating her quite differently. Thus begins the independent value exchange and the empowerment transition.

With grandchildren hatching from coast to coast, I love watching the video with them and noticing their reaction to the Beast's empowerment transition into a lovable creature. He trades his win-lose attitude for win-win. I delight in *his* delight discovering that he's worthy of being loved, and in the young woman's wonder in finding the gentle, vulnerable child beneath his frightening bluster. As they danced together and played hide and seek, I hoped my children and grandchildren got the message:

Look beneath skin-deep commercial values—beyond the tabloid magazines and the *Current Affair*s. Be willing to trade shelter for a rose, or give it to someone in need without a trade. Stop complaining long enough to consider the plight of others. Be willing to look inside the Beast to find its beauty. Be willing to set free those to whom you want to cling, even though you risk losing them forever.

LOVE RETURNS

When the Beast sets Beauty free to go to her father's aid, he knowingly empowers her return. Your children will develop the capacity for independent love in place of dependent need only when you set them free to become adults. And only when you set your romantic and business partners free to be all they can be will you know how attractive and lovable you are yourself, free of the insecurity and self-doubt that spawn envy and jealousy.

LOVE AND MARRIAGE

Commitment to a single partner offers the greatest potential for a win-win life. It combines the natural selfishness of wanting another person to fulfill longed-for fantasies with the chance to be your vulnerable self, able to reveal your innermost thoughts.

One of the most meaningful nonfiction books I ever read is the little-known *Me: The Narcissistic American* by Aaron Stern, a psychiatrist who served as an educational consultant to the United Nations and as a director of the Motion Picture Association of America's Code and Rating Administration. It zeroes in brilliantly on the greatest cause of America's social problems: our narcissistic preoccupation with immediate gratification.

Dr. Stern's understanding of marriage is especially rich. It should, he says, combine "the exquisite excitement of adolescent romance with the ability to assume the responsibility involved in caring for each other. The absence of either of these qualities makes the relationship incomplete. Together they sharpen the sense of fulfillment loving gives us." Dr. Stern believes that every marriage needs some adolescent love as a spice to keep romance alive. But spice is properly added for flavor, not to overwhelm the main course.[1]

In my relationship with my own wife, we can too easily become preoccupied with professional goals, financial matters, and family responsibilities. I sense our longing to play hide-and-seek, to dine and dance in candlelight, to walk on the beach as we did in our courtship. Susan and I have promised each other to keep moving our marriage from position to relationship power. We do more walking and less talking about schedules. We're more spontaneous and less structured. We touch each other and listen to music more, take more evening swims and light more fires in the fireplace. With all the children having flown the nest, we travel together on my business trips. We want to experience each other without interruption, so we set aside more time without phones, manuscripts, faxes, children, or even friends. On our special days, Susan sometimes keeps intruders at bay by setting road blocks with flashing lights in front of our driveway.

Just as it takes effort to nurture children to become independent and to empower employees to assume responsibility, it takes real effort to bolster your commitment to your life partner. Healthy love can't be demanded nor taken for granted. It can only be a continuing give-and-take exchange and dialogue between two independent persons who share many values and responsibilities, yet still feel a childlike magic with each other. That's the deepest message of *Beauty and the Beast:* Love returns when it is set free.

Here are some tips for healthy personal relationships and raising win-win children:

1. Look at yourself through others' eyes. Imagine being married to you. Imagine being your child or your friend.
2. Check to see if you shift roles easily and appropriately from worker/executive and earner to nurturing parent, and from role model to romantic partner.
3. Be empathic in your communications. Knowledge isn't always wisdom, sensitivity isn't always accuracy, sympathy isn't always understanding. Really get inside another person before you pass judgment or offer advice. Ask questions, listen, and discover rather than making assumptions.
4. Listen unconditionally to the significant adults and children in your life. Listening without bias or distraction is the greatest value you can pay another person.
5. Develop a magic touch. Don't assume that money, shelter, and creature comforts are enough to demonstrate your love. Nothing can replace your presence, your hug, your touch—*you.*
6. Be aware of opportunities to add spice and romance to your most important adult relationship: flowers, a greeting card slipped into a briefcase, an unexpected phone call, an overnight bag in the car trunk when it was supposed to be just dinner and a movie.
7. Talk casually and evenly with your children, not as an authority figure. Parents under stress often withdraw from one another and from their children, communicating in a terse, irritated way. To ensure that your children feel accepted, take time to chat with them about anything and everything, a message that says "I'm interested in you."
8. Become enthusiastic about your family members' interests. Young children need their parents' involvement and ap-

proval—but remember that involvement shouldn't mean taking over or becoming their agent and manager.

9. Schedule mandatory family time together, even at the expense of seemingly pressing obligations. Family members often meet coming and going, making the home like a pit stop at the Indianapolis 500. One meal a day together with the television off is a bare minimum.

10. Except where safety may be involved, give your family members the responsibility for the consequences and rewards of their own choices. Don't take over when that will rob them of the experience of the independent action that develops self-trust.

11. Never pay children for doing something for themselves. That form of bribery makes success relate more to external performance than internal values. An allowance should relate to regular household chores at regular times.

12. Build a home atmosphere in which each family member respects the needs, dignity, and individuality of all the others. Make your cornerstones love, caring, trust, and giving.

13. Maintain an atmosphere that encourages free and open communications. Encourage all family members to express feelings and opinions without fear of recrimination or reprisal.

14. Above all, encourage every family member always to take the high road of being a care-giver rather than the low road of being a share-taker from others. Although not *most* traveled, the high road is always the road *best* traveled.

FOURTEEN

❖

SELF-LEADERSHIP AND SERVICE: YOUR ROAD BEST TRAVELED

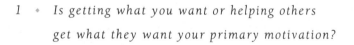

1 ❖ *Is getting what you want or helping others get what they want your primary motivation?*

2 ❖ *Do you, as a matter of principle, do more than is required of you?*

3 ❖ *Are compassion and service key ingredients in your mission?*

TIME NEVER STOPS TO REST, NEVER HESITATES, NEVER LOOKS FORWARD or backward. Life's raw material spends itself *now,* this moment—which is why how you spend your time is far more important than all the material possessions you may own or positions you may attain.

No Replay in the Game of Life

Positions change, possessions come and go, you can earn more money. You can renew your supply of many things, but like good health, that other most precious resource, time spent is gone forever. Each yesterday, and all of them together, are beyond your control. Literally all the money in the world can't undo or redo a single act you performed. You cannot erase a single word you said; can't add an "I love you," "I'm sorry," or "I forgive you"—not even a "thank you" you forgot to say.

You must spend your time wisely, but never try to save it.

THE EQUAL OPPORTUNITY EMPLOYER

Time is the only resource or gift distributed equally to everyone. Each human being in every hemisphere and time zone has precisely 168 hours a week to spend. "Time cuts down all, Both great and small," warned *The New England Primer* three centuries ago. Not Madonna or Queen Elizabeth, not even Warren Buffett, one of the richest men in the United States, can buy another hour. Scientists and computer experts can speed up data transmission to perform millions of transactions a second, but they can't create a single new second.

None of us seems to have enough time, yet we all have all there is or ever will be. It would take a hundred lifetimes to accomplish all we're capable of, but we're given just one for learning and giving as much as we can, for doing our best. If we had more time, there would be less need for books like this one, less need to make plans and set priorities. If we had forever, we could probably wing it every day and still end with immense knowledge, possibly even wisdom. But we're strictly limited to those 168 hours—10,080 minutes—a week, which is why Benjamin Franklin urged us not to squander "the stuff life is made of." (Franklin also coined the famous "Time is money.") And although the celebrated German poet Johann Goethe may have been a trifle optimistic when he promised that "one always has enough time, if only one applies it well," his point is well taken.

ACCELERATING WITH AGE

One of life's great ironies is that time crawls when we're young and flies as we age. When we were children, the ride from the airport to Disneyland lasted forever. It took an eternity for holidays and summer vacations to arrive—birthdays, too, until the twenty-first, which had always been far distant in the unimaginable future. Then, slowly at first, the clock began to accelerate. The thirtieth birthday seemed to arrive inexplicably soon after the twenty-fifth. The fortieth came altogether unexpectedly, and with less than a hearty welcome. The ten years between thirty and forty—a decade of watching children's transformation from toddlers to teens and of often arduous climbing of corporate ladders—passed like three or four.

After age forty, I began linking time to the seasons. There was a blur of time from winter skiing to spring cleaning and onto summer travels and fall commitments. I lived in short swallows of breath, climbing mountains, weathering unexpected storms, enjoying experience and growth—and feeling that six months raced by like a week. After fifty, I realized from very personal experience that time appears to race with the years because we understand how precious and rare it is; we appreciate our remaining portion as if it were pure oxygen escaping from a beautiful balloon that can never be refilled.

ONLY THIS MOMENT IN TIME

Many people live in the past, wishing they could put the clock in reverse, largely to undo mistakes. Most people live in the future, wishing for and worrying about what they want to have and to do but can't—instead of enjoying what they have and doing what they can do, but don't. They put happiness and fulfillment on permanent layaway. We can't relive yesterday and mustn't waste today by living in a fantasy tomorrow. Only the actions we take here and now can create tomorrow's real promise. We will not have this day or moment to enjoy again.

BACK TO THE FUTURE

When we were five years old, one year represented twenty percent of our total lives. At fifty, a year represents two percent, or one fiftieth, of our life experience. No wonder it took so long for holidays to arrive when we were in grammar school—and little wonder also that after age fifty, when a year represents such a small portion of the time we've already spent, it goes by in a seeming blink of an eye. It's a little like a videotape speeding up as it rewinds and accelerating almost wildly near the end of the reel. So goes your remaining time as it dwindles down.

THE ROAD BEST TRAVELED

In our journey into the empires of our mind, we must remember that success is a process, not a destination, let alone a summit. The road best traveled was inspired by "The Road Not Taken," a well-known poem by Robert Frost.

To visualize the road best traveled, you must understand that it's not what you have that counts—not your money, stocks, IRAs, CDs, cars, position, or real estate. What counts is what you now do with what you have. No one can reasonably claim that the choices are easy. I trust I'll never forget M. Scott Peck's great *The Road Less Traveled,* whose opening line consists of three words: "Life is difficult."

No doubt it has always been difficult in various ways, but some stretches are more difficult than others, and America has known far easier, happier periods. In some respects, our nation is spinning out of control. The increase of crime, especially violent crime, is frightening, not only in itself but also for what it says about the underpinnings of our family life, our sense of responsibility, our culture. Many of our children seem destined to live in a world of angry anarchy, with all that means for society as a whole. As we've seen, the middle class must struggle harder and harder to earn its living—whose standard is declining. We worry about our children, in this respect and others. Confusion grows, tempers are raw, relationships are strained, the traditional American optimism has been worn thin. Economic security—security of all kinds—seems to be disappearing. All of this is true, and most of it is rightfully worrying—but at the same time, the opportunities for personal growth and success are unparalleled.

Our society's current condition reminds me of another first line, this one by Charles Dickens. The famous "It was the best of times, it was the worst of times," which opens *A Tale of Two Cities,* could easily serve to summarize our own times. It *is* the worst of times as measured by some aspects of our national life, especially in the demoralized, decaying cities. But age brings perspective, and perspective can offer the refreshing appreciation that things are not quite as bleak as they appear. This is not the first appearance of "the worst of times," even in America. The way out is through personal commitment to individual goals, yours and mine.

> *You must always strive for excellence, but never seek perfection.*

A friend and colleague of mine named Robert C. Larson suggests that an appropriate definition for maturity might simply be fatigue. As we grow older, we recognize that certain battles are no longer worth fighting. Therefore we choose our conflicts carefully, just as we choose the road on which we walk with increasing care. Which road is best? As Robert Frost said, the road less traveled made all the difference. If that's the road you've chosen—never mind whether you're racing ahead, struggling on an upgrade, or resting a moment while you catch your breath—you know that life is not a book that is finished when you've read its last pages. You know that it is more like a garden that changes with the seasons. It grows well in the summer and less well in the fall. What you planted in the spring might die in the winter. But when you plant again, tending the soil and watering the seeds, you will reap again.

You also know that it's not necessary to invite weeds into your garden. They move right in, and in great numbers. No planting is necessary, but getting a life garden to produce flowers of kindness, food for flourishing friendships and success, takes constant attention and vigilance. It demands commitment to the road best traveled.

SHARING THE HARVEST

During many periods of history, farmers left a corner of their crops unharvested so that the less fortunate might use them for food. This ensured that everyone had enough to eat, and also demonstrated the farmers' compassion. It showed that they cared about others and didn't have to have it all in order to feel successful. It was what one did on the road best traveled.

WILLIE JORDAN ON THE HIGH ROAD

Less than a decade ago, a remarkable woman committed herself to spend the rest of her life working among the forgotten people of the streets of Los Angeles. Willie Jordan and her late husband Fred took the inner city's crushing needs personally. They felt they could not stand by while people were being buried by alcohol, drugs, violence, and other abuses.

IT WAS A MAN'S WORLD

In the early days of what is now called the Fred Jordan Mission, it was mostly men who came to its open doors for food, a bed, and a word of encouragement. "Our work was mostly with drunks and those who were simply down on their luck—and they were almost all men," Willie Jordan recalls. "Only on occasion would a woman come to the Mission. It was indeed a man's world, and that included the gutters of Skid Row."

SKID ROW FOR THE FAMILY

Fred Jordan died in 1988. That left the feeding, clothing, and provision of counseling of thousands of street people—including growing numbers of women and children—to Willie. As you read this passage, roughly a thousand men, women, and children are her responsibility, a responsibility she never imagined she could handle alone.

"Just the thought of his death was more than I could imagine," she wrote of her beloved husband in her *Growing Through the Loss of a Loved One.* "I thought . . . I'll be totally devastated, in fact I planned to be devastated. I thought that's the way it should be. I loved him so much, how could I ever live, love and laugh without him?" But Willie Jordan thrived in her giving way. Working with generous local merchants, she arranges for some twenty-five thousand needy children and parents to receive new shoes, socks, shirts, dresses, T-shirts, and underwear each Christmas. Parents who can't find work receive food bags almost too heavy to carry out. And Willie—cradling a child, comforting a mother, praying with a father whose baby was born addicted to crack cocaine—is the center of the outpouring of love.

MOTHER'S DAY AT THE MISSION

"One of the great joys of my life," says Willie, "is what happens around Mother's Day each year. We put out flyers on the streets of Skid Row and invite all the women of the inner city to come to the Fred Jordan Mission for a special day of pampering—when we shampoo and cut their hair, give them manicures and facials, and send them out looking like a million dollars. I don't know who cries more, me or the women, because when they leave the Mission, they're absolutely beautiful!"

Many of those women can't remember when someone has done something so loving for them. The compassion—the tender touch instead of abuse—is literally changing lives.

On Mother's Day, too, Willie and her staff arrange for a sit-down dinner for up to five thousand women and their children. It takes place at the corner of 5th and Towne, in front of the Mission. The sumptuous meal—all the mothers and children can eat—is prepared and served by Mission volunteers. And there is more than food to savor. A freshly picked carnation lies beside each woman's plate—for many, their first gift of a flower. Again Willie is there, not only supervising the feast in the street, but also giving her love and her compassionate ear.

THE PURSUIT OF STEWARDSHIP

Willie Jordan could have used her great intelligence, energy, and leadership abilities for many things. She surely would have made it big had she taken the low road of self-aggrandizement and the pursuit of personal success. It has made a great difference to literally thousands that she took the high road, which is why that's the road best traveled for her.[1]

"In renunciation, it is not the comforts, luxuries, and pleasures to give up," said Mahatma Gandhi. "Many could forgo having meals, a full wardrobe, a fine house, etc. It is the ego that they cannot forgo, the self that is wrapped, suffocated in material things—which include social position, popularity, and power. It is the only self they know and they will not abandon it for an illusory new self—which they may never obtain."

Travelers on the road best traveled are generous to others because they have a strong sense of their own self-worth. They can give freely of themselves without feeling depleted. They know the only thing they can really keep is what they're willing to give away.

These travelers also know that they can never be certain of what lies around the next bend. So they walk in quiet faith, one step at a time, one day at a time, reaching out to one person at a time—starting with their families, then extending to neighbors, and finally to the world at large.

PLANTING SHADE TREES FOR THE FUTURE

These special travelers know too that one of the best ways to spend our tax dollars is to provide truly needy students with scholarships so they can fulfill their dreams and hidden potential. Those who walk the road best traveled make commitments to the next generation, even when that requires sacrifice. They know technology's value as a tool for good and that socially redeeming laboratories that are helping us enrich and extend life must be supported. Still, they do not put their trust in technology alone.

You must do the important, but delegate the urgent.

ASKING THE BIG QUESTIONS

Do you consider the quality of the journey as important as the result? Is your definition of success a million dollars in your bank account and a vault stuffed with stock certificates, or is success taking the high road and placing value on people—your family and others whose goals you can help reach?

If you could balance the demands of your business and personal life with more outside activities, what would you choose? To spend some weekly time reading to the elderly in a community retirement home? Take more walks on the beach or in a park? Volunteer for a drug awareness program for teenagers? If you lived in Los Angeles, would you call Willie Jordan and offer your energies and talents to help the homeless at the Fred Jordan Mission?

I'D PICK MORE DAISIES

While preparing these notes, I found something in my files originally written, I believe, by a cleric named Brother Jeremiah, although it has been borrowed, paraphrased, and excerpted by many authors. "If I had my life to live over again," it reads, "I'd try to make more mistakes. Next time I'd relax, I'd be sillier than on this trip. If I had my life to live over, I'd start barefooted earlier in the spring and stay that way later in the fall. I'd play hooky more, ride on more merry-go-rounds, and I'd pick more daisies."[2]

CARETAKERS, NOT OWNERS

"I'd Pick More Daisies"—the title—is among the most refreshing pieces I've seen. Brother Jeremiah helps us remember that life is to be lived and enjoyed; the time to pick daisies is now. It's easy to be caught in a narrow, constricted perspective, easy to forget that life—like our money, property, jewelry, and antiques—is something we never really own. We've only been entrusted with our possessions, given the privilege of enjoying them for a season, after which we must pass them on to the next caretaker.

EXCELLENCE AS A VERB, NOT A NOUN

Picture yourself investing in a virtual reality pornographic parlor, where men and women would be seduced to spend their money on momentary sensual pleasures. You'd probably make a killing—but also be part of a killing: using the new technology to help destroy dignity, worth, and wonder, to make the world worse. Of course you wouldn't do that, but whatever you *do* do, whatever your business is, ask yourself about your impact on others.

How do you find these roads best traveled? You can't find them in an atlas or on service-station maps. It's harder than that, but also easier. They are roads you build yourself, roads that lead into your own mind. And one way or another, you must travel the road you yourself have designed.

HOW MANY MORE FISHING TRIPS?

In my many years of lecturing and traveling, I've discovered that some of the roads best traveled are in the least known villages, where some of the least publicized people reside. Robert C. Larson recently told me of a trip he took with his son to the High Sierras in California. They sat in their boat on June Lake angling for trout. "You know, Tim," said Bob to his son, "it just struck me. I don't have twenty-five more years to go fishing with you—I may only have twenty-five more fishing trips, period!" Bob's comment hit me hard, knocking a new perspective into my vision. The reality is that my time is dwindling. I've now lived longer than I'll continue to live. All the more reason to keep searching for the road best traveled, keeping my priorities in line.

I don't want to be like the person who said, "If I die, I'll forgive you. If I live, we'll see." Nor do I want a clear conscience to be an indication of a bad memory. With Brother Jeremiah, I want to pick more daisies—not just for myself, but also for those who haven't seen them, like the homeless mothers and children Willie Jordan nourishes on Los Angeles's Skid Row. I hope this is how you want to live your life: serious in your work, playful in your play, and astute enough to know the difference.

THE COURT JESTER WITHIN

Playfulness *is* important. "In each of us," writes Daphne Rose Kingma in a wonderful book called *A Garland of Love* (Conari Press, Berkeley), "there is a hidden court jester, the fanciful spirit that always beholds the humor in life, who will in the midst of any naughty problem or sad tragedy distract us from our troubles by turning somersaults. Staying in touch with the whimsical part of yourself, honoring and developing it, will fill your life with the lightness of spirit that keeps every worry at bay. But court jesters are shy; they won't stick around if they're not applauded, so if you want yours to continue performing, be sure to laugh when he juggles you out of your tears and throw metaphoric confetti each time he whimsies your troubles away."

Here are some action tips as you continue your journey on the road best traveled:

1. The quality of the trip will always be more important than your final destination. You needn't be the world's richest, wisest, best-dressed person. You certainly don't need to be perfect, always judging yourself in comparison to others—which can be a fast track to misery. Instead of blindly pursuing perfection, strive for excellence in all you do. Being a thoughtful, caring person will do it all. Life is a journey. Success is a process, not a pedestal on which to perch.

2. Be willing to learn from and appreciate past challenges. Psychologist Rollo May advised that people should "rejoice in suffering, strange as it sounds, for this is a sign of the availability of energy to transform their characters. Suffering is nature's way of indicating a mistaken attitude or way of behavior, and to the nonegocentric person, every moment of suffering is the opportunity for growth." The opportunity to take the road best traveled where potential dangers lurk around the next bend offers greater potential for growth and success than could ever be accomplished by taking the lower, more traveled path of least resistance.

3. Choose an attitude worthy of you in every situation. Note your way of approaching people and projects and write your thoughts in your daily planner. Devise a rating scale from one to ten, and check on your attitudes at the end of each week. If you need improvement, determine what persuaded you to be less than your best. And on the days when your attitude is triple-A rated, give yourself a pat on the back and say I'm learning to control my attitudes, I'm enjoying the road best traveled.

4. Start enjoying the ripple effect that comes with making a difference. The ever wider concentric circles from a stone thrown into a pond is an appropriate analogy. Today is a good time to start making your waves in your world. Your smallest, seemingly most insignificant action can be of great importance to a family member, friend, or business associate.

5. Enjoy the privilege of doing good. Before he was thirty years old, Millard Fuller was on his way to becoming a self-made millionaire, but his work threatened his health and his marriage, and he began looking beyond money toward a sense of purpose in his life. Millard Fuller is the head of a worldwide organization called Habitat for Humanity, whose goal is to eliminate inadequate housing for the poor. The group raises money and recruits volunteers to renovate and build houses, which are sold at cost, with interest-free mortgages. Habitat now builds and renovates twelve houses a day, providing hope for many who thought they'd come to the end of the line. That is an example of the power of choosing the road best traveled. What example are you prepared to set in your home, community, office, or board room?

WALKING THE TALK

The comment that "Your actions speak so loud I can't hear what you say" is more than a tired cliché. Lech Walesa was right when he spoke of a declining market for words in a speech to the United States Congress. Words without commitment lose their coin; words unsupported by action eventually prompt cynicism and despair. As we move toward the 21st century's challenging demands, preaching alone is less likely than ever before to fill hearts and convince minds. More and more people will make their judgments on the basis of actual personal behavior; fewer and fewer will be enraptured by lofty rhetoric.

One simple truth can never be overemphasized: Success will not be based on your bank account or your earthly possessions. Your sense of fulfillment will always be in direct proportion to how wisely you use your time and how well you maintain your health, both of which will be gone forever once they are spent. Only by nurturing these twin components will your life be balanced, and in the process you will help smooth the ride on your road to opportunity through the empire of your mind.

IF I COULD LIVE MY LIFE AGAIN

I've made a little list of things I'd do more and less of, borrowing Brother Jeremiah's free-verse style from "I'd Pick More Daisies."

> If I could live my life again, I'd laugh at my misfortunes more and at other people's predicaments less. Spend more time counting my blessings, less time scrutinizing my blemishes.
>
> I'd spend more time playing with my children and grandchildren, less time watching professional athletes perform. More time enjoying what I have, less time thinking about the things I don't have.
>
> If I could live my life again, I'd walk in the rain more without an umbrella and listen less to weather reports. I'd spend much more time outdoors in small towns and much less time in tall buildings and big cities. I'd eat more of everything healthy and delicious, less of everything each meal, saving enough on the bill to feed a starving child.

I'd do more listening and less talking so I could learn to understand rather than being desperate to be heard. I'd spend more time looking at trees and climbing them, less time flipping through magazines made from dead trees.

If I could live my life again, I'd get more beach sand between my toes and less friction between myself and others. I'd take more long baths and fewer showers (I can't explain why I've always been in such a hurry to spend my time). I'd spend more time with old people and animals, less time with strangers at clubs and parties.

I'd act the age of my children and grandchildren more and act my own age less. I'd visit libraries, bookstores, and computer networks more and malls and movie theaters less. I'd play the piano more and play fewer mindless games like solitaire. I'd give my spouse and children more tender touches and much less advice.

If I could live my life again, I'd spend more time fully involved in the present moment, less time remembering and anticipating. I'd be more aware of my core values and life mission, and less concerned with the reasons why I might not measure up.

I'd smile more, frown less. I'd express my feelings more, try less to impress my friends and neighbors. I'd forgive and ask forgiveness more, and curse my adversaries less—but most of all I'd be more spontaneous and active, less hesitant and subdued.

When a great idea or spur-of-the-moment adventure popped up—an Easter egg hunt, an open house at school, a game of hide-and-seek, an opportunity to solve a problem at work or to satisfy a disgruntled customer, a hay ride, a chance to build a snowman or paint over graffiti, an invitation to watch a lunar eclipse or a shuttle launch—I'd be less likely to stay in my chair objecting, "It's not in our plan" and more inclined to jump up and say, "Yes, *let's.*"

Although I can't live my life again, I'm still going to live the new way every day. I'll never have all the moments I've missed, but I do have all the time remaining.

You must climb the next mountain, but never reach the summit.

EPILOGUE

❖

One of the greatest lessons I've learned in life is that success is neither the destination nor the journey, but a way of traveling. Destinations and journeys inevitably involve arrivals and endings.

I've always felt the word *retired,* for example, was misspelled. The word should be *retried* or, maybe, *reinspired.* Retired implies tired again or perhaps tired for the final time. A commencement ceremony after one career or major achievement should bring the anticipation of another peak experience ahead, challenging and enriching our bodies, minds, and souls in new, creative pursuits, different from any we may have experienced or imagined before.

I like the idea of life being like an endless range of mountains, with peaks and valleys, inclines and descents, and always more peaks ahead to climb. You and I climb each Mt. Everest in our lives as Edmund Hillary did his, "because it's there," and also for the sheer exhilaration of testing our knowledge, skill, and courage.

When I look for soul-deep meaning as to why I keep building for the future, I recall what has been referred to as the cathedral perspective. The magnificent cathedrals in Europe, built in centuries past, most often took several lifetimes to design and construct. It was impossible to build them like office buildings today, in one short period, as if they were Lego blocks. Cathedrals take generations to build. So do great societies, companies, and families. Life is not something to step back from and admire when completed. It is an ongoing process of design, laying the foundations, forming, erecting, bonding, changing, detailing, refining, and renovating. We never get it quite right. It is never perfect. It is always under construction.

The continuing nature of the life process and our brief mortal encounter with it calls for the cathedral perspective. It calls for us to gain hindsight from all that went before, which is history, with its failures, successes, fashions, and traditions. It calls for us to gain foresight by imagining a better world ahead for all by passing on our trials, errors, and achievements as lessons in leadership. It calls for us to live in the present, longing for neither yesterday nor tomorrow, but rather facing what today offers, boldly, optimistically, and flexibly.

Life, like a cathedral, is not so much to be admired for its external appearance and majesty, although these are attractive and noteworthy. Life, like a cathedral, is more meaningful because of what goes on in the sanctity within.

Hasten not to build your cathedrals or conquer your empires. Seek patiently and persistently to discover them by looking inward.

NOTES

ONE

1. Alvin Toffler, *Powershift* (New York: Bantam Books, 1990), pp. 20–21.
2. Ibid.

TWO

1. Stephen R. Covey, *The Seven Habits of Highly Effective People* (New York: Simon & Schuster, 1989), p. 71.
2. Information on Fred Smith is from an interview with Robert B. Tucker, president of The Innovation Resource, a research and executive development firm in Santa Barbara, California. (Excerpts of Tucker interviews are printed throughout with permission.)

THREE

1. Calhoun W. Wick and Lu Stanton Leon, *The Learning Edge: How Smart Managers and Smart Companies Stay Ahead* (New York: McGraw-Hill, 1993), p. 104.
2. Ibid., p. 94.
3. Ibid., p. 95.
4. Ibid., p. 96.
5. Ibid., p. 97.
6. Ibid., p. 98.
7. Margaret E. Broadley, *Your Natural Gifts* (McLean, VA: EPM Publications, 1972), pp. 3–9.
8. Achievement Technologies Corporation, 4155 East Jewell Ave., Denver, CO 80222. (For information on natural-gift testing services, call 303-595-9219.)
9. "Assessment at the Top," *Human Resource Executive* (March 1994).
10. Winslow Research Institute, Behavioral Testing (800-328-3232).
11. Interview with Robert Hazard conducted by Robert B. Tucker.
12. Interview with John Naisbitt by Robert B. Tucker, and "John Naisbitt Makes Handsome Living Reading Newspapers for Big Corporations," *The Wall Street Journal* (September 30, 1982), pp. 5–6.
13. Information on Florence Skelly from interview conducted by Robert B. Tucker, 1984.

14. Information on Regis McKenna from interview conducted by Robert B. Tucker, 1984.

15. Achievement Technologies Corporation, 4155 East Jewell Ave., Denver, CO 80222. (For information on vocabulary-building programs, call 800-984-6282.)

FOUR

1. Walter Shapiro, reported by Barrett Seaman and Laurence I. Barrett/Washington, with other bureaus, "Ethics: What's Wrong?" *Time* (May 25, 1987), p. 17.

FIVE

1. Sam Deep and Lyle Sussman, *Smart Moves* (Reading, MA: Addison-Wesley, 1990), p. 174.

SIX

1. Andrew E. Serwer, "Lessons from America's Fastest Growing Companies," *Fortune* (August 8, 1994), p. 49.

2. Jim Stovall, autobiography, to be published in 1995 by Thomas Nelson, Nashville, TN. Reprinted with permission.

3. Sam Deep and Lyle Sussman, *Smart Moves* (Reading, MA: Addison-Wesley, 1990), pp. 95–97.

SEVEN

1. *Harvard Business Review* (March–April 1994), p. 165.

2. Paul Harvey, January 4, 1994, Creators Syndicate, Inc.

3. Film reenactment by American Media Incorporated, Des Moines, IA (800-262-2557).

EIGHT

1. Andrew E. Serwer, "Lessons from America's Fastest Growing Companies," *Fortune* (August 8, 1994), pp. 44–45.

2. "Working Against the Odds," *The Wall Street Journal* (July 28, 1993), p. A6.

3. Ibid.

4. Ibid.

5. James C. Collins in *Inc.* (July 1993).

NINE

1. Peter Block, "Reassigning Responsibility," *Sky* (February 1994).

2. Ibid.

3. Richard Chandler, "Pursuit of Excellence" presentation, April 1994.

4. Ibid.

5. Ibid.

6. Carl E. Larson and Frank M. J. Leaseback, *Teamwork: What Must Go Right, What Can Go Wrong* (Newbury Park, CA: SAGE publications, c. 1989).

7. Rochelle Sharpe, "The Waiting Game: Women Make Strides, But Men Stay Firmly in Top Company Jobs," *The Wall Street Journal* (March 29, 1994), p. A1.

8. Lao Tzu, *Tao Te Ching,* various editions.

9. Department of Labor Statistics, 1993.

10. John Huey, "Managing in the Midst of Chaos," *Fortune* (April 5, 1993), pp. 38–48.

11. Information on Fred Smith from an interview with Robert C. Tucker and Denis Waitley, 1984.

12. Information on John DeLorean from an interview with Robert C. Tucker and Denis Waitley, 1984.

13. Carl Jung, *The Psychology of the Unconscious: A Study of the Transformations and Symbolisms of the Libido* (Princeton, NJ: Princeton University Press, 1992).

14. Information on Toyota from a presentation by Denis Waitley to the Toyota Corporation, June 1993.

15. Information on Fred Smith from an interview with Robert C. Tucker and Denis Waitley, 1984.

16. Information on Mo Siegel from a telephone interview with Denis Waitley, 1985.

17. Robert Sobel, *The Rise and Fall of the Conglomerate Kings* (New York: Stein and Day, 1984).

18. Leslie Wayne, "ITT: The Giant Slumbers," *The New York Times* (July 1, 1984), pp. E1, E21.

19. Terrence Deal and Allan Kennedy, *Corporate Cultures: The Rights and Rituals of Corporate Life* (Reading, MA: Addison-Wesley, 1982), pp. 41–43.

20. Joseph F. McKenna, "Close Encounters of the Executive Kind," *Industryweek* (September 6, 1993).

21. *At Work* (July/August 1993).

22. Alan Zaremba, "Communication and Quality," *The Quality Observer* (April 1992).

23. E. James Coates, "Communication and the TQM Process," *The Quality Observer* (April 1992).

24. Dr. Jean Lebedun, *PEPI Update* (June/July 1993), published by the Positive Employee Practices Institute.

25. Kenneth Johnston, *A.S.A.P.* (Fall 1992), published by Business One Irwin.

26. Michael P. Thompson, *Management Communications Quarterly* (August 1993).

27. Tom Kramlinger, "Training's Role in a Learning Organization," *Training* (July 1992), pp. 45–61.

28. *Inc.,* October 1990.

29. M. Scott Peck, *The Road Less Traveled* (New York: Simon and Schuster, 1985).

TEN

1. Jordan E. Ayanis, "The Superhighway and You," *Mind Play,* Vol. 1 (June 1994), Newsletter of Innovative Thinking Network.
2. John Huey, "Waking Up to the New Economy," *Fortune* (June 27, 1994), p. 36.
3. Ibid., p. 38.
4. Ibid.
5. Ibid.
6. Ibid., p. 44.
7. Ibid.
8. Bruce Caldwell, "Missteps, Miscues," *Informationweek* (June 20, 1994), pp. 50–57.
9. Ibid.
10. Ibid.
11. Ibid.
12. Ibid.
13. Ibid.
14. Ibid.
15. Lester Thurow, *Head to Head: The Coming Economic Battle Among Japan, Europe, and America* (New York: William Morrow, 1992).

ELEVEN

1. Hank Whittemore, "Hitting Bottom Can Be the Beginning," *Parade* magazine (March 15, 1992), pp. 4–6.
2. George Raine, "Drug Czar Taps into Delancey Street," *San Francisco Examiner* (November 28, 1993).

TWELVE

1. Andrew E. Serwer, "Lessons from America's Fastest Growing Companies," *Fortune* (August 8, 1994), p. 49.
2. Denis Waitley, "Opportunities Missed," *Being the Best* (Nashville, TN: Thomas Nelson, 1987), p. 115.
3. Interview with Dr. John Shea conducted by Robert C. Tucker, 1984.
4. Gerhard Gschwandtner's interview of Dr. Abraham Zaleznik appeared in the January-February 1984 issue of *Personal Selling Power.* It is reprinted in *Super Sellers: Portrait of Success* by Gerhard Gschwandtner and Laura B. Gschwandtner (New York: AMACOM, American Management Association, 1986), pp. 8–18.
5. Ibid.

THIRTEEN

1. Aaron Stern, M.D., *Me: The Narcissistic American* (New York: Ballantine Books, 1979), p. 111.

FOURTEEN

1. Information on Willie Jordan from interview conducted by Robert C. Larson, 1993. Printed with permission.
2. Brother Jeremiah source came from a handout at a seminar at Bel Air Presbyterian Church, Los Angeles, California, in 1979, attended by Robert C. Larson. "I'd Pick More Daisies" attributed to Brother Jeremiah, unknown cleric.

INDEX

❖

"This book makes it clear that change is constant and inevitable, and to cope we will need knowledge and leadership. In the future we had best attempt projects which release, stimulate, and maximize our potential."

—TONY BASIL, PH.D.
Director of Continuing Education
Ohio State University

"Great motivational book!"

—NANCY KINSEY
Director, Division of Continuing Education
University of Texas at Arlington

"Hopefully, organizational leaders will hear the wake-up call and realize we live in a world of constant change and constant new technologies. These leaders must be flexible, open to new ideas, and understand that people are a resource requiring leadership, not management."

—MICHAEL L. DeLONG
Program/Promotion Coordinator
Center for Organizational Improvement
Oklahoma State University

"He provides a practical and realistic road map to help us accomplish the humanization of the American workplace."

—SUZANNE ALLEGRETTI
Program Coordinator
University College
Creighton University

"The paradoxical proverbs are especially thought-provoking and keep the reader engaged long after the book is set aside."

—ROBERT L. TAYLOR
Dean, College of Business and Public Administration
University of Louisville

"Change is not easy, but Denis Waitley helps companies cope, regroup, and charge forward with his examples and word pictures."

—SUSAN SIEBKE
Director, Drake Business Center
Drake University

"Each of us is responsible for our own performance and we should be proud of how well we do."

—JOHN H. SCHAEFER
Director, Entrepreneurial Center
Xavier University

"This book provides a dizzying array of provocative ideas. It causes us to reevaluate many of our old, and possibly outdated, beliefs."

—CHARLES KUEHL, PH.D.
Director, Division of Continuing Education and Outreach
University of Missouri, St. Louis

"Our mind's eye sets the standards for our performance—mediocrity or more. Empires of concrete or character are the products of our standards. We, as individuals, create or destroy the opportunity to be a builder of an empire of magnificence or mediocrity—either costing millions, and both a result of human performance involving not only ourselves but our entire society."

—JANET T. CHERRY
Director, Institute for Executive Education
University of Memphis

"The most important assets today—our data, information, knowledge."

—KENNETH E. KNIGHT, PH.D.
Dean, School of Business and Economics
Seattle Pacific University

"I loved the 'CEO of your life' concept. I've been a student of leadership for many years and have taught leadership courses and seminars. This book is a wonderful curriculum guide."

—MARY S. JOHNSON
Dean, Continuing Education
Meredith College

"Awareness is the beginning, and a look into the future through Denis Waitley's eyes and experiences adds credibility."

—DONNA HONOLD
Assistant Director, Professional Development Center
St. Ambrose University

"Helps us realize that the ultimate responsibility for our futures lies within us as individuals."

—ANNE GORDON
Associate Director, Center for Professional Development
James Madison University

"Great concepts—loved it! The empires of the mind will be with those individuals who can successfully transmit power and knowledge to each individual within an organization."

—CHERYL M. BURBANO, PH.D.
Program Director, Professional Development Center
University of South Florida

"I think the book alerts us to problems that exist, but guides us to participate in using change positively. In the future, we all must be responsible for improving the quality of life for all and avoid erecting empires."

—NANCY D. GOODE
Director, Continuing Education
Queens College

To order additional copies of

EMPIRES OF THE MIND

please contact your local bookseller
or complete the information below:

Please send _____ cop(ies) of Denis Waitley's EMPIRES OF THE MIND (0-688-14033-5). I have enclosed $23.00 for each book plus $4.50 for the first book and $.50 for each additional title to cover shipping and handling costs.

Payment is by *(check one)*:

_____ American Express   _____ Visa/MasterCard
_____ Check or Money Order   _____ Discover
       (U.S. funds *only,* no CODs)

For credit card purchases:

Account #_____Expiration Date _____

Cardholder signature _____

Ship to (street address only)

Name _____

Address _____

_____

City _____ State _____ Zip _____

Please send the above information to:

Publishers Book & Audio
P.O. Box 070059
Staten Island, N.Y. 10307
or call: 1-800-288-2131

Please allow 2–3 weeks for delivery. Offer based upon availability. Only U.S.A. orders accepted.

Bulk discounts are available for orders of 10 copies or more for businesses and organizations. Please call 1-800-821-1513 for information.
For information about Denis Waitley's seminars, audiotapes, and videotapes, call 1-800-WAITLEY.